# UNLOCKING

## THE MYSTERIES OF
## EATING DISORDERS

A Life-Saving Guide to Your
Child's Treatment and Recovery

**Also from McGraw-Hill and Harvard Medical School**

*The Harvard Medical School Guide to Lowering Your Blood Pressure*, by Aggie Casey, RN, M.S., and Herbert Benson, M.D., with Brian O'Neill

*The Harvard Medical School Guide to Lowering Your Cholesterol*, by Mason Freeman, M.D., with Christine Junge

*The Harvard Medical School Guide to Overcoming Thyroid Problems*, by Jeffrey R. Garber, M.D., with Sandra Sardella White

*The Harvard Medical School Guide to Healing Your Sinuses*, by Ralph B. Metson, M.D., with Steven Mardon

*The Harvard Medical School Guide to Achieving Optimal Memory*, by Aaron P. Nelson, M.D., Ph.D., with Susan Gilbert

*The Harvard Medical School Guide to a Good Night's Sleep*, by Lawrence J. Epstein, M.D., with Steve Mardon

*Living Through Breast Cancer*, by Carolyn M. Kaelin, M.D., M.P.H., with Francesca Coltrera

*Beating Diabetes*, by David M. Nathan, M.D., and Linda M. Delahanty, M.S., RD

*Raising an Emotionally Healthy Child When a Parent Is Sick*, by Paula Rauch, M.D., and Anna C. Muriel, M.D., M.P.H.

*The No Sweat Exercise Plan*, by Harvey B. Simon, M.D.

*Eat, Play, and Be Healthy*, by W. Allan Walker, M.D., with Courtney Humphries

*Healthy Eating During Pregnancy*, by W. Allan Walker, M.D., with Courtney Humphries

*The Breast Cancer Survivor's Fitness Plan*, by Carolyn Kaelin, M.D., M.P.H., Francesca Coltrera, Joy Prouty, and Josie Gardiner

*Hot Flashes, Hormones, and Your Health*, by JoAnn E. Manson, M.D., with Shari S. Bassuk, Sc.D.

*Heal Your Aching Back*, by Jeffrey N. Katz, M.D., and Gloria Parkinson

**Monthly Newsletters from Harvard Medical School**

*Harvard Health Letter*

*Harvard Women's Health Watch*

*Harvard Men's Health Watch*

*Harvard Heart Letter*

*Harvard Mental Health Letter*

For more information, please visit us at health.harvard.edu.

# UNLOCKING
# THE MYSTERIES OF
# EATING DISORDERS

## A Life-Saving Guide to Your Child's Treatment and Recovery

**DAVID B. HERZOG, M.D.**

**DEBRA L. FRANKO, PH.D.**

**AND PAT CABLE, RN**

New York  Chicago  San Francisco  Lisbon  London  Madrid  Mexico City
Milan  New Delhi  San Juan  Seoul  Singapore  Sydney  Toronto

The **McGraw·Hill** Companies

**Library of Congress Cataloging-in-Publication Data**

Herzog, David B.
    Unlocking the mysteries of eating disorders : a life-saving guide to your child's treatment and recovery / David B. Herzog, Debra L. Franko, and Pat Cable.
        p.    cm.
    Includes bibliographical references and index.
    ISBN 978-0-07-147537-2 (alk. paper)
        1. Eating disorders in children—Popular works.    I. Franko, Debra.    II. Cable, Pat.    III. Title.

    RJ506.E18H477    2007
    618.92'8526—dc22                                    2007025519

1  2  3  4  5  6  7  8  9  10  11  12  13  14  15  16  17  18  19  20  21  22    DOC/DOC    0 9 8 7

ISBN  978-0-07-147537-2
MHID      0-07-147537-0

Figures 6.1, 10.2, and 11.3 by Doron Ben-Ami; Figures 6.2 and 6.3 by Scott Leighton; Figure 10.1 courtesy of Harvard Health Publications; Figure 11.1 by Christopher Bing; Figure 11.2 by Ed Wiederer.

McGraw-Hill books are available at special quantity discounts to use as premiums and sales promotions, or for use in corporate training programs. For more information, please write to the Director of Special Sales, Professional Publishing, McGraw-Hill, Two Penn Plaza, New York, NY 10121-2298. Or contact your local bookstore.

This book is printed on acid-free paper.

*To our parents:*

*Muriel and Harry Herzog*

*Geri and Bill Franko*

*Marcia and Austin Cable*

# Contents

Acknowledgments     ix

Introduction     xiii

PART I

Does My Child Have an Eating Disorder?

CHAPTER 1     3

The Nature of Eating Disorders

CHAPTER 2     13

When Does Unhealthy Eating Cross the Line?

CHAPTER 3     29

Spotting the Warning Signs

PART II

Toward Renewed Health: Treatment and Recovery

CHAPTER 4     49

What if She Shows Signs of an Eating Disorder?

CHAPTER 5     65

Setting Up Your Treatment Team

CHAPTER 6     87

Medical Care and Monitoring

CHAPTER 7                                                    105

How You Can Help Support Her Through Recovery

CHAPTER 8                                                    125

Managing and Preventing Relapses

CHAPTER 9                                                    147

Handling the Effects on Family and Friends

PART III

Preventing Eating Disorders and Raising Awareness

CHAPTER 10                                                   169

Examining Risk Factors and Causes

CHAPTER 11                                                   191

Sending Your Child a Healthy Message

CHAPTER 12                                                   215

Eating Disorders Throughout Life

CHAPTER 13                                                   233

Paving the Road to Tomorrow

Resources                                                    247

References                                                   259

Index                                                        275

# Acknowledgments

Our gratitude goes back many years to the mentors and friends who have encouraged and guided us in our efforts to improve the lives of patients with eating disorders. I (Dr. Herzog) first became interested in treating patients with these illnesses back in the 1970s when I was a resident in pediatrics at the University of Wisconsin Hospitals under the superb tutelage of Richard Anderson, M.D. There was disagreement between the disciplines regarding whose role it was to treat teens with anorexia nervosa on the pediatrics unit. The medical doctors claimed that psychiatry should manage the care of this illness, while the psychiatrists believed that these patients were too physically compromised to work on their psychological issues. Neither department really "owned" responsibility for treating these individuals. I wondered what drove these adolescents to lose so much weight. Why were they starving themselves? From this curiosity grew my determination to help individuals with eating disorders and their families.

From Wisconsin, I moved to Boston and, after finishing my residencies, accepted a position at Massachusetts General Hospital (MGH) to set up a program for individuals with illnesses that affected both the mind and the body. I want to thank Tom Hackett, M.D., and Michael Jellinek, M.D., for their support in 1980 to 1981, when I founded the MGH Eating Disorders Unit, which I directed for two decades. In the early 1990s, Joseph Coyle, M.D., then chairman of the Consolidated Department of Psychiatry at Harvard Medical School, helped me create the Harvard Eating Disorders Center, which is now the Harris Center at MGH. Matina Horner, Ph.D., brought to the Center her rich and far-reaching knowledge as professor, researcher in women's achieve-ment motivation, college president at Radcliffe, and mentor. As such, she inspired our summer fellowship program, which pro-vides mentoring and funds for students interested in eating disor-ders research.

I want to thank Peter Slavin, M.D., M.B.A., president of MGH; W. Gerald Austen, M.D., chairman emeritus, MGH Physicians Organization; and Jerrold Rosenbaum, M.D., chief of psychiatry, and Maurizio Fava, M.D., associate chief of psychiatry, for their support in the administrative move of the Center to MGH in 2000 to 2001 and in creating the Harvard Medical School Professorship in Psychiatry in the field of eating disorders at MGH. In 2005, we renamed our Center in honor of our friend and major phil-anthropic supporter, Nancy Harris, to whom we are profoundly grateful.

I would like to express my deep appreciation to Anne Kliban-ski, M.D., professor of medicine at Harvard Medical School and chief of the Neuroendocrine Unit at MGH. Under Anne's leader-ship and expertise and through our collaboration and friendship over many years, the unit—which includes Steven Grinspoon, M.D.; Karen K. Miller, M.D.; and Madhusmita Misra, M.D.—has grown to become a world leader in research on the causes and treatment of bone loss in eating disorders.

—David Herzog, M.D.

I began my journey into the field of eating disorders as a student at the University of Michigan, where I volunteered on an adoles-cent psychiatric unit in the early 1970s and felt mystified by a girl who saw herself so differently than others saw her. I'm grateful to Sherry Hatcher, Ph.D., for encouraging me to pursue my studies in psychology, which led me to McGill University in Montreal. Once there, I found no services for women with eating disorders (in 1980!) and, together with my friend Bonnie Reich Pantel, LICSW, organized the first self-help group at the local YWCA. I'm forever indebted to my dissertation advisor and friend, David

Zuroff, Ph.D., who taught me the meaning of being a psychologist and has mentored me throughout my career.

My colleagues and supervisors at Beth Israel Hospital—Nicholas Covino, Psy.D.; Peter Kassel, Psy.D.; and Fred Frankel, M.D.—taught me the art of psychotherapy and were instrumental in the development of an outpatient eating disorders program. Marian Winterbottom, Ph.D.; Betty North, Ph.D.; and Bob Misch, Ph.D., mentored me from my first day as a psychology intern through my 13 years as a staff psychologist, during which time I had the opportunity to direct the eating disorders program. I thank them for their wisdom and guidance. In 1987 I had the good fortune to complete a postdoctoral fellowship at Massachusetts General Hospital with Dr. Herzog, who invited me to join the Harvard Eating Disorders Center in 1998. I will always be grateful to him—a master clinician, researcher, and teacher—for giving me an appreciation of the hard road that individuals with eating disorders and their families face as they enter treatment. I thank him for all he has taught me during our 20 years of friendship and work together.

—Debra Franko, Ph.D.

Over the years, our patients and their families have been our greatest teachers, enlightening us about eating disorders and showing us the way. We extend our heartfelt appreciation to the individuals and families who participated in this book by sharing their personal experiences of eating disorders and recovery. We were impressed with the candor and clarity with which they told their stories, with their insight, and with their eagerness to help others struggling with these illnesses. All of these individuals and families wished us to assign them pseudonyms for our book, and we were happy to respect these requests.

We are thankful to many dedicated, talented professionals for helping to make this book possible: Cynthia M. Bulik, Ph.D.; Jeanine Cogan, Ph.D.; Susan Frates, M.S., RD, LDN; Mary Gee; Mark Goldstein, M.D.; Thomas R. Insel, M.D.; Lareina La Flair; Daniel le Grange, Ph.D.; Amy Lipsey; Laurie Martinelli, Esq.;

Dianne Neumark-Sztainer, Ph.D., MPH, RD; Janet Treasure, Ph.D.; W. Allan Walker, M.D.; and Nancy Zucker, Ph.D.

We were also blessed with an enthusiastic group of reviewers: Abby Coyle, Kathryn DeVito, Lisa Sussman, and June Tatelman. Each of these women gave generously of herself to make this book reader-friendly and resonant. Their commitments to the book and their chapter-by-chapter feedback have been inspiring. Harris Center research assistants Elizabeth Ong and Kavita Tahilani kept us well-organized, assisted with our reference section, and were consistently helpful.

It was our pleasure to work with Johanna Bowman, our editor at McGraw-Hill, who offered excellent ideas and kept us focused. We want to express our gratitude to Anthony Komaroff, M.D, editor-in-chief of Harvard Health Publications, for inviting us to write this book in the first place. Our thanks to Nancy Ferrari, managing editor at Harvard Health Publications, for helping us get the book started and to Raquel Schott, associate editor, for coordinating the artwork and serving as our liaison with McGraw-Hill.

Last, we thank our spouses, Jennifer Rathbun, M.D., and Danny Kaloupek, Ph.D., for their immeasurable support and our children, Jon and Matt Herzog and Ben and Emma Kaloupek, for their patience throughout the writing of this book.

—David Herzog, M.D.; Debra Franko, Ph.D.; Pat Cable, RN

# Introduction

"Will my child get better? How? When?" If these questions are running through your mind, you are not alone. In fact, more than 8 million people in the United States suffer from eating disorders, and many more have substantially abnormal eating habits that don't meet the formal criteria for classification as illness. The challenges and fears you may be experiencing in coping with your afflicted child can feel overwhelming. Questions such as "Why us?" or "Why this?" lead you to search for explanations for your child's behaviors. Most of all, you are probably wondering how she can overcome her abnormal eating habits and how you can encourage her along the way. This book will help answer your questions.

Eating disorders are complex illnesses that most often strike during adolescence or young adulthood and are more common among females than males. Contrary to popular perception, eating disorders are not just a problem of wealthy, white families. They affect the rich and the poor, cutting across all races and ethnicities. Maybe your child is suffering from anorexia nervosa, the self-starvation disease. Or perhaps she has bulimia nervosa, meaning that she engages in repeated episodes of binge eating followed by efforts to prevent the food she has just ingested from resulting in weight gain. Another possibility is that she is struggling with serious eating problems that border on anorexia or bulimia. If you were to ask a number of people what they first think of when they hear the phrase *eating disorder*, their answers would likely revolve around food and weight. And these responses would be accurate—but only to a point. Abnormal eating is the tangible part of each illness, the part that gives this group of disorders its name. But it is not the only part. Also important are the intangible components of these illnesses—the individual's thought patterns and feelings.

Our decision to write this book comes from our rich clinical experience. Over three decades we have seen and supervised the care of thousands of individuals with eating disorders at Massachusetts General Hospital and Beth Israel Hospital. We have listened to our patients closely, tuning in to their thoughts and feelings, and building on their strengths. The many questions people have asked us have generated valuable research initiatives. In 1994, we created the Harvard Eating Disorders Center, which is now the Harris Center for Education and Advocacy in Eating Disorders at Massachusetts General Hospital. Through the Center, we help train future leaders in the field and conduct research to better understand these illnesses and find effective treatments and prevention strategies. As we seek new knowledge, we strive to share it with the community at large.

Based on a combination of research and clinical experience, we have made the text reader-friendly, without technical terminology. The son or daughter you have in mind when you are reading this book could be almost any age, though our main focus is on school-age children, adolescents, and young adults. For our narrative, we have mostly used feminine pronouns when referring to an individual with an eating disorder; this usage is not to minimize the importance of eating disorders in males but simply to enhance readability. You'll also find first-person perspectives of individuals with eating disorders and families with whom we have worked. To protect their privacy, we have not used their real names. These stories open a window into what it means and how it feels to live with and receive treatment for an eating disorder. Chances are you will identify with the challenges faced by the parents in our vignettes. As you will see, although the young people in these stories have difficulties with food and weight, they often show remarkable capabilities and strengths in other aspects of life.

One reason why eating disorders can be difficult for families to spot is that people with these conditions generally try to keep their behaviors a secret. Those with anorexia often have visible signs of the disorder, such as low weight, but they are reluctant to seek help or admit that anything is wrong. Those with bulimia nervosa are generally normal in weight and look healthy. Part I of this book addresses how to recognize if your child is suffering from an eating disorder. Although every patient is unique, some of the warning signs of these illnesses are common. We talk about the various clues that may lead you to believe that your child has a problem and offer advice about when to seek professional help. It is not unusual for parents to be unsure whether their child has an eating disorder or whether she is at risk of developing one. So we have devoted a chapter to exploring what it means to cross the line from unhealthy eating to illness.

Part II, aimed at treatment and recovery, highlights how important it is for your child to see her primary care physician for an evaluation. You'll learn why a team approach to care is often recommended, how to find the right professionals for your child, and how to navigate the various treatment options. Although eating disturbances afflict people of all ethnic and cultural backgrounds, they may show up differently in different groups. For example, it is not unusual for an Asian woman to manifest all the characteristics of anorexia nervosa but not experience a fear of becoming fat. It is important for care to be sensitive to families' ethnic and cultural identities. The vignette in Chapter 4 brings to life a challenge encountered by many families—arranging treatment for a child who insists she doesn't want it. As puzzling as it is that she is resistant to getting help, this is not unusual among individuals with eating disorders. The experiences of Roberta and her family will shed light on what you can do to encourage your child to give treatment a try.

First and foremost, your child's treatment team—her primary care doctor, her nutritionist, her therapist, and possibly a psychopharmacologist (psychiatrist who specializes in medication)—will strive to keep her medically safe. Perhaps you are aware that anorexia and bulimia can result in serious medical problems. We outline these and discuss how they are managed. Some—but not all—of these negative consequences resolve with the restoration of healthy nutrition, but the goal is to keep them from occurring in the first place. Your child's primary care physician will monitor her closely, educate her about the medical risks of her illness, and encourage her to choose health. The family stories in Chapters 4 and 6 illuminate how you can work with your child's doctor to motivate her to accept help.

What is psychotherapy? What is its purpose? How will it help your child? Will it convince her to change her eating habits? What kinds of issues does it address? If the entire notion of psychotherapy for an eating disorder feels like a mystery to you, Chapter 5 will be of help. In it, we delineate the different schools of thought that inform psychotherapy for eating disorders and talk about the importance of an alliance between the therapist and patient. Throughout the book, the voices of patients capture the experience of talk therapy; that is, individuals describe what therapy was like and whether it helped them. In Chapter 7 we explain that many individuals with eating disorders also suffer from other mental illnesses, such as depression or anxiety disorders. Here, you'll meet 18-year-old Paula, who took a leave of absence from college so that she could get help for her bulimia, her cutting, her dark moods, and her sense of being "not good enough." Her story and many others portray the road to recovery as bumpy and hard to travel rather than smooth or direct.

In addition to giving you an inside look at individual therapy, our vignettes provide a glimpse into family therapy, which offers parents an opportunity to express their concerns, to work on enhancing communication with their child, and to participate in the treatment process. You will learn what kinds of topics are discussed in family therapy and how the parents in our stories used their sessions to increase their understanding of themselves and their children. Chapter 9 introduces you to family-based (Maudsley) therapy, a specific outpatient approach that has shown promise for adolescents who are treated early in the course of their eating disorder. Throughout the book, we offer you tools to help you open channels of communication between you and your child so that—little by little—you can establish a dialogue about her friendships, sports activities, studies, life on the home front, and maybe even about her attitudes toward her body.

Part III, "Preventing Eating Disorders and Raising Awareness," opens with a discussion of the possible causes of eating disorders. Woven throughout the text, and explored in more depth in Chapter 10, is the theme that eating disorders are no one's fault. It is likely that these illnesses stem not from a single influence but from a combination of factors, including biology, culture, personality, and relationships.

Exactly what causes eating disorders is among the mysteries that researchers are trying to unlock. Other questions pertain to treatment. One of our main research projects—our longitudinal study—examines what happens to individuals with eating disorders over time. Who gets better and how? To conduct this study, we are following 246 women who initially sought treatment for anorexia and bulimia. We interview them regularly to find out about their eating behaviors; their emotional health; and their participation in school, work, and social activities. This research project, now in its 19th year, has revealed that the majority of patients improve over time. All of our chapters emphasize that eating disorders are treatable and that individuals and their families can be helped.

The final chapter of the book talks about the progress that is taking place in the field of eating disorders. You will learn how professional and advocacy-based organizations have joined together and established a coalition in Washington, D.C., to call attention to eating disorders as a federal health priority. You will see how the coalition is raising awareness of eating disorders nationwide and garnering support for legislation on behalf of these illnesses. Finally, you will discover what you can do to participate in the advocacy movement.

As you travel the road to recovery with your child, we think this book will guide you, and we hope you will find inspiration in the stories our patients and their families have shared with us.

# PART I

# Does My Child Have
# an Eating Disorder?

## CHAPTER 1

# The Nature of Eating Disorders

"It was 6:00 A.M., and I woke to a familiar noise coming from my 15-year-old daughter's bedroom. Every morning, she had been waking well before dawn to put herself through a strenuous regimen of jumping jacks and other calisthenics. The previous month, after an appointment with her pediatrician, she had discontinued the early morning workouts as advised—but only temporarily. I tried to calm myself as I threw on my bathrobe and headed down the hall to talk with Maureen, hoping she'd stop her calisthenics and rest before getting ready for school. Knocking softly on her door, I sighed at the inevitable 'Wait a sec.' After 'Okay, Mom. C'mon in,' I entered and found her sitting on her bed in shorts and a T-shirt, as sullen and unapproachable as she'd been for the last couple of weeks. My eyes took in the worn exercise shoes that she had most likely flung off only moments before she'd leapt from her exercise mat in front of the mirror to her bed. I wasn't surprised to see a clipping from a magazine on Maureen's dresser; it was one of many weight-loss charts she had collected since beginning her strict diet. As I gave my daughter a good-morning hug and suggested she rest for half an hour before getting dressed for school, I felt like asking her what she wanted for breakfast but thought better of it. I'd give myself a few minutes to figure out how to broach that subject, knowing that Maureen would try to leave the house without eating, just as she'd done every morning for a week."

If you have a child with an eating disorder, chances are you can relate to this mom's worries. Maureen suffered from anorexia nervosa and became our patient a year ago, upon referral from her pediatrician. No matter how many people you have known (or heard of) with eating disorders, the experience of having your own son or daughter in the grip of this type of illness holds an intensity like no other. Even if you have always considered yourself in the know about these conditions, when you face the possibility of such a problem in your own daughter or son, you may find yourself asking, "What is an eating disorder? What's the best treatment? Will my child get better? How can I help?" Based on scientific research and several decades of working with many individuals with eating disorders, we will provide answers to your questions. In addition to helping the families of those who suffer from eating disorders, this book will be useful to teachers, athletic coaches, college residence advisers, youth group leaders, summer camp personnel, and anyone who interacts with vulnerable individuals.

## Identifying the Different Types of Eating Disorders

Eating disorders are serious psychiatric illnesses impacting both the brain and the body. Individuals with eating disorders are afflicted with negative thoughts and intense emotions about their body size and shape; they adopt unhealthy weight control practices and other abnormal eating habits, taking these measures to a dangerous extreme. The most well-known eating disorders are anorexia nervosa and bulimia nervosa. In addition, there is a third category called eating disorders not otherwise specified (EDNOS), which consists of binge eating disorder and other severe conditions that are akin to anorexia nervosa or bulimia nervosa but do not match the official medical definitions of these illnesses.

## Anorexia Nervosa: A Self-Starvation Disease

Maria, the mother you met at the beginning of this chapter, had more to learn about the disease that changed her daughter from a thriving, athletic ninth grader to a shadow of her former self. Known to many as the disease of self-starvation, anorexia nervosa affects about 1 percent of the population at some point in their lives, and the vast majority of sufferers are female. Like Maureen, most individuals with anorexia first fall ill during adolescence or during their early to mid-20s; for many, the disease continues into adulthood. We often do not see people for evaluation and treatment until some time after they develop the illness.

There is a big difference between how people with anorexia nervosa view themselves and how they are viewed by others. While Maria perceived her daughter as painfully thin, Maureen experienced her body as "fat," and in her eyes, fat was "bad." When this 15-year-old insisted she was huge, that her thighs were too big, or that her jeans were tighter than they had been yesterday, she was not just making up the perception or faking it. "She seemed to believe what she claimed about her body," says Maria, "and trying to convince her otherwise felt like an exercise in futility."

Given the nature of this eating disorder, the term *anorexia*—which stems from the Greek terms *an*, meaning "without," and *orexe*, meaning "appetite"—is misleading. Individuals with this illness are so focused on fighting hunger that it is hard for them to acknowledge that they have it; that's where the term *nervosa* fits in. People with anorexia are afraid that if they give in to their appetites and start eating, they won't stop. Maureen felt that her calisthenics took her mind off her hunger. Driven to lose weight and intensely afraid of gaining any, she cut way back on her food intake, first eliminating desserts and snacks, then dropping other foods that worried her, such as meat and bread. When it came to eating, exercise, and weight, Maureen had a set of harsh, rigid rules that she applied only to herself and followed to the letter—even well beyond. She measured everything she ate, checking the measuring

# Self–Starvation in Times Gone By

Self-imposed starvation dates as far back as the early Middle Ages, when the consensus was that girls who refused to eat were possessed by demons and that exorcism was the remedy.

Medieval Europe saw fasting among female saints, one of whom was Catherine of Siena. Born around the middle of the 14th century, she was 16 when she drastically reduced her food intake as part of her religious quest to transcend biological needs. Saint Catherine also engaged in strenuous physical exercise and vomited the meager ration of food that she allowed herself to eat. So tenacious was her fast that no one, not even Church authorities, could convince her to relent. She died of starvation when she was about 32 years old.

In learning about the religious starvation of the medieval saints, some 18th- and 19th-century girls tried to emulate them. Girls with healthy weights who abstained from food yet had no discernable medical problems were viewed as miraculous, but there were also girls whose fasting led to physical wasting and death. Doctors in the 19th century considered voluntary starvation "nervous" in origin; thus, in 1874, the condition was named *anorexia nervosa* and was much like the illness as we know it today.

cup repeatedly to make sure she was not allowing herself too much. In general undernourished individuals are disinclined to engage in sports and other physical activities; with anorexia, the opposite is true. Like Maureen, people with this illness often exercise to an extreme—mostly in the interest of losing weight.

One of anorexia's many dangers is that no matter how many pounds the individual sheds, she is never "thin enough." As soon as Maureen reached one weight goal, she aspired to a lower one, intensifying her self-discipline and guarding against any potential "risk" of weight gain. "At one point, Maureen dropped toast from her breakfast routine," recalls her mom. "Then, in addition to performing her calisthenics, she tried to skip breakfast altogether."

Many sufferers are reluctant to admit they have a problem or need help. "My biggest fear was that my daughter wouldn't accept treatment," says Maria. "What started as voluntary self-starvation became a force unto itself and gained momentum, creating a nightmare for the entire family." Maria's persistence in encouraging Maureen to come in for treatment was a critical first step on the road to recovery.

## Bulimia Nervosa: A Disease with Less Obvious Signs

Sondra, now 23, was referred to us as a college freshman after she had visited the campus health center requesting help for an upset stomach. Initially, she'd been afraid to tell the college doctor about her eating problems. But when he asked her whether she was trying to lose weight and whether she had ever vomited a meal, she told him the truth. Ruth, Sondra's mom, has vivid memories of the days immediately preceding her daughter's evaluation at the college health center:

"The call came on a Tuesday, just after I returned from work. It was Celia, my 18-year-old daughter Sondra's best friend from high school, and the news wasn't good. Celia had visited Sondra at college and found her having difficulties with food. Sondra was going to the dormitory cafeteria at mealtimes and leaving with a huge supply of desserts, which she ate in her room when no one else was there. Celia saw what Sondra's roommate and other students on the third floor had observed repeatedly—Sondra heading straight to the bathroom down the hall, as if nothing in the world would stop her. Celia and the roommate had urged their friend to go to the college health center, which was set up to assist students suffering from eating disturbances, but Sondra wanted no part of it. After Celia's call, I spent the next day getting some books about eating disorders and inquiring further about the college's services for these disorders. Then I was on my way to visit Sondra, hoping to convince her to seek help and to do it soon."

Bulimia nervosa affects approximately 1 to 4.2 percent of people at some time in their lives. The illness tends to begin during adolescence or early adulthood and most often plagues women.

Like individuals with anorexia nervosa, those with bulimia nervosa prize thinness and tend to measure their self-worth in terms of the size and shape of their bodies. Many times, as in Sondra's case, they are of normal weight and show no obvious signs of the disorder. Sondra set very strict weight standards for herself, constantly thought about food, and developed a pattern of binge eating, whereby she rapidly downed a large volume of food and felt unable to stop eating. Her binges were typically high in carbohydrate and fat content, foods that she did not ordinarily allow herself to eat. She went to great lengths to hide her food habits, and in the college dormitory, that was really hard.

Individuals who have recovered tend to look back on their bingeing as temporarily numbing their emotions, shutting out everything except food. Following a binge, Sondra often felt ashamed of herself for eating with such abandon. Adding to her distress was the overwhelming fear that the food she had consumed during the binge would lead to weight gain—a fate she felt compelled to avoid no matter what the cost. In the face of these powerful emotions, she resorted to purging by inducing vomiting, usually in the bathroom of her dormitory. Sondra knew that there are other methods of purging—including the misuse of laxatives, diuretics (drugs that increase the body's rate of urination), or enemas—but she did not try any of these. Some people with bulimia nervosa fast or overexercise after bingeing in an effort to ward off unwanted pounds. Of the various methods patients with bulimia use (often in combination) in desperate attempts to keep their binges from tipping the scale upward, the most common is self-induced vomiting.

Ruth knew from the outset that eating disturbances were serious. "As I set out for my daughter's college," she remembers, "I kept reminding myself not to panic as thoughts about how best to approach Sondra about the problem raced through my mind. When I arrived, I sensed that she had walled herself off from me. Although she seemed to realize she had eating difficulties, she wasn't about to discuss them with me. After expressing my concern to her and urging her to go to the college health center for help, I returned home but was so worried about Sondra that I could barely concentrate on anything. A couple days later, I received a call from the college physician who had met with Sondra and was interested in setting up a treatment plan for her." Ruth's gathering of reading material, her calls to the college health center, and her overall preparedness for talking to her daughter had been instrumental in getting Sondra to come to us for help.

## Eating Disorder Not Otherwise Specified

As long-winded and puzzling as the term sounds, more people who come to treatment centers for help are diagnosed with eating disorder not otherwise specified than with either anorexia nervosa or bulimia nervosa. Patients with EDNOS have various combinations of eating disorder features that fall just shy of the official criteria for anorexia or bulimia but are nonetheless very serious. EDNOS occurs in both genders and is quite common in adolescents.

In females, one of the official determinants of anorexia nervosa is *amenorrhea* (absent menstrual periods). A woman with extreme weight loss, intense fear of gaining weight, and every other feature of anorexia—except amenorrhea—would likely receive the diagnosis of EDNOS. Males and females who have lost a substantial amount of weight but are closer to the normal weight range than those who are diagnosed with anorexia are also in the EDNOS group. Other EDNOS types overlap with bulimia nervosa. Bulimia involves binge eating followed by a behavior to prevent resulting weight gain; according to the official definition of the illness, the binge and subsequent weight-control behavior occur at least twice a week. Someone who binges and vomits once a week would likely be diagnosed as having EDNOS.

In general, the more severe a patient's abnormal behaviors are, the more vulnerable she is to medical complications resulting from the disorder. EDNOS is associated with substantial emotional and medical problems and can be chronic. In addition, those who border on having anorexia nervosa or bulimia nervosa sometimes go on to develop the full-blown manifestation of these illnesses.

**Binge Eating Disorder.** Thus far, the only EDNOS to have a distinct name is binge eating disorder (BED), which has attracted increasing research over the past decade. Named for its major characteristic, BED affects an estimated 0.7 to 4 percent of the population and is more common than either anorexia nervosa or bulimia nervosa. Among those in weight-loss programs, the presence of binge eating disorder is often as high as 20 to 30 percent. While anorexia and bulimia affect far more women than men (10:1), the female-to-male ratio for BED is about 3:2.

Binge eating disorder can be emotionally devastating. Thomas knows about that. Body size and shape were very important to him, and like many people with BED, he was obese. He had been suffering from the illness for a couple of years before he agreed to seek help and was referred to us by his primary care physician. "I was 25 when I first entered therapy," he says now. "I was really overweight and hated myself because of it. I thought about food a lot and considered myself a fat pig because I couldn't resist the temptation to eat. I didn't like the idea of talking about my problem with anyone, but I became so disgusted with my bingeing habit that I would have done just about anything to get over it. So I decided it would be okay to tell my doctor."

Unlike people with bulimia nervosa, those with binge eating disorder do not engage in purging (self-induced vomiting or misuse of laxatives or diuretics) or in other behaviors (compulsive exercise or fasting) aimed at avoiding weight increase after a binge. For Thomas and others with his disorder, the large amounts of food eaten during binges often result in weight gain, which can lead to physical and emotional problems.

Nowadays, obesity and its dangers are often in the news. Obesity is pertinent to eating disorders in important ways, yet it is helpful to understand that some obese individuals have BED (or bulimia) and others do not. Because we have extensive experience working with individuals suffering from anorexia and bulimia, we have focused our book on these two disorders without directly addressing binge eating disorder or other examples of EDNOS.

## Looking Ahead

Until the 1990s, eating disorders were mainly discussed in medical and psychiatric communities. For families who had someone struggling with an eating disorder, accurate information on these illnesses and the dangers they posed was hard to come by, and support services were sparse. Puzzled and worried about their children's relationships with food, parents searched for answers, but more often than not, they came up empty. They fretted, sometimes in silence, sometimes aloud, knowing neither how to approach their children about the problem nor how, when, or where to seek help.

Times have changed. In the last 10 to 15 years, the field of eating disorder research and treatment has expanded, generating new knowledge. Although there is still much to learn, researchers have made valuable inroads into discovering what causes eating disorders, how to detect them, and how to help patients and their families. With the growth of knowledge about how to care for people with these illnesses, the number of professional eating disorder treatment programs—which until 1980 merely dotted the landscape—has multiplied. Professional assistance has become available not only in acute care hospitals and outpatient settings, but also in residential programs, which have more than tripled in number over the past decade.

Threaded throughout this book is the theme that eating disorders stem from a combination of factors. We will explore how mainstream Western culture, certain personality features, and interpersonal relationships influence the onset of a disorder. These factors interact with a biological vulnerability related to genetics and brain chemistry. As the director of the National Institute of Mental Health recently stated, an eating disorder is a "brain disease" and must be taken seriously.

While scientists have made strides in unlocking the mysteries of eating disorders, they have not been alone in planting the seeds of progress. High-profile, renowned public figures, such as singer/dancer Paula Abdul and actress Jane Fonda, have suffered from eating disorders and have begun to tell their stories. Gradually—whether through artwork, journalism, literature, or music—more and more women and men of various ages, ethnicities, and economic backgrounds have started to share their personal experiences.

By the mid-1990s, a number of national nonprofit advocacy organizations for eating disorders had sprouted up, providing families with self-help groups, educational materials, and referrals, and fostering eating disorder awareness programs in schools (see the Resources section at the back of this book). Inspiration for these nonprofits often came from people with anorexia and bulimia and their families, many of whom had learned—through talking with others in their situation—that they were not alone. At the start of the millennium, the roots of the advocacy movement deepened as individual organizations began to work together in a Washington-based alliance (the Eating Disorders Coalition for Research, Policy & Action) to promote federal legislation on behalf of people with eating disorders. Parents active in the Coalition have continually enhanced our appreciation of how harrowing these conditions can be, not only for the person with the illness, but also for her family.

In Chapter 3, we'll examine the clues and signs to watch for with each of the eating disorders we've discussed. However, you'll also want to consider whether your child has really crossed the line to an eating disorder—a question we will explore in the next chapter.

## CHAPTER 2

# When Does Unhealthy Eating Cross the Line?

About four years ago, Joanna, then 22, came to us for help with an eating disorder that had plagued her since her preteen years. Like many sufferers, she had struggled for a long time before seeking help. Now doing very well in recovery, she offered to share her story. "My problems started in the fifth grade," she recalls. "Lots of girls in my class watched their weight. Among them was Gabriella, who put herself on a diet at about the same time I started mine. Her mom was trying to slim down by summer in order to 'look good' in her bathing suit, and Gabriella wanted to do the same. At first, Gabriella was gung ho about dieting, cutting back on snacks and sometimes skipping a meal. But within a couple of weeks, she found food deprivation more uncomfortable than it was worth and spontaneously let go of her diet.

"My experience was different," continues Joanna. "I too wanted the thin look. But once I started dieting, I couldn't stop, soon developing anorexia nervosa. It's not like I woke up one not-so-cheerful morning harboring a big, bad desire to starve to death. I just wanted to lose a little weight. I started a diet and was sucked in by its power."

When we use the term *diet*, we mean a change in eating habits that is aimed at losing weight. Dieting is so widespread in our country and often starts so early in life that many people think it's normal. Periodic dieting, unless prescribed, is one of the behaviors we refer to as "disordered eating." Other examples of disordered eating include the following: eating in secret, avoidance of social eating, and unbalanced eating—such as restricting one of the major food groups. More common in girls and women than in guys, disordered eating behaviors beleaguer people of all ages. The majority of high school girls engage in disordered eating, and the problem is now affecting many younger girls as well. Gabriella's fifth-grade diet was her first but perhaps not her last, and while her mood was fairly stable throughout her weight-loss endeavor, that does not hold true for everyone. Unfortunately, for Joanna and others, unhealthy attitudes and behaviors escalate into illness. We helped Joanna to understand how something that started "simply" had developed into something dangerous.

Among those who travel from disordered eating to eating disorder, there is no black-and-white boundary at which the former ends and the latter begins. There's a gray area, and changes are sometimes subtle. In general, the patient who severely restricts her food intake or binge eats needs to be assessed by her primary care physician. The same holds true for an individual who purges to induce weight loss or prevent weight gain—even if she does so only occasionally. How much do her behaviors influence her life? Can she let go of them? These questions play an important role in determining whether she needs treatment.

Note that dieting is not always a function of being overweight. Some people perceive themselves as too heavy when they are nothing of the kind; others are aware that they are of normal weight but diet nonetheless. The individual on the road to bulimia may appear healthy, and while the person on the threshold of anorexia may have lost weight, her marked undernutrition may not initially be apparent, especially if she wears loose clothing or seems energetic. Nevertheless, these individuals hurt—and hurt deeply.

Some people believe or claim that their food behavior is not serious when, in fact, they are suffering from an eating disorder and don't want to admit it. It's not unusual for a young person to say that she can stop her dieting whenever she wants and doesn't need treatment; however, she does not necessarily have as much control over her behavior as she thinks or would like others to believe. If there's a question in your mind about whether your child has disordered eating or an eating disorder, your best course of action is to consult her pediatrician or primary care physician.

## Have I Gained Weight? Is That the Question?

When disordered eating spirals into an eating disorder, an individual's thoughts about body size and shape become increasingly irrational. Gabriella never had that problem, but Joanna did. "The more weight I lost, the more my fear of gaining weight grew," she says. "I went from a well-balanced lunch to cottage cheese, grapes, and water; as time passed, I left out the cottage cheese, eating only the fruit."

As your daughter's eating disorder takes hold, she is apt to perceive "Have I gained weight?" as the one and only question. She is likely to ask it many times a day, often in the form of tangible, food-related worries. It is not unusual for a patient to categorize foods as either "safe" or "unsafe," allowing herself only the former in regimented amounts. While such rigidity lightens the burden of food and portion selection, it does not make her feel better in the long run. Because the nutritional value of these regimes is woefully inadequate, near-constant food thoughts—an inevitable outgrowth of starvation—break through her steely fortress of self-discipline.

The brain plays an important role in triggering these overwhelming food thoughts. In a well-known 1940s research study, Ancel Keys and his team restricted the food intake of a group of healthy volunteers and observed what happened to them. In addition to the striking physical effects brought on by starvation, there were major changes in the participants' thought patterns. The men became preoccupied with food, reviewing recipes and deliberating the ins and outs of various cooking techniques to the point where they thought and talked about little else. Anorexia nervosa leads to the same sorts of obsessions as those observed in the starving volunteers but also involves more complicated issues.

While some individuals become slaves to self-imposed eating regimens, some experience and eventually give in to food cravings, some eat on impulse, and still others agonize about what they will eat long in advance of each meal. It is not unusual for someone to engage in more than one of these patterns. Food- and weight-related worries grow urgent and all-consuming, begging for closure yet resisting it at the same time. "What-ifs" and "what-have-I-dones" seem to strike out of nowhere and hammer away at the individual from the inside. Some of these pounding thoughts may be self-accusatory and stern, demanding penitence for perceived infractions: "I vowed I wouldn't snack, but I did, and now I have to pay for it by running twice my usual number of laps." Although these indictments have the same common denominator—food and weight—the individual does not recognize them as familiar; instead she experiences each one as new and painful. Over the years, many of our patients have described such thought patterns.

Once these toxic thoughts set in, they are difficult to dispel. Ultimately, the only way the individual feels that she can halt the mental torment is to engage in an eating- or weight-related behavior, but no sooner does one worry fade than another takes its place. While her question of "Have I gained weight?" reigns supreme, she either doesn't notice or won't admit that she is losing more than pounds—her vivaciousness, her creativity, her intellectual curiosity, her time with friends, and even her alertness behind the wheel of a car are all gradually diminishing. Each food worry is draining in itself, but the cumulative effect of many can wear her down to the point where she derives little, if any, enjoyment from life. Whether she is watching a movie, listening to music, doing homework, working out, or tidying her room, her food and weight worries take precedence, impeding her concentration and causing her distress. For a while, she can continue to earn high grades in school, but doing so requires more and more effort.

Unlike mild forms of dieting, an eating disorder has a profound effect on interpersonal relationships. Most social activities revolve around food and are just about the last things in which people with eating disorders—especially those with anorexia—want to take part. That was certainly true of Joanna. Looking back on middle school and high school, she says, "There was a part of me that longed for connection with others. But with my eating disorder, my anxiety about being with other people grew fiercer than ever, following me from one grade to another and making me a prisoner of my own thoughts. At lunchtime, when I was in the ninth grade, I used to head for the school coatroom, which was in the basement and empty at that time of day. There, I'd hide and eat my small cup of yogurt in tiny spoonfuls. After scraping the container clean with my spoon, I'd run my finger along the inner surface of the cup to catch every last drop. I could only imagine how embarrassed I'd be if someone came along and 'caught me' licking my fingers."

As we've often seen, a person struggling with bulimia likely realizes that her food habits are abnormal, but this is not always the case for those suffering from anorexia. When you express concern about the health of a child with anorexia, she is likely to insist that she's fine. Among the many feelings you might experience when she refuses food is an impulse to interpret her reluctance to eat as defiance. "Why doesn't she listen to us when we tell her she's too thin?" you want to know. "Does she really believe she's too heavy?" Yes. When she says, "I am not underweight" or "I'm fat," her words are true to her experience; at the same time, your questions are valid and natural reactions to the mismatch between your perceptions and hers.

Despite what your daughter would have you believe, whether she has gained weight is not her only question, but rather the only one she recognizes. Inside her lie other questions—difficult ones—that are unlikely to involve food. With professional care, she can explore her inner world and learn, with practice, to stop those painful food thoughts in their tracks.

## Looking at the Food and Beyond

There is more to eating disorders than first meets the eye. These illnesses consist of multiple layers, food-related behaviors being one. The first goal in helping your child with anorexia or bulimia is to prevent the medical complications that can result from unhealthy eating habits. To accomplish this, it is important for her to reach a healthier nutritional state.

To feed one's child—to help her grow into a strong, thriving adult—is a basic parental instinct; thus, upon seeing a child in dire nutritional straits, the first impulse can often be to address unhealthy food behaviors. While your eagerness to halt the problem is totally understandable, the process of helping someone to relinquish her food behaviors is complex and fraught with potential pitfalls. What's more, abnormal eating behaviors often have a disruptive impact on family life. A household hullabaloo over the child's eating habits frequently aggravates them. Tension mounts, making those unproductive "You will–I won't" types of quarrels hard to avoid, despite your best efforts. Any urging, cajoling, or coaxing aimed at convincing your child to stop her abnormal behaviors seems to fall upon deaf ears. That's one reason we suggest that you seek professional guidance. Working with a treatment team can give you the tools and emotional support necessary to approach your child and her eating disorder. Your child's clinicians will talk with you about what roles you will play in the treatment process. For adolescents in the early phase of the disorder, family-based (Maudsley) treatment, which helps parents take charge of nutritional restoration, has showed promising results and we will describe this intervention in more detail in Chapters 5 and 9.

Although the patient's safety (the prevention of medical complications resulting from the eating disorder) is paramount, it is also important to address the thoughts and emotions that can perpetuate the disorder. Weight control practices are an outward sign—an embodiment—of underlying emotions. Over time, no matter which treatment approach is prescribed, your child's reluctance to change her eating patterns makes it all the more crucial for you to remind yourself that food is only *one part* of the problem.

## Weight Worries Often Begin in Adolescence and Young Adulthood

Each stage of life comes with a wide range of challenges involving body image and self-esteem. Healthy children develop at different rates, with puberty (the time period in which they grow to sexual maturity) beginning in girls anywhere between the ages of 9 and 13. This is when the pituitary gland (a part of the brain) signals the ovaries to secrete estrogen and other hormones, which are instrumental in changing a girl's body into that of a woman. During puberty, girls reach nearly their adult height and develop curves. Breasts bud and grow, hips widen and become more rounded, and the body accrues some additional fat.

Many girls who prize thinness worry about the weight increase that accompanies this stage of life. When you talk to your daughter about this, it is wise to underscore that gaining weight at her age is normal and necessary for good health. Go ahead and tell her how you felt about bodily changes during your own teen years. As long as you are careful to take your daughter's concerns seriously, adding humor to your personal stories can help her relax enough to talk openly about her own feelings. Some girls compare their own developing physiques (usually negatively) with those of their peers. If your daughter has this tendency, you can help her appreciate that girls grow at different rates, that women are different shapes and sizes, and that all body contours deserve equal respect. Other girls are concerned about premenstrual weight gain, and to address this, you can explain that the few added pounds are due to fluid retention, an experience shared by many women.

Without adequate nutrition, a girl's body is unable to initiate menstruation. If she has already passed through menarche (first menses) when her nutritional status begins to suffer, her periods can stop or become less regular. Thus, in the event that your daughter is underweight and not menstruating, it is important that you consult her doctor—the sooner, the better.

Boys enter puberty a couple of years later than girls, accounting at least in part for some preteen girls being taller and seeming more grown-up than their male counterparts. During puberty, boys shoot up in height. While female puberty leads to an increase in fat—particularly in the abdomen, hips, buttocks, and thighs—males put on muscle mass, and their shoulders get bigger in comparison to their hips. Boys who start puberty later than their peers are vulnerable to feeling inadequate, especially if they are teased by other guys and rebuffed by girls.

Adolescence is a time of intense emotions and fleeting moods. In addition, growth in the brain enables a teen to search for her own values and lifestyle, which are not necessarily the ones her parents had in mind for her. Academic commitments and friendships often hold center stage in her life as her thirst for independence pulls her one way and her need for security pulls her another. Parent-child tiffs about the use of the car or about how late she can stay out with friends are typical at this stage. While the journey of adolescence is trying under the best of circumstances, it can become harrowing when laced with additional stress, such as the death or illness of a family member, parental divorce, or family financial loss.

Eating problems run rampant on college campuses, where many young adults are living away from home for the first time. Meeting people, getting along with one or more roommates, peer pressure, academic requirements, and perhaps competition on the playing field or working a part-time job can leave many students isolated, overwhelmed, and vulnerable to developing an eating disturbance.

The tradition of eating at structured times and locations has waned in this country in favor of downing small portions in various locations throughout the day, depending on one's schedule,

## What Is Body Dysmorphic Disorder?

Body dysmorphic disorder is a mental condition involving preoccupation with an aspect of physical appearance that does not involve body size and shape. An individual with this disorder may constantly worry about her skin, hair, nose, eyes, or teeth. As you know, patients with anorexia and bulimia have difficulties in the way they experience their bodies and suffer from repeated thoughts and driven behaviors. So do people with body dysmorphic disorder. Perhaps, for example, your daughter is ashamed of her complexion, checking her face in the mirror many times a day and declaring it "hideous." Although no one else considers her "ugly," chances are she is unable to take in reassurance. Instead, her obsession with her "defect" takes charge of her life. Some individuals who dwell on a perceived physical imperfection decide to have it "fixed" through plastic surgery; often, however, they are dissatisfied with the results of their first surgery and opt for more. A higher percentage of males are afflicted with body dysmorphic disorder than with anorexia or bulimia. Some people have both an eating disorder and body dysmorphic disorder.

and this trend is pronounced on college campuses. If a student is disinclined to eat in the dormitory cafeteria, she can order take-out or have pizza delivered, even in the middle of the night. For someone with unstructured eating patterns and round-the-clock access to the foods of her choice, it becomes all too easy to lose track of what is healthy and thereby fall prey to an eating problem.

## What Are Her Food and Weight Worries Accomplishing?

Individuals with eating disorders channel emotional turmoil into worries about calories and grams of fat or carbohydrates. This funneling of emotional issues into weight struggles is not necessarily a function of conscious deliberation. Some patients in the throes of an eating disorder, particularly those with anorexia nervosa, don't have a clue that their agony over eating a meal reflects conflicts or emotions about something else; due at least in part to the effects of starvation, they are unlikely to acknowledge the *existence* of an underlying "something else," much less identify it. People with bulimia nervosa, as well as those with binge eating disorder, tend to be aware of some of the emotions that lead to a binge but nevertheless feel powerless to change their behaviors. During the course of treatment, many patients become increasingly attuned to their inner selves and able to reflect on the feelings underlying their food and weight concerns.

We have learned a great deal about eating disorders from people who have recovered and shared their insights. Because every individual's situation is different and complex, we find it useful to talk about the potential functions of eating disorders in terms of themes that have emerged from professional work with patients and their families. Within the framework of each theme is a great deal of individual variation.

## Keeping Difficult Feelings at Bay

An eating disorder can function to take the person's mind off difficult emotions or decrease the intensity of these emotions. For example, consider an adolescent girl who is sometimes excluded by her friends. In an effort to be accepted, she may start to diet; disordered eating behavior could represent her attempt to escape the disappointment or anger she feels about her troubled friendships or her effort to fit in with what others are doing. If her dieting takes on increasing importance to her and serves as a way for her to cope with her feelings about friendship, it might evolve into an illness.

For some people, an eating disorder can offer diversion from a whole cauldron of emotions or from emotions that may have accumulated or festered, unacknowledged, over time. Even well-adjusted adults sometimes find it trying to come to terms with mixed or conflicted feelings. For teens—who have not yet developed an adult repertoire of intellectual and emotional skills—sorting out ambivalence can be enormously difficult and made all the more challenging by the mood swings and irritability that are part of adolescence. The experience of inner emptiness, which is often intense and enduring, can be particularly hard to recognize and name, much less fill in a healthy way.

For boys and men, our culture has traditionally prescribed strength, bravery, accomplishment, and initiative. From a very young age, boys absorb expectations such as "Men don't cry," and "Don't be a mama's boy"; for many, expressing sadness, fear, or hurt is to risk ridicule, if not rejection. Societal pressure to conform to an image of invulnerability can leave men feeling alone and unsupported, and some dwell on their bodies to avoid what is going on within.

## Feeling Worthy

Individuals with eating disorders are dissatisfied not merely with their bodies but, more often than not, with other aspects of themselves as well. Some people with these illnesses seem to dislike themselves through and through, right down to the deepest core of their being. In helping patients explore their feelings, we sometimes reflect their words back to them; thus, if a patient calls herself "a nothing," we'd query, "You think of yourself as nothing?" The authenticity of patients' self-statements was driven home by one young woman we were seeing who retorted, "I didn't say I'm nothing. I said I'm *a* nothing." Through her eyes, her nothingness was finite, absolute, and nonnegotiable.

A person's feelings of inadequacy can target one area of her life or many. For example, it is not uncommon for a girl who is struggling to make friends to also perceive herself as inept in the classroom, in her after-school job at the clothing store, or on the soccer field. Sometimes viewing oneself as inferior or incompetent snowballs, spreading from one skill set to another. For an individual who feels she is "not good enough," weight loss often represents an effort to show that she is capable or worthy. Although she isn't necessarily aware of it, her disorder can serve as a way to feel special, to keep her family united, to compete with her siblings or mother, or to connect with her mother or father.

## Becoming One's Own Person

In navigating the journey between childhood and adulthood, adolescents strive to establish their individuality. A question every boy or girl has heard from early childhood—"What do you want to be when you grow up?"—now carries new meaning. What makes "me" me? What is my niche? How do I get there? Processing the feelings involved in charting one's future has never been easy. Ironically, the increasing number of opportunities that have opened to many women over the last couple of decades can make it harder than ever for a girl to set realistic academic and job-related goals.

As trying as it is to map one's educational and career future, it is just as difficult to adjust to one's new sexual maturity, to cultivate healthy relationships, and to weather the waves of inner conflict that come with increasing independence from parents. Given all the changes girls face during adolescence, it is not surprising that some diet as an attempt (albeit not necessarily a conscious, premeditated one) to slow down the clock and get relief from the demands that seem to bombard them from all directions. If a girl's weight loss continues and becomes relentless, she might become more childlike, perhaps as a way of saying that she needs more time to get her bearings before moving forward in her journey toward adulthood.

During adolescence, boys also face challenges related to sexuality and relationships, and some turn to body concerns in an attempt to cope. Boys, however, tend to focus more on building muscle than on losing weight, and for most, this is a positive way to care for their bodies and feel stronger. For a few, however, the drive to gain muscle goes too far. The last 15 to 20 years have seen the emergence of muscle dysmorphia, which almost always affects men. Many who suffer from this condition are accomplished

# What Does History Tell Us?

The last half-century has seen more eating disorders than any other period in history. Researchers from various disciplines are making progress in analyzing this trend. Some of our clues have come from looking at how our culture has evolved.

Today's American lifestyle differs markedly from that of a century ago, when rotund, matronly bodies were the norm. Back then, girls started menstruating at age 15 or 16 and remained virgins until they married, usually in their early 20s. Today girls typically experience menarche just after they turn 12 and, on average, become sexually active shortly before age 16. While physical growth has sped up, rates of intellectual and emotional development have not. Today's sixth- and seventh-grade girls often look grown-up, but like children, they still think in concrete terms, sometimes see the world only from their own perspective, and don't always apply the levels of discernment needed to ensure well-being.

In the 1960s and 1970s, sexual taboos began to lift, making girls vulnerable not only to unwanted pregnancy and sexually transmitted diseases, but also to consumerism and glorified images of sex on TV and film.

Congress's 1972 approval of Title IX, which prohibited discrimination on the basis of gender, afforded women unprecedented professional, educational, and athletic opportunities. This success heralded a fitness movement, as well as a cultural emphasis on women being more autonomous than ever before. Girls and women who were inclined to control their weight had two culturally accepted ways to do so: diet and physical activity.

Today, the adolescent search for identity is laced with additional hurdles associated with substance abuse, a powerful mass media, and commercialism. By learning how to navigate the journey of an eating disorder with your daughter or son, you and your family have an opportunity to confront these challenges directly.

bodybuilders who perceive themselves as too small and become obsessed with the pursuit of muscle, often subjecting themselves to extreme workouts and ingesting unusually large amounts of protein. In addition, some boys and men with muscle dysmorphia take anabolic steroids (synthetic hormones derived from testosterone); although these drugs are highly effective in building muscle, they are also addictive; have a negative impact on the liver, heart, and reproductive systems; and often lead to irritability or aggression.

## Strengthening Your Relationship with Your Child

We sometimes find that a child's need and her parent's response to it are not neatly aligned. Often the question is not whether a parent tries or cares but whether the youngster perceives parental efforts as meeting her needs. When it comes to your interpretation of what your daughter is feeling, is there a communication gap? As you interact with her on a day-to-day basis, think about the following: What do her words and behaviors tell you about her inner world? Depending on her age, what questions can you ask her to get a clearer sense of how she is feeling emotionally?

Intuition plays a role in gauging your response to fit your youngster's need. As an example, consider an elementary school child who comes home distraught because her classmates are excluding her from recess activities. Your first reaction might be to phone the school. Although your call would be well intended, it is likely that what your child really wants—whether or not she says so verbally—is for you to listen to her; to help her sort out what is happening at recess; to work with her on solving the problem; and to affirm that she is a valuable, competent individual who deserves to have friends. As we work with parents, we help them strive for a closer match between what their youngster is asking for and the responses they can offer.

Your empathy can make a huge difference in the way your daughter sees herself and copes with challenges. Let's say, for example, that your eighth grader comes home after tryouts for the school play, eats very little dinner, and finally divulges that she had wanted to audition but "chickened out" just before it was her turn. Empathic responses include the following:

- "I'm sorry. I know you really wanted a part."
- "I imagine it felt scary to think that everyone would be watching you."
- "It's understandable that you were jittery. Standing up alone on stage is really, really difficult, and this was your first time trying."
- "That sensation of butterflies in the stomach is a tough one."
- "Watching your best friend audition right before you must have been really hard."
- "I know it was not easy to tell me what happened, but I'm really glad you did."

Perhaps you can share with her some fear you have felt, whether it involves stage fright, social shyness, or anxiety about trying something new. By disclosing your own life experiences, you can help bring her out of her shell and learn more about her inner world.

## What if She Has Disordered Eating but Won't Tell Me?

People with eating problems are very sensitive about their food-related behaviors and do not like to discuss them. Although you see your child's food habits as dangerous, she clings to them tenaciously, perhaps as a last-ditch effort to cope. Someone who binges and purges tend to feel disgusted with herself, her body, or both, and goes to great lengths to keep her behaviors a secret. One reason a child with anorexia resists advice to eat more is that she feels more disciplined or more accomplished as she loses weight, but this perception is likely to fade as her illness progresses. In addition, her thinness can at first garner positive feedback from peers: "You've lost weight. You look terrific. How'd you do it?" Yet as her weight plummets, the compliments will end.

If you suspect your child has disordered eating, you should continue to educate yourself about eating disorders, to become aware of potential resources for help in your community, and to quietly observe and monitor the intensity of her unhealthy attitudes and behaviors. We find that some children *will* talk to their parents about their eating patterns. Has your youngster been dieting? What weight-loss methods does she use? Is she distraught about her body size or her food habits? Often, the severity of her eating behaviors (restricting her intake or bingeing and purging) becomes the factor that determines whether she needs professional treatment. If her attitudes about her body and her food behaviors are interfering with her ability to concentrate, see friends, and enjoy life, a visit to her primary care physician or pediatrician is in order.

Perhaps your daughter will tell you next to nothing about her food habits. Or you might be unsure whether she has given you all the information you need in order to determine whether to seek outside help. Please don't take her reticence personally; whether or not she tells you everything is not a commentary on your merit as a parent. Nevertheless, some eating disordered individuals find it easier to confide in someone outside their family, such as a teacher, school nurse or guidance counselor, or doctor. An evaluation by a primary care physician often includes a referral to a nutritionist. Some families seek nutritional counseling before going to a primary care physician, and this is workable as long as there is communication between the two professionals.

People with eating disorders struggle profoundly with issues related to body size and shape, but they are not the only ones who have food and weight concerns. Many individuals face some of the same challenges as those with anorexia and bulimia but to a lesser degree. We've explained that the burgeoning of an eating disorder does not involve behavior alone but many thoughts and emotions as well. Thus, you'll want to know about the warning signs of these illnesses, a topic we'll address in the next chapter.

## CHAPTER 3

# Spotting the Warning Signs

If you have a hunch that your child may have an eating disorder, knowing what to look for is key. The signs of these illnesses vary from one individual to another. Some of the potentially frontline clues—such as changes in weight and eating behaviors—can be harder to recognize than one might expect. That's why it is also helpful to be aware that other characteristics, such as perfectionism, mood issues, and anxiety, are associated with eating disorders. In this chapter we will outline the various warning signs of anorexia and bulimia and introduce some of the thoughts and feelings that are likely contributing to your child's behavior.

## Trying to Interpret the Signs of Anorexia

Early in the school year, Victor and Adrienne came in to tell us about their 13-year-old daughter, Shelley. "She's a straight-A student with a wonderful sense of humor," began her mom. "She has always loved to draw, and two years ago, her animal cartoons stole the show at a local arts and crafts festival. She now keeps a sketch pad in her backpack so that she can capture special moments for her school newspaper. Until recently, she was a healthy eater. But over the summer, she changed. She'd never been overweight, and though I was puzzled when she announced she was going on a diet, it never occurred to me that it would reach such an extreme."

Adrienne went on to explain some of the challenges inherent in recognizing an eating disorder. "At first," she recalled, "Shelley took pride in her weight loss and received a ton of praise. Other moms in the neighborhood kept telling me she looked 'great.' At that time, I didn't know all the signs of eating disorders. But soon it became frighteningly clear that my daughter was too skinny. A couple of my longtime friends expressed concern that Shelley might have anorexia, and a few days later, the pediatrician confirmed my worst fears."

Although weight loss is an important warning sign of anorexia, the course of the illness varies from one person to another and is not always obvious. Some patients look strikingly thin when we first meet them, whereas others are severely ill without appearing skeletal. Healthy children grow at all different rates. Due to increases in height, anorexia can initially show up not as weight *loss*, but as a delay in weight *gain*. Changes in height and weight are often less obvious to family members who live with the child than to relatives who see her infrequently, so it is important to be alert to both weight changes and other signs of anorexia.

Victor recalled clues that he had observed in his daughter. "She used to eat the foods on her plate in the same order at every meal—when she ate meals, that is. Often she'd pick at her food but eat very little. The strained expression on her face as she arranged and rearranged her food worried me; this seemed very different from the 'picky eating' that lots of children show and usually outgrow. Shelley would spread jelly on a slice of toast, scrape it off, and reapply it, repeating this process 15 times before she'd take a bite. It was agonizing to watch. I remember making pancakes for breakfast. Shelley put one on her plate, cut it up into miniscule pieces, and took more than an hour to eat them." Many parents we've seen report these kinds of behaviors in their children with anorexia.

## Does She Want to Be Around Food but Not Want to Eat It?

"One summer evening," said Victor, "I invited both of my daughters out for ice cream. Shelley seemed very enthusiastic—that is, until we arrived at the dairy bar, when she ordered nothing. Had that been an isolated incident, I might not have worried. But there was more and more evidence that Shelley was not herself. She'd never expressed a whit of interest in going to the supermarket; now she was eager to help with the shopping. I'd wheel the cart up and down the aisles while Shelley handled one product after another, checking each label for calories and fat grams. Once, I noticed 'goose bumps' along her arms. With her weight loss, she had become very sensitive to cold, and while the store's air-conditioning was a relief to many shoppers, it was too much for her. As I was about to suggest that she wear a jacket next time, I was struck by her undivided attention to cereal boxes, even as she shivered. I offered to buy whichever brand she preferred, but she said she wanted none of them."

Adrienne noticed something else about her daughter that was way out of character. "Shelley had a newfound fascination with cooking and talked a great deal about recipes. Absorbed in my cookbooks, she'd circle dishes that looked appetizing and fun to make. I remember once, when she made lasagna for dinner, she encouraged all of us to eat our fill but said she wasn't hungry and didn't want any. It was the same way if she baked desserts. When we hosted holiday dinners, she immersed herself in preparing for these events, something she never did when she was healthy. And once the guests arrived, she kept incredibly busy, heating this or that in the microwave, serving the various foods, and assisting with cleanup. If she did join the others at the table, she moved her food around on her plate, eating next to nothing." In describing these events to us, Adrienne and Victor realized that Shelley's helpfulness around food was likely masking her reluctance to eat.

## Does She Eat with Anyone?

Adrienne found it troubling that Shelley began to shun her friends if their plans included food. "There was this Sunday morning when Shelley was excited about going to a movie with a couple of class-mates. But upon learning that her friends were planning to stop for pizza afterward, Shelley changed her mind about the matinee and stayed home. She also had a change of heart about sleepovers. Until three months ago, she considered them fun. As far as I knew, she seemed comfortable with the popcorn and other treats that went along with these occasions. Once the anorexia set in, however, it was a different story: she wanted nothing to do with overnights."

Over the years, we have found that many patients with anorexia do eat—albeit very selectively—but have great difficulty doing so in the company of other people. The preference for solitude dur-ing meals results, at least in part, from the embarrassment these individuals feel about how and what they ingest. Some patients, perhaps as an outgrowth of semistarvation, experience unusual taste preferences and therefore eat foods or combinations of foods that are considered odd. Other potential habits include licking the plate, foraging, shredding a quarter of a muffin and ingesting it bit by bit, or perhaps picking out the raisins to eat and leaving the rest. Individuals allow themselves so little food that they tend to savor every bite and avoid anything—including conversation—that is likely to distract them from these few precious moments of plea-sure. Hence, many eat alone.

## Is She a Vegetarian?

One Saturday, Victor grilled hamburgers for dinner. "His barbecue 'specials' had always been a hit with both our daughters," recalled Adrienne. "I figured that if there was one meal Shelley would eat, this would be it. I was wrong. It didn't surprise me when she refused to come to the dinner table. That had been going on for at least a week. So I delivered the meal to her room, but she said she wasn't hungry. When I offered to keep her hamburger warm in the oven for her to eat later, I was flabbergasted when she replied, 'I don't eat meat anymore.' "

It is not unusual for an individual with an eating disorder to say she's a vegetarian. She'll be quick to remind you that vegetarian diets are healthy or she'll say she's committed to animal welfare and objects to the slaughter of livestock. What she probably won't tell you is that she has an additional or different reason for becoming a vegetarian; that is, because of her intense anguish about gaining weight, she is trying to avoid the calories and fat grams she associates with meat. If she is struggling with food and weight worries, the likelihood is that she'll be reluctant to replace animal-derived calories with plant-derived ones.

Does every vegetarian develop an eating disorder? Absolutely not. Your child becoming a vegetarian is no cause for alarm but simply for increased watchfulness. If her vegetarianism is accompanied by other signs of eating disorders, you should seek medical evaluation.

## Will She Be Honest with Me About Not Eating Enough?

Victor and Adrienne began to notice that their daughter was less than truthful with them about food. "I was aghast that my own daughter was lying to me," said Adrienne. She and Victor agreed that coping with Shelley's dishonesty was one of the most stressful parts of their journey. "If allowed to eat breakfast without supervision," reported Victor, "she would drop one or two flakes of cereal into a bowl, add milk, and depart for school, leading us to believe she had eaten. Other mornings, she'd promise to have breakfast on her way to school but never follow through."

Adrienne, too, felt duped. "Until I discovered my daughter's tricks," she said, "I assumed she was having lunch at school, but that wasn't happening, and I grew terribly worried. Finally, Shelley's best friend, her mom, and I collaborated to track Shelley's habit of skipping her midday meal. Upon hearing through the grapevine that Shelley had not eaten at school, I'd try to talk with her about it, but she'd then concoct her own version of the story, trying to make me believe it was a one-time occurrence."

If circumstances make it impossible to avoid meals with other people, those with anorexia often sit at the table and "pretend" to eat. Shelley kept her utensils busy, at times raising a forkful partway toward her mouth and then lowering it. Other people shuttle food—often by way of a napkin—into a pocket, up a shirtsleeve, or into the folds of a blanket on their laps. By the end of a meal, these individuals have managed to empty their plates without ingesting a single morsel.

The tendency to distort the truth, create false impressions, or lie about food intake is common among many with anorexia. Individuals describe a fear of weight gain so overwhelming that any perceived threat of losing control of the disordered behaviors becomes frightening, even unbearable. Therefore, patients resort to frantic efforts to continue their pursuit of thinness.

We encouraged Victor and Adrienne to aim at understanding their daughter's dishonesty and to avoid pressing her to "fess up." If there's anything more painful to these individuals than admitting to their food disturbance, it's admitting to the disturbance *and* to lying about it. Some are ashamed of themselves or afraid their parents will brand them a failure for their disordered eating, their dishonesty, or both. Some stretch the truth because they do not want to hurt people or because they cannot yet acknowledge—to themselves, much less to anyone else—that they have a problem. If your child is fibbing, you'd be wise to create an atmosphere based on mutual respect in which to talk with her about her unhealthy habits. Keep in mind that building a dialogue is a gradual process, and try to be patient with yourself as well as with her. However, if you suspect that she is engaging in severe restriction of food intake or is suffering from medical complications such as fainting spells, then it is important to seek help, even if she does not agree.

## The Challenges of Recognizing Bulimia

Carol first came to see us a couple of years ago, shortly before her daughter became our patient. "Robin was a superb student and wanted to become a historian," said her mom. "I found out about her eating disorder when she was a rising college sophomore. She had always loved sports and was spending the summer at home coaching a children's soccer team in addition to working in the public library. When she first moved home from the dorm, she looked as fit and athletic as ever. She said she was on a diet and ate rather lightly at mealtimes, but that was nothing unusual for her. When cousins came over for dinner, she participated in the conversation and seemed to eat as much as she ever did, but something seemed different about her that I couldn't quite pinpoint. She'd always been on the reserved side, but now there was a sullen, irritable edge to her quietness. The more I tried to talk to her to find out if anything was wrong, the more she seemed to shut me out.

"I'll never forget the Friday when I discovered her bulimia. It was a light day at work, so I headed home an hour early. As I fumbled through my purse for my house keys, I glanced through the glass pane on the back door and was dumbfounded. The kitchen looked like a cyclone had struck it. Standing at the counter was Robin, eating. She didn't see me, and I quietly left to do errands. I returned home a couple of hours later to a spotless kitchen and a daughter glued to the television, as morose and isolated as she'd been every evening for a week. I didn't broach the subject of her eating because I didn't know what to say.

"That was the only time I saw Robin in the course of a binge. However, a couple of days later, large amounts of food seemed to vanish from the fridge, and there was no doubt in my mind that my daughter had eaten them. It wasn't just the bingeing I worried about. It was also her hurried visits to the bathroom, particularly after meals. I had a hunch that Robin was vomiting. I figured that she might be engaging in more than one kind of purging behavior, so I kept my eyes open for empty laxative and diuretic containers but did not see any.

"I didn't like playing the role of detective within my own home, so I went to see a therapist to sort out my feelings and put together an approach to my daughter's disorder. It was unnerving to me that, until I'd glimpsed the binge, I'd had absolutely no idea that my daughter had the problem. How long had Robin been suffering from her disordered eating? Had she told anyone about it, or had she suffered in silence?"

## Should I Have Discovered Her Bulimia Sooner?

Carol is not the only parent who has asked us this. In fact, it is one of the questions most frequently raised by moms and dads whose children have a bingeing and purging problem. Our answer for the most part is "no." Multiple factors make this illness very elusive. Parents who have personal concerns about food and weight often have a hard time recognizing the same problem in their children. Some parents feel proud of their children for losing weight, particularly at the beginning of a "successful" diet. Carol can attest to that. "Robin was overweight as a child and well into her teens. In the 10th grade, she was lonesome and hoped that losing weight would be a ticket to popularity. I was pleased that she had the gumption to stick to her diet. After she trimmed down and joined the swim team, she continued to watch her food intake; I think she was afraid that added weight would trigger the teasing and rejection she'd suffered in the past."

When a young person embarks on a weight-loss effort, it is extremely hard (if not impossible) to predict what course it will take. Many diets are short-lived. When a diet does head in a dangerous direction and eventually becomes a way of life, as it did for Robin, the changes can happen gradually and be well hidden. Occasionally individuals leave clues, such as a mess in the bathroom, but these are difficult to pick up on. In fact, because of their shame and embarrassment, people who binge and purge are careful to keep any signs of the disorder hidden from others. Individuals with bulimia can develop scars or bruises on the back of their hands from induced vomiting. Some patients, however, describe vomiting "almost at will," without using their hands. Others ingest a substance such as ipecac to stimulate vomiting.

As hard as it is to detect a child's problem when she lives at home, the challenges for parents multiply if she is away at boarding school or college. It is not unusual for an individual to have both anorexia and bulimia, either at the same time or separately. Some patients start out with anorexia and eventually develop bulimia. Cigarette smoking is not unusual among adolescent girls who want to be thin and may signal a potential risk of an eating disorder. Robin relates to this. "From 10th through 12th grades, I restricted my food intake," she says. "I was really serious about curbing my appetite and staving off unwanted pounds, so I started smoking cigarettes in my senior year and never told Mom. Just before entering college, I stepped up my smoking as an 'insurance policy' against gaining weight.

"When I arrived at college, the dormitory felt worlds apart from life at home. My diet led to bingeing, and my bingeing led to vomiting. Initially, I was pleased to have found a way to eat what I wanted without gaining weight. So began a vicious cycle that I hid for eight months and would have continued to conceal had my mom not seen me bingeing on that fateful Friday in June."

## Are There Signs of Turmoil?

An individual who feels overwhelmed does not necessarily want her parents or others to know it. It is not unusual for someone experiencing emotional difficulties to go for months or longer without confiding in anyone. At least for a while, she'll continue to perform well in school or at work so that to all outward appearances she's fine.

A number of problems, either individually or in combination, serve as signs of turmoil. The binge–purge cycle is one; stealing is another. An individual who feels almost beyond hope might repeatedly take money, food, or objects unrelated to food. Also indicative of turmoil is the habit of cutting; the individual pierces her skin—perhaps her inner wrist, thigh, or abdomen—with a sharp object, often causing a bit of bleeding but not serious harm. Maybe she perceives her cutting as an outlet for pent-up anxieties, anger, or other emotions that she has difficulty dispelling in healthier ways. Maybe she feels down on herself, alone, or empty inside. Cutting, which sometimes coexists with eating disorders and sometimes with other mental illnesses, can be a call for help but is generally not an attempt at suicide. With treatment, patients who cut themselves often let up on this behavior as they learn healthier ways to cope with stress.

Some express turmoil through alcohol or drug abuse. An eating disorder results not only in emotional pain but also in grave health and safety risks; the same is true of substance use disorder. To suffer from both illnesses, whether simultaneously or sequentially, is a formidable challenge to overcome.

## Warning Signs of Eating Disorders in Guys

If you are the mom or dad of a boy or young man with an eating disorder, you are not alone. An estimated 10 percent of individuals with anorexia or bulimia and 40 percent of those with binge eating disorder are male. Homosexual males are more likely to develop eating disorders than their heterosexual counterparts. Eating disorders are as perilous for men as for women; in fact, the signs of these illnesses and their medical consequences are similar in both sexes.

Is your son critical of his physique? Disliking one's size or shape can help set the stage for unhealthy behaviors to develop in boys as well as girls. Males who berate their bodies (and many do) are apt to focus on their chest, shoulders, and biceps. Many aspire to the lean and muscular look that defines our mainstream culture's idealized image of masculinity. Some boys who are overweight diet, while those who are below average in weight often wish to get bigger. Because anorexia and bulimia are commonly perceived as a women's illness, many boys and men understandably feel stigmatized and are highly secretive, making their problems all the harder to recognize.

## Signs Common to Anorexia and Bulimia

It is so hard to know if your child is headed toward developing an eating disorder. Unfortunately there is no sure way to predict her path, but a number of signs, in addition to her food-related behaviors, provide some clues. If any of these are a concern, it would be best to share your observations with your child's most trusted clinician. Having her checked sooner rather than later can allow the illness to be detected and treated before it becomes severe.

## Does She Exercise Too Much?

Chances are you're familiar with the lifelong benefits of physical activity; exercise reduces the risk of heart disease and some cancers, helps keep bones strong, and promotes an overall good mood. For many, playing on a team or striving to achieve an athletic goal can be very rewarding. Some have difficulties knowing how much physical activity is enough and often push themselves unreasonably hard. Excessive physical activity is often solitary, and if an at-risk individual plays on a team, she is likely to spend considerable time working out by herself in addition to participating in games and group practice sessions. Overwhelmed by unwanted "I have to exercise" thoughts, she tends to feel that the only way she can relieve the anguish of such demands is to meet them. For every goal she accomplishes, she sets her eyes higher, continually increasing her activity level as her "train harder" mind-set begins to consume her life. Is your daughter exercising longer or more frequently than she has in the past? Is she able to stop? Does she get uncomfortable if a workout is delayed or if the necessary equipment isn't available? Is she reluctant to skip a day or two of exercise to make time for other opportunities? Has she refused to go out with friends because she "has to" run? Does she try to work out even when she is ill or hurt? All of these attitudes and behaviors are worrisome.

Excessive, driven exercise is not, by itself, a sign of an eating disorder but rather a red flag that your child's doctor needs to know about. These behaviors are a signal that your concerns have reached a point where professional assessment is advisable. The individual who has begun to engage in too much activity may look healthy. And because she does not see her exercise as a problem or doesn't want anything to interfere with it, she's likely to play it down. In fact, upon hearing your daughter insist that she's fine, you may find yourself thinking, "Maybe my worries that she's exercising too much are silly. After all, she's a straight-A student and an excellent athlete." Although such self-doubts are understandable, please don't give in to them. Instead, try to reassure yourself that your concerns about your child's activity level are reasonable and that it's time to share them with her clinician. If your daughter is an adolescent or adult with a primary care provider of her own, you won't necessarily be invited to her appointments, and there's a chance she'll have a physical exam without mentioning her exercise habits. In such situations, you would be wise to provide the clinician with information that will help her make an accurate assessment.

At particular risk for eating disorders are women and men who compete at the top level in activities that attach special importance to body shape and size. These include gymnastics, figure skating, dance, and crew; wrestlers compete within weight categories and are also vulnerable. Even those who participate at more amateur levels of these sports can run the risk of developing eating disorders.

Whether or not they are competitive athletes, girls and women who exercise to an extreme may compromise their health. Overtraining, combined with poor nutrition, can set off a complex series of hormonal changes that interferes with menstruation and potentially leads to bone loss, meaning that the athlete's bones become fragile, weak, and prone to fracture, a condition known as *osteoporosis*.

Overexercise often goes along with disordered eating. Now 28, Robin describes how physical activity became a kind of torment. "Initially, swimming on my high school team was pleasurable, but the more I worried about food and weight, the less I liked the sport. When I arrived at college, I started a rigorous early morning jogging routine and continued to swim to stay in shape. By Thanksgiving, I dreaded my daily laps, which I'd tripled in number since early September. To accomplish that entire distance felt grueling but absolutely nonnegotiable; something inside me mandated that I swim every lap with no excuses. I was afraid that if I slacked off on my exercise—even for one day—I'd gain weight, a 'risk' I experienced as intolerable."

## Is Nothing Ever Good Enough?

One quality common among many people with eating disorders is a tendency toward perfectionism. These individuals impose extremely high personal expectations and standards on themselves. As a result, they strive to be the best in everything they do, often to the point of enormous personal cost. The world of perfectionism, where rules are strict and mistakes intolerable, can be a hard place to live. Individuals tend to think and behave in all-or-nothing terms instead of selecting a middle ground. Through their eyes, achieving anything less than 100 percent spells failure.

Many perfectionists are people pleasers, who are eager for approval and go to great lengths to earn it. So focused are they on accommodating others, they are apt to overlook their own needs. Furthermore, the constant strain of pleasing other people can eventually grow wearing or overwhelming. Much can be said for compliance in children; however, if they comply to the point of agreeing with everything requested of them and are unduly careful to do no wrong, then the question is whether they are capable of making their own decisions.

Because perfectionists shoot for unrealistic goals and operate only in high gear, they often set themselves up for disappointment; their tendency to measure their self-worth based on their achievements makes them all the more vulnerable to feeling down on themselves. In addition, many are highly sensitive to criticism and sometimes personalize or overreact to benign feedback. Even if you are not demanding, a child inclined toward perfectionism can construe your comments as such. Thus, if you praise your track star for doing well in practice, she may interpret "well" as not well enough.

Charlene knows about perfectionism firsthand. She came in to talk to us a few days before we started working with her son, who suffered from anorexia and bulimia. She opened by pointing to

Alan's many strengths, including his high intelligence, his affinity for math, and his helpfulness around the house. As a 10th grader in a competitive school, Alan took all honors courses, and his grades were outstanding. "He studies very hard," said Charlene, "and gets mad at himself if he can't do something right the first time. In the fall, he earned all As except for a B+ in Spanish. I considered this report card superb and told him so, but he disagreed, claiming that he was 'stupid' in languages."

We are not, by any means, saying that all young perfectionists develop eating disorders nor that only eating disordered individuals are perfectionists. These illnesses are complex and most likely arise from a combination of factors, personality being only one. What is important here is your awareness of the potential association between perfectionism and eating disorders. Observing perfectionism in your child is not, by itself, a call to action but rather a gentle heads-up. When perfectionism is present alongside one or more of the other characteristics of eating disturbances, or in tandem with problematic eating behaviors, seeking a professional opinion is in order.

## Is She Cautious? How Cautious?

Some people with eating disorders are apprehensive and constrained. It is not unusual for someone to follow a structured daily routine, experiencing any interruption in her schedule as highly stressful. Even before our patient Sonya developed her illness, she struggled with ruthless anxiety. "I was always afraid without knowing exactly why. As a child, I used to engage in a lot of counting routines. When putting away laundry, I had to fold so many pieces one way, so many another way, and always in the same order—first blouses, then pants, then socks. At night, I'd become afraid that the stove was still on. Only through checking it 16 times at precise two-minute intervals would I believe that the house wouldn't catch fire."

Although Sonya was exceptionally bright, she was painfully inhibited and reluctant to join other children in play. "I felt like my body as well as my personality were out of bounds and that I had to rein myself in," she says. "In elementary school, I used to spend recess tense and panicky. While the other kids romped on the playground, I stood on the sidelines, waiting intently for the bell to ring so that I could return to the safety of my desk."

Anxieties such as Sonya's are common in individuals with eating disorders and are often present prior to the onset of starving, bingeing, or vomiting. She started to diet in sixth grade and kept right on going, funneling her anxieties into an obsession with calories and weight and subsequently developing anorexia.

It is important to remember that most anxious children never develop eating disorders. Girls and boys experience fears and insecurities of different kinds and to all different degrees; preschoolers often have security blankets or bedtime rituals to help themselves feel safe. Shyness also occurs on a continuum, with some people experiencing more than others. Who hasn't felt self-conscious in a social situation, especially during adolescence? If you have an anxious child and begin to notice problematic eating behaviors, seek professional evaluation for an eating disorder.

## Has She Become More Moody?

As painful as it is to suffer from both an eating disorder and low moods, the combination is not unusual. That's what 19-year-old Theresa was facing when she came to us for help. "As a child, I was terribly insecure," she recalls, "and I experienced emotions—such as sorrow, hurt, anger, guilt, and powerlessness—very intensely. My negative thoughts and feelings about myself went deeper and lasted longer than the transient 'funks' that happen to just about everyone now and then. In high school, accomplishing even the smallest tasks and making even the most minor decisions felt overwhelming. Despite problems concentrating, I managed to earn fairly good grades and participated in sports. But my dark moods and mixed-up feelings affected every aspect of my life. In addition, I developed the binge-purge cycle, which followed me to college."

Depression, which often accompanies anorexia and bulimia, can start prior to the eating disorder or vice versa. Has your child

43

become more irritable or self-critical? If she has generally enjoyed spending time with friends and family, has that changed? Does she dislike her body or feel worse about herself than she has in the past? Some characteristics of depression, such as withdrawal from friends and feelings of inadequacy, are also features of eating disorders. When a person suffers from both illnesses and at least part of her wants help, it's possible she'll tell a family member, teacher, college residence adviser, or doctor about her depression without mentioning her unhealthy food habits. For that reason, among others, your mindfulness that depression and eating disorders often travel together will stand you and your family in good stead.

## Warning Signs in a Nutshell

Here are the frontline clues that say, "My child may have an eating disorder and needs to see her doctor for evaluation."

### Key Signs of Anorexia Nervosa

- She is extremely fearful of gaining weight, even if underweight.
- She strictly limits her food intake.
- She appears markedly thin.
- She shuffles food around on her plate without eating it, hides food in her napkin, and/or cuts food into tiny pieces.
- She is reluctant to eat with other people.
- She exercises to an extreme.
- She no longer has menstrual periods.
- She exhibits sensitivity to cold.
- She makes negative comments about her body size or shape.
- She suffers from insomnia.
- She is reluctant to be weighed.
- She has difficulty eating in a social setting.
- She exhibits increased school absenteeism.
- She is socially isolated.
- She has changed her diet (for example, is a new vegetarian).

### Key Signs of Bulimia Nervosa

- She is extremely fearful of gaining weight.
- She exercises to an extreme.
- She rushes to the bathroom after eating.
- She has scars on her hands (from self-induced vomiting).
- She makes negative comments about her body size or shape.
- She is reluctant to eat with friends or family.
- Food disappears from the refrigerator or cupboards.
- Food wrappers are hidden in her bedroom.
- Laxative wrappers and/or diuretic (water pill) containers are found in the house.

Some individuals show signs from both lists and suffer from aspects of both anorexia and bulimia.

## Putting the Clues Together

Whether you spot one sign of an eating disorder or many in your child, they do not confirm that she has an illness; that's where your doctor comes in. Generally speaking, no one warning sign in itself foretells an eating disorder; rather, it becomes part of a larger picture. We are often struck by the many issues and risk behaviors that are present in the patients with whom we consult. An illness consists of a number of dimensions, each of which the doctor will take into account as she blends the clues you have recognized into her findings to determine your child's diagnosis. In the next chapter, we will discuss how to find a physician to assess your son or daughter and what to expect from this health professional.

# PART II

# Toward Renewed Health: Treatment and Recovery

## CHAPTER 4

# What if She Shows Signs of an Eating Disorder?

"It was really scary," says Roberta, of the August before her daughter Serena's ninth-grade year. Now 24 and well on the road to recovery from anorexia, Serena also has vivid memories of that time period. Recently, mother and daughter looked back on that tumultuous summer, sharing their thoughts with each other and with us.

## Roberta's Perspective

"Serena always loved the outdoors. Until she was about 10, we used to go camping for a week every summer; she was quite the adventurer. She earned stellar grades in school, and though she was quiet, she'd open up with kids she knew well. In eighth grade, she befriended three classmates, and when she asked to spend July with them at a sleepaway computer program, I was excited for her. But when she came home, I could barely believe my eyes, much less think straight. What had happened to my beautiful, smart Serena? She'd been lean to begin with; now she looked entirely too skinny. The possibility that she had an eating disorder began to haunt me. I kept hoping there was some sensible explanation for the weight loss or that it was only a bad dream.

"It took me a couple of days to get my wits about me. It was wrenching to know that my daughter was hurting, yet when I reached out to her—telling her I loved her and asking how she was feeling—she was anything but talkative. Meanwhile, she ate like a bird and showed no interest in going outside, preferring to stay in her room. She was due to start high school in a few weeks, and I couldn't imagine sending her there in the condition she was in. Finally, she agreed to a medical checkup. 'Okay, if I have to,' she relented. 'But my health is fine.'

"I made an appointment with the pediatrician for the following day. Meanwhile, I went to the library and borrowed some books on eating disorders. I knew little about these illnesses and was afraid of what I might learn. What I did know was that now was not the time to give in to my fears. Serena needed help, and my first priority was to make that happen."

## Serena's Perspective

"It's hard to put that summer's experiences into a neat package, because that's not how they happened. Even now, they haven't completely fallen into place in my mind. Actually, my feelings were so jumbled that even if I'd wanted to sort them out, I wouldn't have had the vaguest idea how to go about it. Emotions were not on my radar back then. I really didn't know I had them, much less how to name them or what to do with them.

"Three classmates and I signed up for a sleepaway computer program in July. When camp started, I thought these girls were my friends. To this day, I don't know why they turned against me. When they joked around, I often missed the drift of their sarcasm. There was a fair amount of bantering and joshing, and they all knew how to make good comebacks. But I didn't, and I sensed that was because I was stupid. I didn't fit in; at least not the way they wanted me to. It was all very confusing. Looking back, I'd guess that my insecurity somehow drifted to thoughts about my body, even though I wasn't aware that this was happening.

"At the beginning of my diet, I wasn't married to it. In fact, I didn't feel strongly about it one way or another. At the time, I was grabbing at straws for anything that might account for the friendship problem or, better yet, correct it. For want of a better explanation, I somehow latched on to a half-baked idea that maybe I was too heavy. I had no idea how much I weighed when I started my diet, but that was beside the point. Looking back, I devoted so little forethought to the idea of reducing that I can scarcely call it a 'plan.' Being overweight seemed as good a guess as any for why they were treating me like an outcast. And if there was a chance—even a remote one—that a diet might make me popular, maybe it was worth a try.

"At the end of camp, there was a long bus ride home. My three former friends were in the bus too, but I didn't sit with them. Mom met me at the station. When she saw me, her jaw dropped. At the time, I hadn't a clue that I was developing an illness. I didn't start my diet with an intention to hurt myself; instead, I conceived it as a way to fix what was wrong with me. I wasn't sure exactly what was wrong with me; I just knew it was a lot."

## Getting a Medical Evaluation

If your child shows signs of an eating disorder (such as weight loss, dieting when there is no need, binge eating, purging), we suggest that she see her primary care physician or pediatrician for evaluation. Ambivalence about getting help is understandably common in patients with eating disorders, and some may even resist. They may deny they have a problem or admit to feeling unwell but continue to defend their eating habits. Many feel ashamed—of their food behaviors, their bodies, or both—and this can be a deterrent to seeking help. It is not unusual for eating disorder sufferers to consult a doctor for a sports injury, stomachache, sore throat, or depression without volunteering a word about food or exercise patterns. Although presenting to a physician for help is a sign of strength, it is not often viewed this way by the patient herself.

Sometimes trying to give her that message can help her understand that seeking help is an important and courageous step to take.

In addition to performing a physical exam and blood tests, the doctor will ask your child about symptoms, offering compassion and aiming for a positive rapport. Questions are likely to include the following: How often do you worry about your weight or about food? Do you eat large amounts of food quickly within a brief period of time? Do you induce vomiting? Do you take laxatives or diuretics (pills to increase urination)? How frequently? Since your child may feel embarrassed in the face of these questions, you'll want to address this with her prior to her medical consultation in a gentle and empathic way. For example, you can offer such statements as "I know you don't like to talk about your eating" or "Anticipating embarrassment is really hard" or "I'm sorry, this must be such a hard time for you." This type of dialogue will help reinforce the notion that it's important for her to be honest about her habits so the doctor can determine how best to help her and will also remind her how much you care and recognize that she's hurting.

Meanwhile, you're likely to have many questions for the pediatrician; in fact, you will want to make a list to bring to the appointment: Will she be okay? How serious is her condition? What ramifications will the illness have for her everyday life? Can she continue to attend school and play sports? What kinds of treatment are available for eating disorders, and which of these will be most effective for my child? How do I go about getting her into treatment? What can I do at home to help the situation?

Looking back on her visit to the pediatrician, Roberta thinks of it as a positive turning point in her life. But back then, her feelings were mixed. "Until our visit to the pediatrician, part of me refused to believe Serena had an eating disorder. That last shred of hope crumbled when I heard the diagnosis. I desperately wanted to help Serena but didn't know how. Over the next couple of days, I realized that she and I were operating on different understandings of the word *help*. She vehemently disagreed that improved nutrition or talk therapy [talking to a therapist or counselor] would help. When I'd ask her what would, her replies ranged from 'I don't need help' to 'Being good at something.'"

## Enhancing Her Motivation to Change

For an individual with an eating disorder to acknowledge that she is ill and needs help is often very difficult; that's one of the many reasons some postpone treatment until the disease worsens, perhaps opening the door to medical complications. It is not unusual for a person who suffers from anorexia or bulimia to progress in her thinking from "I'm fine" through various stages of "Maybe I'm not fine" before reaching "I have an eating disorder and need treatment." Sometimes a person's intellectual side tells her that she wants to get well, but her emotional side is unsure; it can take a while for the two sides to agree. The process of contemplating change and reconciling ambivalence often continues well after the patient has entered talk therapy.

Some individuals try to avoid treatment by insisting that they are not "sick enough" or not "thin enough" to necessitate professional care. In fact, they tend to compare themselves to other unusually thin people or even to other eating disorder sufferers who appear more underweight. These comparisons can serve to minimize the illness in their minds, thus further delaying treatment.

Motivation for treatment emerges at a different pace for everyone. Many patients who have recovered describe their readiness to change less as a "lightbulb moment" than as glimmers of awareness that grew brighter and steadier over time. For some, the progression toward readiness is not linear but more suggestive of the two-steps-forward-one-step-back principle. Thus, your child's level of motivation may fluctuate; sometimes she'll feel able to take on the challenge of change, and other times she'll feel more vulnerable. The good news is that you can, through your words and actions, encourage her to become more open to treatment.

## Discussing Medical Risks

"Soon after my appointment with the pediatrician," recalls Serena, "I decided that I did not want talk therapy. The appointment with my medical doctor had been hard enough. Now I had to see a psychiatrist? No way. But then Mom told me about certain health problems that can result from anorexia. One of them was infertility. At the time of the conversation, I acted indifferent. But days later, I started to worry that I'd never be able to have a baby."

Like Serena, some patients who have recovered recall that learning about the medical risks of eating disorders provided an incentive for them to get better. However, it is not unusual for an individual to dismiss the physical dangers with thoughts such as, "Medical crisis? That won't happen to *me*." In fact, she may take pride in her ability to do well day after day despite a low weight, almost as if she's won a bronze medal and will now shoot for the gold. Some patients hit rock bottom before realizing they want to get well.

To approach your child about medical dangers, call on your empathy skills, perhaps opening with an acknowledgment of how uncomfortable it might be for her to talk about her eating disorder. Trying to put yourself in her place will help her feel that you understand. You can then address factors that contribute to her resistance to treatment. For example, you'll want to recognize how hard it must be for her to believe she's ill when she doesn't feel it all the time. She may have had a normal physical exam and lab tests, particularly if she's in the earlier stages of the illness, and draw the conclusion that nothing's wrong. We know that potentially life-threatening medical events, such as abnormal heart rhythms, sometimes strike suddenly and that a person can coast for a while without complications only to suffer a catastrophe in the end. However, it is often difficult for those with eating disorders, particularly adolescents, to take these risks seriously.

If your child responds to your concerns with "No one else notices a problem," realize that many people are uneasy about approaching someone they suspect has an eating disorder (particularly if she's in the early stages of the illness), even though they care about her. Some don't know what to say, some are nervous they're wrong, some are concerned they'll be intrusive, and others are worried they'll cause a problem. When asking for a friend's opinion about whether she's too thin, your child will be more likely to approach someone she knows will agree with her than someone who will tell the truth. She is likely to search desperately for any feedback that can be perceived as supportive of her claim that she is healthy. Such attempts can further obscure her ability to believe you when you tell her that she has a disorder and needs help.

In discussing amenorrhea (absent menses), you'll want to explain that to maintain normal periods the female body needs a healthy intake of food. If a woman does not eat sufficiently, the hormonal signals responsible for stimulating menstruation are interrupted. Thus, her monthly menstrual periods may halt or become increasingly irregular. Amenorrhea can result in bone loss, a problem that affects 90 percent of women with anorexia nervosa and places them at a higher risk of fracture and resulting disability. For more than a decade, we've been studying bone loss in anorexia and observed that participating in this research can help motivate some patients to eat more healthfully.

Many people are not aware that some dangerously low-weight women continue to menstruate but experience every other characteristic of anorexia and are severely ill. Thus, someone who retains her menstrual cycles may say and believe she's healthy when, in fact, that is not the case. To an individual suffering from an eating disorder, even the question of what constitutes low weight can feel like complicated business. One reason she tends to dislike going to a clinician is that it reminds her she's ill. Perhaps she'll insist "I don't have a disorder. I'm naturally this thin."

In presenting medical consequences as preventable, it is important to avoid statements that your child might perceive as criticism and to focus instead on what she is doing *well* in taking care of herself, such as getting some rest, setting a limit on an exercise session, or venturing out of isolation to see a friend. It is advisable to approach the topic of heart and bone health from a positive standpoint, underscoring how getting help for her eating disorder will increase her likelihood of enjoying a variety of intellectual, social, and physical activities now and for years to come.

## Discussing Body Image

We often use the term *body image* to refer to how a person thinks and feels about her size and shape. Individuals with eating disorders typically perceive themselves as heavier than they actually are; some see themselves as overweight even when they are strikingly thin. You'll want to discuss with your child how perplexing it must be for her that friends and family insist she's too thin when she thinks she's fine or maybe even a little overweight. Eating disorders are complex, and your mission here is not to correct her misperceptions about her body, but to begin to understand her turmoil and pave the way to revisit the issue in the future. Point out that, with treatment, she can learn to appreciate her body more and to address the mismatch between how she views herself and how others view her.

Encouraging your child to discuss her body image can help her build a bridge to therapy, but it can also put you in closer touch with your feelings about your own body size and shape. When you self-reflect, try to do so in your gentle, nonjudgmental voice, reminding yourself that pressure to be thin is so prominent in our culture that it's hard not to be affected by it, even if only slightly. When it comes to body size concern, the question is less whether one has it than to what degree. Realizing that no one is to blame for his or her own or anyone else's body dissatisfaction, you'll want to ask yourself what factors may have played a role in yours. When you were growing up, were you unduly influenced by ultrathin fashion models? Were you teased about your size or shape? Did you compare yourself negatively to peers or family members?

Whether you're listening to your child talk about her body image or reflecting on your own, remember to give yourself well-deserved credit for broaching these sensitive and challenging issues.

## Discussing Social Activity

If your child has an eating disorder, chances are she goes to great lengths to avoid eating socially; she probably shuns opportunities to be with friends even if the plans don't include meals. The social withdrawal that often accompanies an eating disorder can gradually impact the individual's life in ways she never imagined before her illness struck. Your efforts to paint a picture of talk therapy as a road to feeling more comfortable in social situations can help motivate your child, particularly if she previously found friendships rewarding. For a son or daughter who declines an invitation to a formerly enjoyable activity, try opening a dialogue with a comment such as "It must be so hard when something inside you holds you back." The idea of initiating discussion about her social life (or lack thereof) is not to change or "cure" her, but rather to try to understand why these situations have become so difficult for her.

As it is, worries such as "I've eaten too much" or "I will eat too much" or "I'm gaining weight" might pummel a person with an eating disorder continually; on top of these feelings, the prospects of socializing tend to call forth a number of additional concerns. Particularly challenging is the threat of embarrassment. For example, if your child is invited on a day outing with friends, she's likely to worry about how she'll finagle her way out of eating with them. It is not unusual for an individual with anorexia to worry that others at the table will look at her plate to see what she has or has not eaten. Chances are she feels embarrassed going to a restaurant with friends but ordering nothing; if she shares a table with only one other person, she's apt to fear that her own abstinence from food will make her companion uncomfortable.

If the individual with anorexia feels pressured to eat, she typically decides to fake it, often by pushing her food around on her plate or hiding some in a napkin. However, executing these maneuvers is stressful, and no matter how much she likes the people she's "eating" with, her preoccupation with her no-eating strategy diminishes her ability to enjoy their company or concentrate on the conversation.

# Reaching Out to Your Student

If you are a teacher, athletic coach, school nurse, or residence adviser, you can play a key role in helping students who are struggling with an eating disorder. Naomi, a residence adviser at a large university, has reached out to many kids. Several parents we've seen have credited Naomi's nonjudgmental, calm manner not only for seeing them through a trying time, but also for mobilizing their children into treatment. The following is Naomi's account of her journey with Sophie, who recently became our patient.

"It started with a brief message about 'roommate problems' on my telephone answering machine. Later that evening, I saw the student who had called me, and she expressed concern that Sophie had recently begun to gorge on food and then traipse straight to the bathroom. I never doubted this roommate's good intentions. But sometimes a student who reports a friend's behavior is also worried about her own, so I explored that possibility and ruled it out. When I asked the roommate whether she wanted our conversation about Sophie to remain confidential, she replied, 'Yes, though I told her I was coming to you—and she's really mad at me.'

"Like many with bulimia nervosa, Sophie looked healthy. But she seemed sullen. She was aware that her eating habits were problematic, and I approached her several times about seeing a doctor, but she wanted no part of it. Early in the course of my discussions with her, I made it clear that I would contact her parents if her condition worsened. Within the next few weeks, her mood went downhill and her eating problems continued. Much to Sophie's dismay, I phoned her mom:

Naomi:  Hello, this is Naomi, the residence adviser in Sophie's dorm. Have I caught you at a convenient time?

Mom:  Is Sophie okay?

Naomi: Until recently, she seemed fine. She's keeping up academically, but she's been having difficulties with food, and she's not her enthusiastic self. I explained to her that I'd be contacting you.

Mom: She hasn't mentioned anything about food.

Naomi: Students with eating disorders often keep their problem a secret. Sophie seems to have a habit of binge eating and vomiting, and I've been encouraging her to see a doctor for evaluation, but she's hesitant to do that.

Mom: Of course she needs to see a doctor! Whew, this is all so unexpected.

Naomi: I'm sorry. I can only imagine how overwhelming this news feels to you. It must seem very sudden. I've come to know Sophie as a very bright young woman with good friends, and I believe she can feel much better. The student health center right here on campus is equipped to help people with eating disorders, and as I've told Sophie, I'd be happy to go there with her. If she prefers to see a primary care physician she's known in the past, that's fine as well.

Mom: I'll start making some calls. Can I get back to you later today or tomorrow?

Naomi: Of course. You can call me anytime. Please know that what you and I talk about will be confidential. Also, I can fax you some information on eating disorders if you wish.

Mom: Yes, I'd like that information. Thank you, Naomi. We'll talk soon.

"It didn't surprise me that Sophie resented me for calling her mom," said Naomi. "The message I tried to send her was 'I care about you, and I did it for your safety.'"

Several features of bulimia nervosa make it very hard to spend appreciable time with others. When an individual who suffers from the binge-purge cycle finds no way out of a social meal, she tends to sit down with others and eat but feel tormented by the questions of where and when she'll purge. Were she to venture on a slightly longer outing, such as an overnight, the logistics of her bulimia (how, when, and where to obtain food, binge eat, and purge) would likely be problematic. To engage in these habits around friends who know about her disorder is embarrassing, but being furtive is also a strain. Furthermore, the inordinate amounts of time involved in planning and engaging in the behaviors leave the individual limited opportunities to take in anything else about the outing. In the long run, a person with an eating disorder often considers social eating such a burden that she gives it up completely.

You'll want to explore with your child which friends, if any, she would feel comfortable with. Are some social situations more feasible for her than others? In any event, dialogue about socializing is potentially a difficult one for both you and your child, so pace it, offering her ongoing reassurance and ending each discussion on as positive a note as possible.

## Informing Others That She Has an Eating Disorder

You and your child do not necessarily want every relative and friend to know that she has an eating disorder. Before you tell others about the diagnosis, you need to talk this over with your child. Who will communicate what to whom? The answers to this question vary widely from one family to another, depending on the age of the patient and the quality and styles of relationships among family members. Serena and her mom looked back on how they managed challenges related to privacy.

### Serena's Perspective

"I wasn't fussy about which adult relatives knew about my eating disorder. What worried me was how kids at school would react.

I didn't tell any of my ninth-grade classmates about my problem. Now I realize that most of them knew anyway. They didn't give me a hard time about having anorexia. They mostly stayed away from me and vice versa. I wanted to know why my three former friends had dropped me but was afraid to ask them. Back then, I could not come close to describing how alone I felt.

"At about that time, a childhood friend came back into my life. Until Ricky and I were 11, his family had lived in the apartment down the hall from us. Ricky and I did a lot of bike riding back then; we were good buddies. But then his family moved about an hour away. Ricky and I stayed in touch, but we didn't see each other often. One afternoon in ninth grade—when my eating disorder was at its worst—I'd just started the walk home when a yellow bus pulled up to the school's athletic field and members of a visiting team filed out, among them Ricky. I wanted to run away before he saw me, but it was too late. We exchanged greetings. It felt surreal. He phoned me that evening, and I told him I had anorexia. As we talked, I sensed that he didn't just want me to look better, he wanted me to feel better, and that meant a lot to me."

Understandably, many individuals fear that their eating disorder will draw ridicule from peers. You should warn your child, as Roberta did, that it is not unusual for young people to promise they'll keep a secret but then tell others, perhaps thinking, "I'll just tell her a tiny bit about it," or "She won't mind if so-and-so knows." Thus, your child needs to be judicious regarding which friends she tells about her struggles.

## Roberta's Perspective

"When Serena's eating disorder struck, I'd been divorced from her father, Russ, for four years. But he'd stayed in the area and maintained positive ties with Serena. He and I were on fairly good terms as well. Though I harbored unspoken fears that Russ might blame me for Serena's illness, she and I both felt strongly that he should be the first to know. That turned out to be a good decision. Though Russ and I had some awkward, intense conversations during that time period, for the most part, my fears proved unfounded. I have to say that Russ totally came through for us; in fact, he was the one who finally convinced Serena to try talk therapy, and he was supportive to her throughout treatment. Plus, he kept everything confidential. Unfortunately, I can't say the same for every adult relative we told. But I suppose some gossip was inevitable, and it seemed to bother me much more than it did Serena."

Once you decide whom to tell, you'll want to think about what to tell them. How much detail will you include? Will you play the illness up—or down?

"We had numerous relatives spread out over several states, and as a general rule, we tended to play the problem down, keeping the news brief and reassuring folks that Serena would be fine. One reason I took this approach was to spare them worry; another was to avoid becoming a target of family gossip. Frankly, I was in no mood for getting an onslaught of family phone calls. I had no doubt that such calls would be well intended, but I feared they'd feel overwhelming, not only to Serena, but to me as well. I didn't want to answer relatives' questions nor listen to unsolicited advice.

"In addition to Russ, there were a couple of people to whom we offered more details. One of them was my sister Alyssa, who lived nearby. Serena had always been one of her biggest fans and vice versa. It didn't surprise me that my daughter wanted Alyssa to know what was happening. However, I worried about putting my sister in an awkward position. For example, I was aware that my daughter might try to enlist Alyssa's support for declining talk therapy. Though that was a tense situation, Alyssa's input on the therapy conflict was valuable. But I feared future mother-daughter spats would find Alyssa in the middle, and that didn't seem fair to her. I wanted to initiate a dialogue about this, but I kept procrastinating."

There are times when it is fine for you to share information about your child, whether or not you have her permission. For example, the likelihood is that you'll need to talk with a close friend about your turmoil; we encourage you to do so and to request that she keep everything you've told her confidential. Similarly, you're likely to have contact with your child's teachers, her school psychologist, or—if she lives at boarding school or in a college dormitory—her residence adviser. These professionals are usually respectful of client privacy, but you'll want to remind them, just to be sure.

## What if My Attempts to Convince My Child to Accept Treatment Aren't Working?

Despite your best efforts to persuade your child to accept professional attention, it's possible that she'll continue to resist. At this point, you'll want to ask your pediatrician to help you formulate a plan for motivating her to enter therapy. Another option is to seek guidance from a therapist. Bring your partner but not your child to the consult. After helping you devise an individualized strategy aimed at encouraging her to accept treatment, the therapist will then follow up with you regarding her condition and whether she's becoming more willing to see a doctor.

If your treatment-reluctant child is physically weakened or unstable, if she's very depressed, or if her food restriction is extreme, you'll need to get help despite her objections. Even if she is not in medical crisis, you may need to insist that she give therapy a try. Under such circumstances, you should remind yourself that your child's recalcitrance is neither her fault nor yours, but rather part of an illness. Your role in getting her the help she so desperately needs is an admirable step, even though it may feel extremely difficult in the face of her opposition. Although she may not be able to understand your intentions now, you can take solace in knowing that your initiative in getting her help will be pivotal in affording her the opportunity for better health in the long run.

Now that we've addressed the challenges of encouraging your child to accept help, you're likely wondering what professional care for eating disorders is all about, a topic we'll introduce in the next chapter.

## CHAPTER 5

# Setting Up Your Treatment Team

About 18 months ago, Wes came to see us about his son Mike, an athletic high school senior. "Mike lives and breathes sports," Wes reported. "Right now he's into varsity crew. One night, I thought I heard him vomiting in the bathroom. My suspicion that he had an eating disorder grew stronger and stronger, but he was reluctant to talk about it. To make a long story short, Mike finally went to his primary care doctor, who confirmed that he had bulimia nervosa and explained treatment options to both of us. He felt it would be best for Mike to work with a team of professionals. There were so many details to consider that I could barely sort them out in my own mind, much less figure out how to discuss them with Mike. I felt like I was drowning in uncertainty."

Perhaps like Wes and many other parents we've talked to, you feel ill-equipped to make decisions regarding your child's care. Individuals with eating disorders often function well in specific areas of life and, in fact, are quite capable. It can be overwhelming to discover that a son or daughter whom you think of as accomplished or even gifted is hurting so much inside. Given the many dimensions of the illness, your apprehension is understandable and expected. Before exploring the "who, what, where, and when" of treatment, you'll want to consider the bigger picture of what professional care for eating disorders hopes to accomplish.

The general aims of treatment are closely entwined. One priority will be to address medical problems created by your child's abnormal eating habits. Another is to restore her to good nutritional health. Her health providers will strive to motivate her to work on modifying habits such as starving, bingeing, and purging. In addition, they will try to help her become more at peace with herself, less self-demanding, better able to avoid extremes, and more comfortable in her relationships with peers and family. All treatment goals will be tailored to your child's individual needs.

Because eating disorder treatment involves different aspects of the problem, patients often respond best to a team approach consisting of medical monitoring, talk therapy, nutrition counseling, and (potentially) medication. To set up your team, we recommend starting with your child's primary care provider, as Wes did. After evaluating Mike, the doctor offered him referrals to treatment programs and to individual psychotherapists and nutritionists who he knew worked well together. Some families find it helpful to contact a national eating disorders organization for referrals (see the Resources section at the end of this book).

Your child's reluctance to accept care may understandably make your effort to find treatment all the more stressful. Don't hesitate to call on her primary care physician to reinforce the need for treatment. The doctor's compassionate yet firm approach will allow you to position yourself as the understanding parent with comments such as "I know you don't like the idea of therapy, and I see this is terribly hard on you, but we need to do what the doctor recommends."

## How Do I Choose Professionals?

Whether to interview more than one nutritionist or mental health provider before making a decision is a matter of personal preference; some parents want second opinions, while others don't see the need—each of these approaches is reasonable. If you live in a rural area, however, there tend to be fewer health care facilities than in a larger city, and your choices are likely to be limited.

When evaluating practitioners, it is important to consider their credentials and experience treating eating disorders. Is the practitioner affiliated with a clinic or health care system? Give some thought to his or her location. Is it too far from home? Note whether the practice is aimed at adult patients or at adolescents and children. For some families, the provider's gender or age matter as well.

You may want to ask your health insurance company for a list of providers whose services are covered. Review the list with your child's primary care physician or even with a mental health professional who works outside the field of eating disorders and can offer you advice about doctors in the community. Perhaps, for example, there are practitioners who are not covered by your insurance plan but are more expert. If so, find out how soon they can see your child. Given her condition, is the wait time feasible and safe, or is her need for care more urgent?

Communication between the members of your child's professional care team will be the cornerstone of treatment. Having providers in the same setting makes collaboration more likely. Who will be in charge of the team and ultimately make decisions? Either the primary care provider or the psychotherapist serves as "team leader." The idea is to have a point person on the team whom the family can turn to and consult with throughout the course of treatment.

## Where Will My Child Meet with Her Team?

Eating disorders are treated in a number of settings: the acute care hospital, residential care, partial hospitalization, and outpatient care. The one that's right for your child depends on a number of factors, including the severity of her abnormal eating behaviors, her medical status, her level of motivation to regain her health, and the availability of practitioners in her geographic area. Many individuals need treatment in more than one setting during the course of their illness.

## Will She Need Hospitalization?

If your child's eating habits pose a risk to her safety, she may require admission to an acute care hospital. Chances are she'll say that she doesn't want to go, insisting that she isn't ill. Given the heat of her protests, you are likely to worry she'll hate you forever if you send her to the hospital. We suggest that you strongly encourage her to enter an inpatient unit if that is what her physician prescribes. We are certainly not minimizing your anguish under such circumstances, but we must point out that a number of teenagers with eating disorders who are initially reluctant to be hospitalized become more accepting of their need to be on an inpatient unit within a couple of weeks after admission.

Your child's length of stay in the hospital will range from a few days to a couple of months. In considering hospitalization for your child, the doctor will take both her physical and psychiatric states into account. Inpatient treatment can take place on a medical unit or a psychiatric unit, depending on the circumstances. It is not unusual for a patient to be dangerously thin on admission to the hospital. However, the question of hospitalization depends not only on how many pounds she's lost but also on the rate at which she's lost them. Fast drops in weight, particularly in children, often warrant inpatient treatment.

Another indication that your child needs hospitalization involves her vital signs, meaning her body temperature, heart rate, and blood pressure. An undernourished individual can experience a substantial drop in body temperature. She will frequently present to her doctor with a slowed heart rate, which can trigger dangerous heart rhythms and therefore needs careful monitoring. A heart rate below 40 beats per minute in an adult is highly concerning. In a child or adolescent, a daytime heart rate below 50 beats per minute or nighttme heart rate below 45 beats per minute is potentially problematic. As blood is pumped through the body, it exerts a force against the walls of the blood vessels; hence, the term *blood pressure*. Malnutrition is often accompanied by low blood pressure. A blood pressure less than 90/60 mm Hg in an adult and less than 80/50 mm Hg in an adolescent or child is very worrying. A nurse or doctor will take the patient's heart rate and blood pressure while she is sitting and then ask her to stand up for a second reading; a significant rise in heart rate or drop in blood pressure associated with the change in position is cause for concern.

Another risk requiring medical vigilance involves essential electrolytes (such as sodium and potassium) that travel in the blood serum and are critical to several functions of the body. Electrolyte imbalances can result in serious or even life-threatening medical complications such as abnormal heart rhythms. Although electrolyte disturbances are very worrisome in eating disorder sufferers who are underweight, they are not the only ones at risk. Individuals with large ups and downs in weight are also vulnerable to such problems and may require hospitalization. While your child is an inpatient, the doctors will keep a close eye on her vital signs. She is likely to have periodic blood tests and may receive intravenous fluids to correct electrolyte problems.

If your child is underweight, a primary goal of her hospitalization will be to increase her food intake. Her nutritionist will help her plan balanced, healthy meals, while the nursing staff will lend her support at mealtimes and set limits on potential attempts at overexercising or purging. The general approach is to encourage patients to take in food orally. For those who don't eat adequately on their own, nasogastric feeding is sometimes necessary. A slender tube is inserted through the individual's nose into her stomach, a process that feels strange or mildly uncomfortable but is not painful and does not involve surgery. Once the tube is in place, liquid feedings are introduced and carefully monitored to give her body the sustenance it so urgently needs.

Some acute inpatient settings offer group meetings at which your child can talk with the professional staff and other patients about her feelings as she comes face-to-face with treatment. Understandably, the food-related changes that she is encouraged to undertake in the hospital may be upsetting and even frightening for her. You can help her cope with emotional hurdles with statements such as "I can see how much you don't want to be here. I'm sorry, I know that eating is very frightening to you." If she does increase her food intake, you'll want to acknowledge this as a courageous and admirable step. Stay in touch with your child's treatment team throughout her hospitalization so that you can best serve as her advocate. Meanwhile, keep reminding yourself that you are not the cause of the illness, that your child is in the care of experienced professionals, and that her hospitalization can be a turning point in her eating disorder.

## What if She's Not in Medical Crisis but Still Seriously Ill?

Many patients don't require the intense medical and nursing care of an acute care hospital but are undernourished or engage in abnormal eating to the point that they cannot hold their behaviors in check without staff support. That's when residential treatment—24/7 care in a structured environment—can be helpful. Although a stay in residential care ranges from one month to a year or more, a period of 30 to 60 days is typical.

May, who is Chinese American, spent eight weeks in residential treatment for anorexia and bulimia when she was 16 years old. Six years later, she recounts her mixed feelings about the experience. "Apart from a few stomachaches, I didn't think anything was wrong," she recalls. "I didn't want to go to any institution, so I would have balked no matter which one was chosen. Plus, I was worried that treatment would bring shame and embarrassment to my family, especially since in my culture one was not supposed to talk about family issues with 'strangers.' But the residential center I went to looked more like a comfy house than a hospital—that part I liked. I felt that everything I did there was under a microscope and monitored by staff—that part I didn't like. My days were organized around groups, meetings with therapists, academic classes, and meals. Art therapy was part of the program as well.

"Every day at the residence seemed emotionally charged. The first two weeks were especially hard, because I didn't trust any of the therapists and it didn't feel 'right' to talk about my family relationships or my feelings. Besides, none of the staff looked like me—how could they relate to what I was going through? I was afraid to tell them how terrified I was right before mealtimes. I felt torn apart about doing what I'd vowed I'd never, ever do—gain weight. And there was never any doubt in my mind that I was the fattest patient there and that if I started to eat, I'd never be able to stop. I compared myself to everyone. After eating, I'd feel that parts of me were inflating like a balloon, and that was upsetting—at times, almost more than I could handle. Sometimes I wanted to vomit, and I knew some tricks to use—that is, ways to get past the staff's 'checks'—but I didn't think I could succeed without getting caught. By about the third week, I'd started to build a good rapport with one of the nurses and didn't want to disappoint her.

"Another problem was that I liked to stay very busy and wasn't good at handling downtime. My therapists understood when I complained about boredom. They said that unstructured time could open the door to uncomfortable feelings and that the idea was to experience them rather than to run away from them. They tried to help me think about a 'game plan' for how to cope with onslaughts of 'I'm not good enough,' 'I'm ashamed of the way I look,' 'I'm embarrassing my family,' and other bad feelings. At the time, that seemed complicated, and I didn't get very far with it. Part of me wanted to run away from the center, but then I'd disappoint my parents even more.

"Yet another part of me said to stay for the whole program. I'd never have admitted it back then, but there was at least one moment when I realized at a very gut level that I'd be okay. It felt weird because I had never experienced anything like it; it came over me while I was doing something completely ordinary and vanished in a flash, leaving me with a sense that I could actually feel better someday. This twinge of confidence and security was very new to me—I wasn't used to trusting my experiences or feelings. Maybe that's why this moment of well-being made a lasting impression on me."

In evaluating a potential residential treatment facility for your child, you will want information about the following areas.

**Whom Does the Center Treat?** Most all residential facilities admit individuals with anorexia or bulimia, and many also include those with binge eating disorder. All of them treat females; among those that accept both genders, several offer units only for males. Some programs admit mainly adolescents, others mostly adults. Few accept individuals who are suffering from both an eating disorder and substance abuse.

**How Individualized Will Your Child's Treatment Plan Be?** Does the center expect every patient to stay for the same amount of time? Is a minimum length of stay required? If she is a vegetarian or has other dietary idiosyncrasies, will the facility accommodate her, or will she need to follow "the program"? Will her treatment include a spirituality component? Is the staff knowledgeable about and sensitive to ethnic and cultural considerations? Some programs have bilingual staff members or interpreters, but the number of such facilities is limited.

**What Medical Services Are Offered?** How often will your child see a medical doctor and a psychopharmacologist (a psychiatrist who specializes in medication)? If your child suffers from diabetes or another chronic medical problem along with her eating disorder, is the facility equipped to serve her needs? If she uses a feeding tube at home, can she also have it at the residence? What is the center's proximity to a hospital?

**Will the Facility Involve You in Your Child's Program?** Are you welcome to visit while you are exploring options for treatment facilities? What is the center's policy regarding patient-family contact? How open will the channels of communication be between you and your child's treatment team? Will you have a primary contact person at the residence? How often will you receive updates on your child's progress? Does the facility host family educational or support programs?

**Will Health Insurance Pay?** This question arises not just for residential care, but across all inpatient and outpatient treatment settings. Insurance companies base their payment decisions on "medical necessity." For the most part, finance departments of hospitals and residences don't know up front how much of an individual's stay will be covered. One reason is that insurance companies tend to approve an initial few days and then make determinations about a continued stay proactively based on the patient's condition and progress.

An insurer's decision to stop coverage before you and the treatment team feel it is safe for your child to leave may pose an emotional and financial challenge to you, as it does to many parents. As one mom explained, "When my daughter's insurer cut off payment, the residential facility expected me to pick up the tab for the remainder of her stay. I felt like she was being kicked out. It boiled down to deciding whether to take out a second mortgage on my house to pay out-of-pocket expenses for a treatment I'd been told 'is not guaranteed.' I shuddered at the thought of paying for the balance of this stay only to see my daughter return to the residence for another bout of treatment in the future."

Prior to your child's admission to residential care or soon thereafter, you'll want information about how the facility responds when an insurer refuses to pay. Plan how you'll proceed should your child's insurance company cut off further payment. There is an appeals process through which you can attempt to overturn the insurer's denial. (See Chapter 13.) When evaluating a prospective residential care facility, feel free to ask, "Do you help families appeal denials of payment by insurance companies, and if so, how?"

**Is There Aftercare?** Although many patients improve in residential care, few recover. After discharge, most will need continued treatment. Some facilities have day programs with housing to give patients transitioning out an opportunity to live independently before going home. May's discharge from her residential unit remains fresh in her mind. Although her facility did not have transition housing, her family lived just six miles away. So the plan was for her to move home and spend most of each weekday at the center's partial hospitalization program until her pub-

# What Will My Child Do All Day While She's in Treatment?

If your child is in partial hospitalization, residential care, or even an acute care environment, her daily care will revolve around structured therapy activities. A hallmark of these programs is group therapy, which offers patients the opportunity to support each other under the leadership of a mental health provider. All meals are monitored by staff.

Here is the schedule of a typical day. Note that evening activities don't apply to partial hospitalization patients.

| | |
|---|---|
| 8:00 A.M. | Community meeting |
| 8:30 A.M. | Breakfast/relaxation session |
| 9:30 A.M. | Assertiveness training (group) |
| 10:30 A.M. | Snack/relaxation session |
| 10:45 A.M. | One-to-one talk with member of nursing staff |
| 11:15 A.M. | Weathering change (group) |

lic high school opened in a month, at which point she'd shift to therapy appointments a couple of afternoons a week. "Throughout my entire stay in residential care, all I'd wanted was to leave," she recalls. "I'd been looking forward to August 1 ever since I'd known it was my discharge date. When that day arrived, my feelings were topsy-turvy. What would happen if I went home and couldn't sustain the changes I'd made? I didn't want to end up back in residential care."

## What Is a Partial Hospitalization Program?

Also known as day treatment, this setting, which can be part of an acute care hospital or residential facility, is often beneficial to those who don't require constant monitoring but are not well enough for outpatient care. Like May, many patients live at home and com-

| 12:00 P.M. | Lunch followed by relaxation session |
| 1:00 P.M. | Educational video (documentary on body image) followed by group discussion |
| 2:00 P.M. | One-to-one meeting with psychotherapist |
| 3:00 P.M. | Snack/relaxation session |
| 3:30 P.M. | Group discussion of how to structure free time |
| 4:30 P.M. | One-to-one talk with member of nursing staff |
| 5:00 P.M. | Dinner/relaxation session |
| 6:00 P.M. | Women's group/men's group |
| 7:00 P.M. | Reading/journal writing/receiving visitors/talking with other patients |
| 8:00 P.M. | Snack/relaxation session |

mute to partial hospitalization programs lasting up to eight hours a day and including at least two meals and snacks. Patients generally spend one week to several months in these programs; four or five days a week are prescribed for some individuals, two or three days for others. At "partial," patients take part in groups that focus on topics such as assertiveness skills, body image, friendship, family relations, coping with transitions, or recognizing emotions. Some programs provide guidance in practical skills such as cooking or grocery shopping.

## What Does Outpatient Treatment Involve?

For individuals who are medically safe, clinicians generally recommend outpatient treatment. The *intensive* outpatient setting consists of several hours of care per day; for example, if your child is busy with school or work activities until late afternoon but needs help around dinnertime, evening programs provide it, with group therapy afterward. An individual typically receives intensive outpatient care for one week to several months. For those who do not need the intensive level, an outpatient program of one or two hours a week is usually recommended. Some individuals need years of outpatient psychotherapy, while others require less time.

For Wes's son, Mike, treatment included outpatient talk therapy and nutrition counseling. Although he was unhappy about taking time off from varsity crew during treatment, the decision stood him in good stead. "Slowly I began to cut back on my bingeing and vomiting, though I did have setbacks," he recalls. "It was very hard to limit my workouts. After I quit crew, I'd practice on the rowing machine longer than ever because something inside told me I had to. I'd lift weights until very late, even if I had exams the next day. Somehow I managed to keep my grades up; I hadn't recovered by June of my senior year but was able to graduate with my class."

Looking back, May admits that her first few weeks out of residential care were rough. "When I returned home, neighbors I hadn't seen in a while would open conversations with 'You look terrific.' To me, *terrific* meant 'fat.' It set off an automatic alarm system in my mind." Despite her fears, May did well in day treatment and felt ready to take another step forward. A month after discharge from residential care and just a few days after good-byes at "partial," she ascended the front steps of her public high school to greet the new academic year.

## How Can My Child Benefit from Psychotherapy?

Provided mainly by psychiatrists, psychologists, and social workers, psychotherapy helps your child work toward changing her behaviors while learning to feel better about herself and her relationships with others. A patient can attend therapy on a one-to-one basis, as a member of a group, or with her family. Many patients receive therapy in more than one of these contexts.

There are various schools of thought in both individual and group psychotherapy. Between these theories lie areas of common ground. Instead of basing our treatment of eating disorders purely on one ideology, we—like many therapists—draw something from all of them to meet individual patients' needs. Often conducted on a one-to-one basis, *psychodynamically oriented therapy* builds on the nature of the patient-therapist relationship to help the individual understand herself; this will often include, for example, a discussion of why she considers herself "not good enough." *Interpersonal therapy* focuses on helping the person discover how complex interactions with important people in her life influence her eating habits. Talk generally revolves around the patient's current situation and explores ways she can change her behaviors and improve her relationships. *Dialectical behavior therapy* teaches the individual skills for coping with emotional pain without engaging in unhealthy behaviors; this form of therapy is generally used with patients who are chronically ill and struggling with problems in a number of different areas, including relationships, identity, and mood. *Cognitive behavioral therapy* (CBT) involves strategies that modify a patient's thoughts and behaviors. Nicole, who developed anorexia at 14 and bulimia several years later, received components of CBT that were suited to her specific needs. Recently she and her mom, Patrice, looked back on their arduous journey and shared their insights with us.

"When Nicole's pediatrician discovered she had anorexia, he wanted to see her every week," says Patrice. "She agreed to that. But when he added that he'd like her to start talk therapy, she refused. So he broached the subject again the following week, and this time she didn't object—not right there in his office anyway. Her first therapy appointment was a day later, and I practically had to drag her there. In the car, she kept repeating that nothing was wrong with her and that this entire 'therapy thing' was stupid. While therapy was meant to help her, she seemed to perceive it as a punishment; that troubled me. As I pulled into the parking lot of the therapy office with my angry, yet fragile daughter, I felt drained. She and I had been fighting since early morning—first about going to therapy, then about breakfast, then once again about therapy. The strain seemed endless."

Nicole, now 27, remembers that first therapy session as if it were yesterday. "I was certain that therapy had one purpose and one purpose only: to fatten me up. That, I figured, was why Mom had made me come. For weeks she'd been claiming I was too skinny, but I felt she had that all wrong. I wished she'd leave me alone about the entire subject. One of the only comments I made during my first therapy session was 'If Mom thinks I'm too skinny, she's the crazy one, not me.'"

Like Nicole, many of our new patients—especially those with anorexia—don't walk into our office eager and ready for therapy. Family members, roommates, or athletic coaches bring them. To the individual with an eating disorder, the idea of spending 45 to 50 minutes talking about herself often feels foreign and uncomfortable. Typically, she is not trusting; from her standpoint, the therapist is out to make her fat. Thus, our primary goal is to forge a trusting alliance with the patient. It is only natural for you to want your child's therapist to persuade her to eat again as soon as possible, but try to be patient. Behavioral change can only take place once a trusting relationship has begun to develop, and that may not happen immediately. As important as it is to build a partnership with a patient, her medical safety is our first and foremost concern. For this reason, we establish ground rules: "We'd like to use these sessions to get to know you, but we can't continue if your weight falls out of the safety zone."

In the early stage of alliance building, we try to find a language in which to communicate with our patient. For example, to approach the topic of body image (how a person thinks and feels about her body), we may ask a patient to draw two self-portraits, the first to represent how she looks now and the second to show how she wants to look. As you'd expect, the individual with an eating disorder tends to depict the current size and shape of her body as larger than her ideal, and this can help pave the way to meaningful patient-therapist dialogue.

For the patient who insists she's fine and wishes Mom and Dad would stop bothering her about her eating (or lack thereof), we ask her to keep a log of everything she eats for a couple of days as a way to help us understand what the food feud in her household is all about. This record can serve as a springboard for patient-therapist talk. For example, if her documentation reveals that she binge eats, we ask her what thoughts and feelings she associates with the episodes and what steps she can take under similar circumstances to avoid bingeing. As a follow-up assignment, we suggest that she write down not only what she eats but also the thoughts and emotions she experiences at the time. In talking with the patient about her food-thoughts-feelings record we try to convey our appreciation and understanding of the challenges she's up against. Sometimes log-related talk can evolve into a discussion about the individual's relationships with her peers and family. In fact, much of our role involves coaching patients through interpersonal issues and encouraging them to try new approaches to life's stresses.

The record keeping we've described is part of cognitive behavioral therapy. Building a log benefited Nicole in that it helped identify her unhealthy attitudes in an organized way. Instead of addressing only emotions and conflicts, CBT—one of the most common psychological treatments for eating disorders—aims to help the patient reduce her food restriction, binge eating, and purging. Based on the results of research studies, we are in favor of incorporating CBT into individual and group therapy for adults with bulimia. Structured and goal-oriented, this approach helps the patient reconstruct the negative thoughts and belief systems that may have led to her food restriction, binge eating, or purging. For about 50 percent of adults with bulimia who complete CBT, the treatment is effective. Among patients with anorexia, CBT tends to help those who have returned to a healthy weight but not those who are underweight. Originally formulated for adults, CBT for eating disorders may also be useful for adolescent patients.

Mike's therapy for bulimia nervosa included a strong CBT component. "I used to think that I had to be one particular weight all the time," he admits. "I feared a gain in weight would make me a loser in every other respect. Therapy helped me to reevaluate what makes a person a winner or a loser and to draw some new conclusions. One was that a person's weight is not connected to his worth. Another was that a person isn't either all 'winner' or all 'loser,' but somewhere in between."

Mike found that CBT challenged his use of binge eating as a way to release pent-up feelings. "In CBT, I was supposed to find non-eating ways to deal with tension. Listening to music sounded like a good alternative but was very hard to put into practice. I've made some progress, and I'm still working on it. One of the most helpful facts I learned during therapy is that purging doesn't completely get rid of the calories eaten during a binge—most of them stay in the body. To me, that felt like a compelling reason to change."

In studying the process of getting well, we have learned a great deal from our patients who have recovered. When we asked individuals what had "worked" and what hadn't in therapy, most pointed out that it had helped that we participated actively in the sessions, offering clarification about eating disorders, coaching, and emotional support. Many patients cited honesty, consistency, reliability, and flexibility as vitally important qualities for a therapist; in their eyes, the "ideal" therapist would be trustworthy, nonjudgmental, and empathic but capable of being firm when necessary. The majority reported that therapy had helped them discover their emotions and gain self-confidence. Many valued advice regarding how to interact with other people but cautioned that such guidance needs to be grounded in the therapist's understanding of the patient's individual temperament and needs. Woven throughout the responses was the theme of patients wanting to be understood as individuals in their own right.

Individual psychotherapy needs to operate in conjunction with medical monitoring, family sessions, and nutrition counseling. A patient's reluctance to change often persists well into treatment. In fact, motivating the patient to persist in her recovery efforts is often an integral part of the therapy process. For some patients, treatment can take years.

## How Can Group Therapy Help?

Group therapy for eating disorders offers patients an opportunity to discuss their concerns and support each other under the leadership of a mental health practitioner. Particularly prominent among the more intensive treatment settings, groups are also offered on an outpatient basis. These sessions, which are less expensive than one-to-one meetings, can follow a psychodynamic, interpersonal, dialectical, or cognitive behavioral approach. For adults with bulimia, CBT is often helpful and is as effective in groups as in a one-to-one context.

Many patients experiencing the binge-purge cycle feel ashamed of their problem and don't want to talk about it with friends or family. For such individuals, outpatient groups can lessen the sting of isolation. For example, one woman we treated for bulimia often referred to herself as a "freak." When she began to participate in a professional outpatient therapy group, she realized that many other people also suffer from binge-purge cycles and associated self-disgust. The nonjudgmental group environment helped her discuss the nitty-gritty of living hour to hour with tormenting thoughts about food and weight. During the course of therapy, she discovered that several members of the group took prescribed medication for depression. Her doctor had recommended an antidepressant for her, but she'd firmly declined. However, when group members told her that medication helped them feel better, she gradually summoned the courage to give it a try.

Some patients are more receptive to groups than others. Concerned that her daughter had become a recluse, Patrice sought referrals to professional outpatient eating disorder therapy groups, found one that included members of all different body sizes, and hoped that Nicole would consider giving it a try while continuing individual therapy. "At the time, she wasn't the least bit interested," admits Patrice. We find that some patients who refuse group therapy at one point in their illness become more receptive over time.

Sometimes working on a one-to-one basis with a psychotherapist can improve a patient's readiness to participate in groups.

Support and self-help groups, such as those led by advocacy organizations, often reach out to communities to provide information about eating disorders, referrals for treatment, and emotional support to individuals and their families. Some of these groups are led by individuals who have a history of the disorder and often include a professional as well. Such forums can help alleviate your child's loneliness by giving her the opportunity to talk with people who have overcome their own disorders.

## How Can I Be Involved in My Child's Treatment?

Recommended for adolescent and some adult patients, family therapy is a forum in which you can discuss how you are affected by your child's illness. The topics addressed during these sessions vary from one family to another. One theme that often comes to the forefront is how to manage meals at home. For example, you might ask, "What should I do at dinner? Shall I let her choose what she'll eat? Should I guide her food decisions? How much guidance should I give her?" The larger question becomes what roles you will play in your child's nutrition program; this is a topic you'll want to discuss with your child's treatment team.

Over the past couple of decades, increasing attention has focused on the "Maudsley" approach to family treatment, which has demonstrated good results for adolescents with anorexia nervosa (particularly those who enter treatment early in the course of their illness) and is also beneficial for those with bulimia nervosa. A professional assessment will help you determine whether the Maudsley approach might be useful to your family. At the heart of this family-based method is parental participation on the treatment team. Thus, under the guidance of a therapist you initially take charge of your adolescent's eating with the goal of restoring her to a safe nutritional base or modifying her binge-purge behaviors. Family-based therapy sessions give you and the rest of your family the tools and confidence to work together. For example, you and your partner are coached to back each other up on decisions around food; if you have other children, their role in the treatment process is to help fortify their eating disordered sibling's will to recover. Once weight gain and/or binge-purge reduction is progressing well, your family sessions focus on transitioning the responsibility for eating back to your adolescent. When she is in charge of her own eating, staying at a healthy weight, and no longer restricting her food intake, bingeing or purging, family therapy may turn from a focus on illness to concerns that arise in most all adolescents, such as sexuality and independence.

Whether or not your child's doctor prescribes Maudsley treatment, challenges related to growing up, transitioning to college, and leaving home are appropriate for discussion in family therapy. Other topics include efforts to improve parent-child communication skills and how to cope with change. It is not unusual for an individual with an eating disorder to have trouble defining herself as a person separate from her mom and dad; Patrice is one of many parents who have found family therapy a good place to discuss that topic. "These sessions helped both Nicole and me sort out our feelings about independence. I needed to let go a little bit and let her grow up, and she needed to learn to be comfortable with separating from me."

Patrice felt that one of the most valuable tools she learned during family therapy was to think of the eating disorder as separate from her child. "That made good sense," she recalled. "At times, Nicole's eating habits threw family activities off track with resulting arguments about who was to blame. When talk in family therapy turned to these incidents, all of us were encouraged to stop seeing Nicole and her anorexia as one and the same. Instead, we were to view them as separate; thus, rather than finding fault in ourselves or in each other for food-related disruptions, we were to blame them on the illness. This way of thinking made life on the home front easier." While Nicole learned to separate herself from her illness in family meetings, other patients are introduced to this skill in one-on-one therapy or in groups.

While family, group, or individual psychotherapy—or some combination thereof—will focus on relieving your child's obsession with food and weight, she'll also need to learn what foods support a healthy, well-balanced lifestyle. That's where her nutritionist comes in.

## What Is Nutrition Counseling?

Your child may claim that she doesn't need to see a nutritionist because she's already well informed about food and calories. In response, try to explain that she can increase her knowledge and learn how to use it effectively by seeing a nutritionist. This important member of your child's treatment team will provide her with facts about healthy eating and help her develop a balanced meal plan, outlining the nutrients needed and ways to increase her intake gradually. The nutrition counselor will offer your child positive ways to think about food and invite her to challenge certain misconceptions. For instance, your daughter may divide foods into "safe" and "unsafe" categories, partaking only of the former; as a way to gradually counter her fears, the nutritionist would reassure her that all foods are safe and encourage her to widen her range of choices. Other roles of the nutritionist include discussing energy expenditure, teaching social eating skills, and helping the patient recognize hunger and satiety cues.

## Has She Seen the Dentist Lately?

If your child induces vomiting to control her weight, she is vulnerable to dental problems. The stomach contents that travel up the esophagus into the mouth include digestive acid, which erodes dental enamel (the hard external layer of the tooth), leaving the dentin (inner part of the tooth) susceptible to decay. Some people who induce vomiting are not aware of the potential for enamel erosion; some fear erosion but avoid the dentist due to embarrassment about having an eating disorder. Others see the dentist for checkups without mentioning their eating behaviors. In spotting worn enamel as a possible sign of purging, the dentist can be a frontline player in detecting an individual's eating disorder, encouraging her to seek medical evaluation, providing her with compassionate dental care throughout the course of her illness, and communicating with the other professionals on her team.

## Understanding the Teamwork Component

It is common for a patient to express very high regard for some members of her treatment team and intense negative feelings toward others. Although all of her health care providers are striving to improve her life, the individual does not necessarily see it that way. Often, she will focus her criticism on the professional who sets limits on her behaviors. This can be a reaction to feeling controlled or it can suggest that the patient is not ready to acknowledge that she has an eating disorder or to give up her behaviors.

Your awareness of the possibility that your child will view some of her clinicians as "good" and others as "bad" will see you through potentially perplexing moments. In listening to her concerns, avoid criticizing her in favor of separating her from her illness and feel free to contact her health care providers with questions. Close communication among the members of your child's treatment team—her primary care physician, her nutritionist, her psychotherapist(s) and her family—is a crucial part of her care.

In Chapter 6, we will talk about the medical care and monitoring of patients with eating disorders, describe potential complications of these illnesses, and explore avenues for treating them.

# 6

# Medical Care and Monitoring

Will she get better? How? Those questions weighed heavily on Lucinda's mind when she first came to talk to us about her daughter, who had developed anorexia nervosa and soon became our patient. She described Anita, then 16, as a very good student who worked as hard academically as she did on the swim team and had set her mind on becoming a marine biologist. Six years later, mother and daughter recall the turbulence that dominated their lives during Anita's 10th- and 11th-grade years.

"When Anita first showed signs of anorexia, she'd insist she felt fine," remembers Lucinda. "She'd say, 'How *could* I have anorexia? I eat.' Or 'So-and-so is skinnier,' or 'I could eat more if I wanted to.' As much as I wanted to believe that she was well, I didn't. Actually, I wasn't at all sure what was wrong with her. For all I knew, some other illness could have been causing her weight loss. That's why I pressed her to see her primary care physician."

Lucinda's point is key. When someone experiences unexpected weight loss, she might have an eating disorder or she might have another condition such as diabetes mellitus, thyroid disease, or inflammatory bowel disease. Sometimes an eating disorder can occur along with one of these other illnesses, and thus it is crucial for your child to see her primary care physician, pediatrician, or adolescent medicine specialist for an evaluation.

"After Anita's primary care doctor examined her, he confirmed my worst nightmare," Lucinda continues. "Anita had anorexia nervosa. He explained to both of us that malnutrition can progress to the point of harming every organ of the body, including the heart. He was clearly concerned about her weight loss. Her pulse and blood pressure were on the low side, and he felt this went along with her semistarved condition. The doctor assured us that Anita's blood test results would be available within 48 hours and requested that we return to see him in seven days. Meanwhile, he wanted her to take the week off from swim practice and to start eating breakfast before leaving for school."

"Those two recommendations did not sit well with me," admits Anita. "To my way of thinking, my heart rate was slow not because I was ill, but because I was physically fit. A couple of days after my medical evaluation, Mom called the doctor to check on my blood work and learned that it was all normal. When I heard the news, I said, 'See, Mom? There's nothing wrong with me.' What I didn't tell her was that I'd gone running in place of swim practice that afternoon and intended to do the same every day for the rest of the week. Something inside kept telling me to exercise harder."

Like Anita, many patients in the early stages of anorexia and bulimia have normal laboratory results, which they perceive as evidence that they don't have an eating disorder. Furthermore, these individuals often feel fine. In fact, a person may report feeling more accomplished or better disciplined as she loses weight. This preliminary sense of well-being is likely to reinforce her resolve to continue her food-related behaviors, particularly if peers or others are complimenting her thinness.

Lucinda says, "When I phoned the doctor about Anita's reaction to her lab report, he explained that it generally takes time for an individual with an eating disorder to admit she has a problem and that he would work with me on keeping her medically safe and on increasing her motivation to get well. By seeing Anita every week, he would monitor her health and weight, and at the same time, try to help her see the need for treatment for her eating disorder."

"I dreaded those weekly appointments," recalls Anita. "Every week Mom and I would fight about whether I was going. I'd say, 'Mom, I feel okay. These appointments are so *stupid*.' I'd be furious at her for making me go. Each visit started with a weigh-in and a vital sign check followed by a talk with the doctor. He would take my pulse and blood pressure while I was lying down and then ask me to stand up so he could check them again. The weighing sent my thoughts spinning. I was so upset about the number on the scale that when the doctor tried to talk with me, I couldn't concentrate on what he was saying. And I didn't want to."

Lucinda remembers those quarrels about the appointments all too well. "As hard as I tried to avoid arguing with Anita, I could not let her skip her visits to her doctor," she says. "His diligence in sharing his findings and reasons for recommendations with me—as well as with Anita—helped equip me to reinforce his suggestions at home. Early in his treatment, the doctor observed that Anita often looked chilled in the examining room. 'I'm cold a lot,' she admitted. He gently explained that when the body does not get sufficient nutrients, fuel that would normally heat the skin is used to sustain the heart and other vital organs. In addition, a body that is too low in fat has difficulty retaining heat, thus leaving the person feeling cold. Improving Anita's nutrition would help keep her warm. Aware that she had probably tuned out, I figured that, for the time being, I'd be satisfied if she could begin to absorb the doctor's compassion and understanding. As for the information per se, I'd have it to call on whenever she grew ready to hear it."

"That readiness didn't happen for quite some time," notes Anita. "I came away from the discussion convinced that the doctor was out to make me fat. He told my coach that swim practice was off-limits for a while. He spoke to my school nurse as well. I snuck in some laps one weekend during the pool's family hours; I shivered too much in the water to enjoy myself, but that didn't matter. Neither did my jitters nor the trouble I had falling asleep at night. I'd missed several menstrual periods but was only marginally aware of that; what's more, I didn't care. As my illness progressed, I grew proud that I didn't have periods; losing them felt like a real accomplishment."

Many individuals who have recovered from an eating disorder have told us that their drive to be thin was so overpowering that they'd resort to anything to meet that goal, even if it meant tricking a parent or health professional into thinking they'd gained weight when they really hadn't. One young woman recalled arriving at her first appointment with a paperweight deep within each side pocket of her baggy jeans, only to learn that her physician wanted her weighed in an examining room gown. It is not unusual for a patient to secretly drink large amounts of water prior to a weigh-in so as to tip the scale upward. This is worrisome from a medical standpoint because water overload, combined with a low level of sodium in the individual's blood serum, can place her at risk for seizures. Physicians monitor for water misuse by testing the patient's urine for specific gravity.

Due to the nature of eating disorders, it may sometimes be hard—for you and even for the doctor—to know how your child is doing with her eating behaviors. Moreover, a person struggling with an eating disorder tends to experiment with a variety of behaviors throughout the course of her illness. For instance, someone who deprives herself of food may become so hungry that she eats and then panics that the food she has ingested will result in weight gain; in an attempt to rid herself of unwanted calories, she may induce vomiting. A person with bulimia who is stuck in a vicious binge-purge cycle often retains some of this behavior well into treatment. If her doctor has laboratory evidence (such as abnormal electrolytes and chemistries, especially potassium and bicarbonate) suggesting that she is vomiting, she is likely to retort, "I am not."

Whether or not there's clarity regarding your child's behaviors, the idea is for you to strive to understand why she hides them and to avoid putting on your detective's hat to prove her wrong. Perhaps she is ashamed of her eating disorder or unable to admit that she has one. It's possible that she's concealing her behaviors because she is worried about the impact on you and is trying to safeguard you from becoming frightened or distressed. Maybe she's dishonest about purging because she fears it means that she's "failing treatment" or that you will view it as such. Instead of turning her possible vomiting into a "gotcha" mission, you are better off keeping the lines of communication between the two of you open. In talking to her primary care doctor or pediatrician, let safety be your guide; if she is medically safe, you may have to tolerate occasional purging episodes.

"About six weeks after we started seeing the doctor, Anita lost a couple of pounds," recalls Lucinda. "I was a worried wreck. 'I *am* eating more,' she'd insist. The doctor told me that anorexia may distort an individual's interpretation of what constitutes 'more.' He also suspected that she was exercising more than he had recommended and that, like many young athletes, she might have the misconception that the less she weighed, the better she'd perform. In talking to us about sports, he highlighted the role of nutrition in sustaining energy and in keeping the muscles strong. He explained that when the body confronts a fuel shortage, it may burn muscle to meet energy needs. Underfed muscles may get smaller, weaker, and less capable of meeting athletic challenges. He added that restricting Anita's exercise was not a punishment; its purpose was not to deprive her of sports, but rather to make sure she was well enough to participate."

One reason primary care doctors and pediatricians monitor patients with anorexia and bulimia closely is that acute medical problems stemming from these illnesses can strike suddenly, without warning. Anita's doctor discussed the heart as a muscle that pumps life-sustaining oxygen and nutrients throughout the body. Just as the muscles of the arms and legs get weaker when undernourished, so can the heart. Gesturing toward a plastic anatomical heart model on his desk, he addressed the topic of pulse. While it is true that a low heart rate can be a part of physical fitness, a rate that is healthy for one person can be less so for another. That's why it is important for a patient with an eating disorder who exercises regularly to talk about her pulse with her primary care doctor; sometimes a cardiologist is involved in this discussion as well. When a heart beats too slowly or when a potassium level is abnormally low, life-threatening heart rhythms can develop. Levels of potassium and other electrolytes are followed closely in patients with eating disorders. Electrocardiograms (EKGs), which record the rhythm of the heart, may be performed and monitored as well. Some with eating disorders misuse ipecac and similar medications that induce vomiting. Ingesting large amounts of these substances places individuals at risk for muscle weakness and unpredictable cardiac events.

In addition to the life-threatening aspects of eating disorders, a number of other medical consequences exist. Using imaging techniques, such as magnetic resonance imagery (MRI) and positron emission tomography (PET), scientists have identified abnormalities in brain structure and function in individuals with anorexia. Some patients demonstrate problems with attention, concentration, and memory, and these often resolve with improved nutrition. Regarding her schoolwork, Anita recalls, "Projects that other kids completed with ease came harder to me when I had anorexia. I compensated by working lots of extra hours to keep my grades high. But all that studying took a lot out of me and kept me from having fun on weekends."

Many of our patients have reported abdominal discomfort. When Anita began to eat more, she was troubled by bloating and constipation, which her doctor attributed to a slowdown in the movement of food through her stomach and intestines as a result of malnutrition. "He felt that with continued healthy eating, these discomforts would go away," says Anita. "My vital signs had improved and were now normal. He told me that if I kept up the good work, I'd be strong enough to participate in a one-day group scuba-diving adventure that I'd found out about. I definitely wanted go on that expedition, but I didn't want to gain any more weight. In fact, I wouldn't have minded losing a few pounds."

Individuals who induce vomiting are subject to inflammation of the lining of the digestive tract and esophagus due to acid that backs up toward the mouth along with stomach contents. As our patient Rose, now 25 and doing well in recovery from anorexia and bulimia, recalls, "My heartburn, my sore throats, and my swollen salivary glands all went away when I cut back on my bingeing and vomiting. My strange taste preferences faded as I gained weight. My periods had stopped because I was so skinny. About six months after I reached what my treatment team called my 'goal weight,' my menstrual cycles started up again. Unfortunately, there was one problem that didn't go away, and that involved my bones."

## Discussing Bone Health

Healthy puberty brings about a growth spurt. Young people who develop anorexia before reaching their genetically programmed adult height may end up shorter than they would be if they were nutritionally healthy. Boys grow for about two years longer than girls and thus are more prone to shortened stature as a result of anorexia. Through improved nutrition, these individuals are often able to make up for some of their lost growth, but they may never reach their full height potential. Semistarvation disturbs the body's hormone system. A hallmark of anorexia nervosa, amenorrhea (the absence of menstrual periods) stems from a combination of poor nutrition, reduced body fat, overexercise, low weight, and emotional stress. Insufficient body fat, in particular, is an important reason why girls with anorexia nervosa do not get their periods. If your daughter's anorexia begins prior to or early in puberty, her first menstrual period and the development of other features of sexual maturity will likely be delayed. If she falls prey to anorexia after menarche (first menses), she will find that her monthly cycles become irregular or stop.

Amenorrhea and low estrogen set the stage for bone loss, a condition known as *osteopenia*, which can develop early in the course of anorexia and advance to the more serious condition of osteoporosis. More than 90 percent of women and 50 percent of teenage girls with anorexia sustain some loss in bone density. As a result, their bones become fragile, weak, and particularly susceptible to fracture. Due to a combination of bone loss and inadequate bone formation, people who develop anorexia during adolescence are more vulnerable to osteoporosis than those who develop the eating disorder later in life.

Bone loss occurs in many boys with anorexia as well. The good news is that advances in x-ray technology have made it possible to detect bone loss (or risk thereof) in its early stages. Painless, noninvasive, and with minimal radiation, a bone density test (also known as densitometry) measures the amount of mineral in a bone. (See Figure 6.1.) The skeletal areas most often tested are the lower spine (lumbar vertebrae) and the hips. Higher density bones are stronger and more resistant to breakage than lower density ones. (See Figure 6.2.) Looking back on her initial bone density study, Anita notes, "It was really easy and fast. Less than a year after the first test, my doctor recommended a second one to see if there were any changes." The suggested interval of not more than a year between a first and second bone density scan is particularly important in the teenage years, which represent a key period of growth. Bone formation is greatest between the ages of 11 and 14 in girls and 13 and 16 in boys. Ninety percent of a person's total bone mass has developed by late adolescence or early adulthood.

**FIGURE 6.1** Bone Density Test

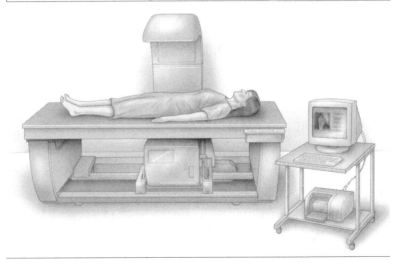

**FIGURE 6.2** Normal Healthy Bone vs. Osteoporotic Bone

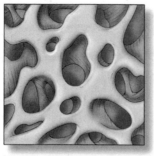

Normal, healthy bone

Osteoporotic bone

For a girl to bring back her periods, she needs to regain weight, with a healthy proportion of it consisting of fat. The patient with anorexia who overexercises is often very anxious about putting on pounds in the form of fat. She may regain the suggested amount of weight, but because not enough of it is fat, a delay in the return of her periods is possible. It is not unusual for an individual to perceive thinness as more important than the restart of her menses, especially if she competes in a sport that ties weight to performance. If your daughter is reluctant to put on fat, you need to be patient, realizing how emotionally charged this topic is for her. Offer her empathy with statements such as "It took a lot of courage and hard work to meet your weight goal, and you've done a tremendous job. Now that you've regained the weight, it must be so difficult to hear that your body fat is too low." It's a good policy to link discussion of body size and shape to health and safety. Thus, gently remind her that the body requires a certain amount of fat to maintain its hormone system, which in turn helps keep bones strong and resistant to injury.

When an individual with anorexia regains a healthy nutritional state, her bone density increases but—at least in the short term—doesn't recover completely from its loss. Girls with anorexia need to take in about 1,300 to 1,500 milligrams of calcium (a key component of bones), as well as 400 international units (IU) of vitamin D daily. Vitamin D helps the body absorb calcium. Because girls with osteoporosis are particularly vulnerable to fracture, it is important for them to avoid high-impact sports. You have probably read that exercise is thought to increase bone density; while this is generally the case, it does *not* hold true for individuals with anorexia nervosa. Muscle and fat tissues, as well as a normal menstrual cycle, play a major role in the growth of strong bones. When teenage girls with anorexia overexercise, their supplies of muscle and fat decrease, and this might further hamper bone formation. That's one of the main reasons doctors encourage patients with anorexia to limit their physical activity. Individuals with bulimia who have stayed within the healthy weight range are generally not in significant danger of bone loss. Normal-weight patients with bulimia who have suffered from anorexia in the past often need careful bone health monitoring.

For more than 10 years we've worked alongside Massachusetts General Hospital neuroendocrinologists Anne Klibanski, M.D.; Steven Grinspoon, M.D.; Karen K. Miller, M.D.; and Madhusmita Misra, M.D., on an internationally renowned study of osteoporosis in anorexia nervosa. Although we have established no definitive treatments, we are making headway and have found some promising clues. Research is in progress on bisphosphonates, such as risedronate (Actonel) and alendronate (Fosamax), which have been helpful in treating bone loss in postmenopausal women. The hormone testosterone is also under investigation for the treatment of osteopenia in individuals with anorexia. There is no evidence that birth control pills will reverse bone loss for this group of patients.

# Medical Dangers of Eating Disorders

The number-one priority of your child's treatment team will be to help her reach and maintain medical safety. While the physical complications of anorexia result mostly from self-starvation, those associated with bulimia derive from purging behaviors. The severity of each complication varies from one person to another. While the following lists are not all-encompassing, they will alert you to many of the problems that your child's treatment team is trying to prevent.

### Medical Consequences of Anorexia

- Heart abnormalities (slow heart rate, abnormal heart rhythm)
- Low blood pressure
- Low body temperature
- Bone loss, risk of fracture
- (For teenagers) Slowed growth, delayed sexual development, short stature
- Loss of menstrual periods
- Infertility
- Impaired concentration
- Anemia
- Muscle wasting, weakness
- Long-term constipation
- Loss of hair from scalp
- Brittle nails
- Halitosis (bad breath)
- Reduction in breast size
- Sallow skin
- Bloating
- Abdominal pain

### Medical Consequences of Bulimia

- Electrolyte imbalance (low potassium)
- Dehydration
- Irregular menstrual periods

- Swollen salivary glands
- Erosion of tooth enamel and cavities
- Inflammation in the lining of the digestive tract and esophagus
- Gastrointestinal bleeding (vomiting blood, blood in stools)
- Seizures
- Anxiety
- Mouth sores
- Heart rhythm disturbance
- Aspiration pneumonia
- Collapsed lung
- Chest pain

## What Medications May Help My Child?

Whether your child may benefit from psychiatric medication warrants close evaluation by her primary care physician or a psychopharmacologist (a psychiatrist who specializes in medication). Thus far, most research on the use of psychiatric medications for eating disorders has been conducted on adults. Many medications that the U.S. Food and Drug Administration (FDA) has approved for the treatment of anxiety and depression are now prescribed for individuals with eating disorders. Having said that, we want you to understand that there are no magic bullets; that is, no drug has proven consistently effective in the treatment of these disorders.

One of the most promising developments involves the role of antidepressants in individuals with bulimia nervosa. Chances are you associate antidepressants with their mood-lifting ability; what you may not know is that these medications can also serve other functions. For example, many people with bulimia who have taken an antidepressant have reported that it helped them cut down on their binge eating episodes. The selective serotonin reuptake inhibitors (SSRIs) tend to be tolerated better and result in fewer problems than the older generations of antidepressants and are most frequently prescribed for bulimia. More research is needed to determine how SSRIs and other antidepressants reduce binge frequency. It is likely that a multitude of factors play a role. A number of chemicals in the brain impact eating. Some of them (such as serotonin, dopamine, and norepinephrine) are known as neurotransmitters, and their function is to transport information between brain cells. (See Figure 6.3.) Research shows that people with eating disorders tend to have an imbalance in the neurotransmitter serotonin, which influences mood, anxiety, and the sensation that one has eaten enough. Normally, after serotonin delivers a message, it travels back to the brain cell from which it came. An SSRI blocks this reuptake (return passage), keeping more serotonin active in the system to make up for what the patient may not be producing on her own.

**FIGURE 6.3** How Neurons (Brain Cells) Communicate

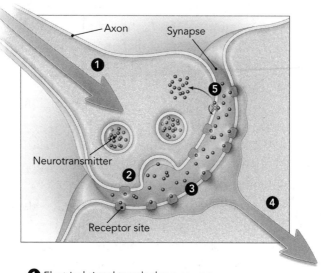

❶ Electrical signal travels down neuron.

❷ Chemical neurotransmitter is released.

❸ Neurotransmitter binds to receptor sites.

❹ Signal continues into new neuron.

❺ Reuptake occurs; neurotransmitter is transported back into the cell that released it.

Among the SSRIs is the well-known Prozac (fluoxetine), the only medication approved by the FDA for the treatment of bulimia nervosa. Individuals taking Prozac often do well on 60 milligrams per day, which is higher than the dose typically prescribed for the treatment of depression. If your child's doctor recommends an SSRI, he or she will probably start her on a small dose and increase it gradually while monitoring her response. The helpful effects of SSRIs tend to kick in by about six weeks.

SSRIs tend to ease the mood problems and anxiety that often accompany bulimia. Of her experience on this type of drug, our patient Tara, now 24, reports, "I started treatment as a college senior. About seven weeks into outpatient psychotherapy, my team of health providers suggested that I start an SSRI. I wasn't enthused about the idea of medication, but I figured I had nothing to lose. The first effect I noticed was a small but growing improvement in my overall wretchedness. In time, I became better able to bounce back from emotional upsets and to roll with the punches of everyday life. The combination of therapy and medication helped me binge and purge less frequently; but I have still not been able to stop those behaviors completely."

Like Tara, many patients with bulimia do well when receiving both antidepressant medication and psychotherapy. In general, SSRIs are very well tolerated. "I didn't have any negative effects," says Tara. Alternatives to SSRIs include a number of other antidepressants (such as Effexor, generic name venlafaxine) that can help patients manage anxiety, excessive activity, or idiosyncratic thoughts. Regardless of which antidepressant is prescribed for your child, she'll be professionally monitored, not only while she's initially adjusting to the medication, but for as long as she's on it. If her doctor starts her on one antidepressant and it doesn't "work," he or she may recommend that she switch to another from either the same class or a different one. She may need to try several drugs before finding an effective one. The dose of antidepressant required varies. While taking medication, your child should avoid drinking alcohol.

During the past few years of the 21st century, the possibility that antidepressants increase the risk of suicide in adolescents stirred considerable controversy and led to caution in prescribing these medications for this age group. Meanwhile, scientists analyzed extensive data about safety of antidepressants in young people and found the risk of suicidal thoughts and behavior to be much lower than anticipated. This is excellent news. If your child's doctor prescribes an antidepressant, he or she will monitor her during the early phases of treatment and talk with you about the advantages and safety of the medication. By reducing anxiety and improving mood, an antidepressant may allow a patient with an eating disorder to better accept therapy and, at times, to use it more effectively.

Whereas antidepressant medication has been helpful to many individuals with bulimia, its role in the treatment of anorexia nervosa is less clear. Although SSRIs have not proven effective in promoting weight gain, they are commonly prescribed for individuals with anorexia nervosa; seem to be well tolerated; and often have a positive effect on mood, anxiety, and obsessive-compulsive tendencies (persistent, uninvited thoughts, and behaviors resulting from obsessions). SSRIs do not seem to prevent relapse in patients with anorexia who have just been discharged from the hospital after gaining weight.

Anita recalls how the sense of well-being that marked the earliest phase of her anorexia waned. "Food- and weight-related pressures started to bombard me from all sides; each guilt trip that I'd eaten something 'fattening' would prey on my mind until a new, similar worry would come along to take its place. Before meals and snacks, my fears would go through the roof. My primary care doctor prescribed a low dose of an SSRI for me and explained that it would not take effect for several weeks. For the interim, he suggested a low dose of Ativan [lorazepam], a short-acting sedative that would help ease my anxiety about taking in food."

An individual with anorexia can benefit from a family of medications that originated as a treatment for schizophrenia and is now used to alleviate obsessions and compulsions, agitation, and idiosyncratic thoughts. The association of this group of antipsychotic drugs with weight gain sparked interest in their use in the treatment of anorexia patients who are entrenched in the illness and unable to see that they have a problem or need treatment. Zyprexa (olanzapine) and other medications in this class tend to improve an individual's mistaken belief that she is obese or that one meal will make her fat. With this class of medications, ongoing medical monitoring is essential.

Don't be surprised if your child is reluctant to take medication for her eating disorder. Whether she wants to recover herself (without meds) or fears that her medication will make her fat or control her thinking, it's possible that she'll refuse a prescription. Many patients are opposed not just to trying medication but to *any* change. Some are unable to admit that they are ill or that medication is warranted and others worry about side effects such as constipation. Concerns such as these call for patience and understanding. Remind your child of the ways her eating disorder "gets in the way" by keeping her from sports or making her cold and tired; point out that medication can help her feel less down and thereby make it easier for her to work on her eating difficulties.

Try to establish a dialogue around how difficult it must be for her to keep hearing medical recommendations that she wants no part of and how puzzling it must be that measures intended to help her don't feel helpful. Your nonjudgmental approach and your focus on not pressuring her can open her mind to follow-up discussion and give her the space she needs to reconsider the possibility of trying medication. You and the other members of your child's treatment team will continue to share ideas about how to encourage her to take steps, such as trying medication, that are hard but potentially rewarding.

## Continuing Care

Your child's primary care physician will remain a valuable resource not only during her initial weeks of medical stabilization, but throughout the entire treatment process and into recovery. As your child's health improves, her primary care doctor won't need to see her as frequently. However, he or she will be in communication with the other members of the treatment team. Feel free to call on the primary care physician or any other team member as your questions arise. They understand what you are going through and will welcome your calls.

In Chapter 7, we will look at some of the emotional illnesses that can accompany eating disorders.

## CHAPTER 7

# How You Can Help Support Her Through Recovery

"Paula's generosity of spirit is very special," says her mother, Rita. "She's bright, diligent, and resourceful. She's always been an avid reader; even as a young child, she loved stories and was fascinated by rhyme. She chose a career in social work and is doing so well in it. I wish *she* knew how capable she is."

Paula had first come to see us as a college freshman, when she was suffering from bulimia. At the time, her firm belief that she was "not good enough" was ruling her life, leading to unhealthy habits and making it difficult for her to pursue her studies and reside in her dormitory. Paula's situation was not unusual. Most individuals with eating disorders also struggle with other mental health challenges, such as dark moods or anxiety. In this chapter, we will describe some of these difficulties, explore how they may be treated, and suggest ways you can assist your child in her journey. Rita and Paula, now 28, kindly offered to share their story with you.

"When Paula left for college, we were on good terms," remembers her mother. "I phoned her in her dormitory every weekend or so. At the beginning of the academic year, she seemed herself; but gradually, a cloud came over her, and she had very little to say. She answered my questions in one word. How are you? 'Fine.' How is freshman English? 'Okay.' How are your roommates? 'Good.' Sometimes her voice was monotone and other times snippy, as if she'd rather not talk to me. Every time I tried to reach out to her, she shut me out."

"I shut *everyone* out," acknowledges Paula. "When my family asked me what was going on, I always answered, 'Nothing,' which meant that I hadn't a clue. Back then, I didn't have the words to describe my inner experience. I felt that I wasn't good at anything. The kids in my dorm were good at hanging out and meeting new people; I thought I was terrible at that, always the awkward one. I went running three times a week on my own and wanted to get involved in college sports but felt I wasn't athletic enough. I'd played lacrosse in high school but always struggled with skills that other players seemed to grasp with ease. When I saw how 'good' my teammates were and how 'bad' I was, I freaked. I practiced the skills superhard on my own so that I could catch up with the others before they and the coach found out how clumsy I was.

"If I'd been particularly good at one thing in high school, I wouldn't have minded being second-rate at others. But that wasn't the case. When it came to hobbies and extracurricular interests, one kid in my class was a really good actor, another loved photography, and a third was musically talented. I envied a girl who had a special way with animals. I had a special way with nothing. It was similar with schoolwork. Some students were good in biology, some in math, others in history; I was mediocre across the board. The only reason I earned top grades in high school is that I spent my whole life studying, or so it seemed. If I hadn't worked so hard, my grades would have slipped and everyone would have discovered how stupid I really was.

"I couldn't get my bearings in college. I felt lost in an emotional whirlwind that never seemed to stop. I had no idea where that sensation came from or what to do about it. Once it gained momentum, it became so much a part of me that it seemed to have always been there. Somewhere within that tornado was my sense of never being good enough. Looking back, I can say that my feelings and thoughts spun around so much that they seemed to cancel each other out and leave my mind blank.

"When I wasn't in class, I wandered the campus aimlessly or hibernated in the library with my books. Although I was no longer interested in learning, in reading, or in the content of my courses, I needed good grades and felt safest in the quiet and anonymity of the library. What's more, it seemed like I didn't have anywhere else to go. It took everything I had to keep going without adding the hassles of interacting with other people. I wasn't sure why, but many students seemed to enjoy being with others. I didn't consider myself a candidate for friendship, much less for a romantic relationship. I wondered what was wrong with me that I wasn't more like other students.

"Because my mind felt empty, it was hard to manage certain academic projects, especially those that required decision making or 'out-of-the-box' thinking. In freshman English, one assignment was to choose a poem and write a review of it. Selecting the poem felt like a tremendous ordeal. I found one I sort of liked but didn't think would pass muster with the professor; so I went on to consider another and another, unable to make a decision for many hours. Once I finally settled on one, writing the review was equally hard. I felt thankful that I didn't have to write a poem of my own. That would have bowled me over completely; I wouldn't have been able to handle it.

"In mid-October, I went on a diet. I'd never been heavy but feared that I would be if I weren't careful. The women who struck me as well liked, accomplished, and happy looked thin. Now I realize that the thinness-equals-perfection assumption is false, but back then I bought into it. At first, I lost weight. The problem with my diet was that I'd become famished toward the end of every day. I picked up the habit of downing a huge amount of food frantically, unable to stop. After eating, I'd feel disgusted with myself. My stomach hurt. I cried and reminded myself to keep my habits secret. The pressure of the waistband of my jeans against my stomach kept reminding me that I was fat and bad; that feeling was unbearable. I wanted to crawl out of my skin. I'd panic that the food I'd just ingested would pile on the pounds. To get rid of the unwelcome calories and calm down, I'd make myself vomit. So began a cycle that I didn't like but had to continue because something inside expected me to.

"Although concealing my bingeing and vomiting was of major importance, I also had something else to hide. Now and then I'd get a powerful urge to cut myself and feel driven to act on that impulse, as if I had no choice. After ensuring my privacy, I'd use a razor blade to carve small cuts on the inside of my wrist. I'd wince at the sting but, at the same time, accept it as punishment. The piercing of my skin produced slight bleeding and a release of indefinable emotional pressures. Afterward, I'd feel at peace. I realized that if other people were to find out about my cutting, they'd insist I never do it again; what's more, they'd think I was crazy. And they might misinterpret my cutting as a suicide attempt. I wasn't trying to kill myself. But I had to do something to calm myself, and since cutting created that effect, it was well-worth repeating, as long as I could keep it secret; that's why I always wore long sleeves. Though the calm following each cutting episode proved short-lived, it was better than none. And at that point, I was willing to take whatever emotional peace I could get."

In everyday functioning, it is not only whether and to what degree a person feels she isn't good enough that matters, but also how she manages that feeling. Some ways of dealing with such perceptions are healthier than others. Productive approaches include efforts to recognize and talk about negative inner experiences and to devise short- and long-term strategies aimed at feeling better. Binge eating is a counterproductive way of dealing with emotions. So are cutting, stealing, excessive sexual activity, suicide gestures, and misuse of alcohol or drugs. Cigarette smoking, which people use to relieve anxiety, assist with weight control, or feel "cool," is a form of substance abuse and is addictive. All these behaviors carry serious health risks. It is not unusual for someone with an eating disorder also to suffer from one or more of these other self-defeating habits, as Paula did, in an effort to manage tumultuous and painful emotions.

People with eating disorders come from a range of early life experiences. While some patients describe their childhoods in positive terms, others report trauma. Past physical, emotional, or sexual abuse is not unusual among those with eating disorders. The impact of early trauma can follow a person into her teenage years and beyond, increasing her vulnerability to a host of emotional problems, including eating disorders, depression, or anxiety. For the individual with a history of abuse, recovery from an eating disorder tends to be particularly arduous. Ties between her trauma and her eating disorder often depend on a number of factors, including the following: the kind of abuse, how old she was at the time, how frequently it occurred, the nature of her relationship with the abuser, and what consequences were threatened if she told anyone about it. The eating disordered individual who has suffered abuse is prone to developing one or more additional self-defeating habits in attempts to cope with intense negative emotions arising from the trauma.

The paths that lead to "I'm not good enough" differ from one person to another. Furthermore, an individual's negative feelings about herself can come from a combination of many places. Some people have a tendency to defer to the outside world for reassurance that they are good enough. Lacking an internal sense of "I'm good," they gauge their worth based on feedback from others. Paula describes a childhood free of trauma and speaks of how "I'm bad" can snowball. "When it first occurred to me that I was inept, I began to avoid athletic and social activities that might have challenged that belief and helped me to feel better about myself. Ultimately 'I'm bad' became a fixture in my mind. But as a college freshman, I was unaware of how my perceptions of myself were shaping and coloring my experiences. Back then, each day felt like a struggle for survival."

Given Paula's wall of silence, Rita could not have known the extent of her turmoil. "My daughter's curt telephone manner told me *something* was wrong," she says, "but I had no idea what that was. Back then, the possibility that she had an eating disorder never occurred to me. Sure, she'd dieted at home—so had her 15-year-old sister and most of their friends. Neither of my daughters had been fanatic about losing weight. Paula's diets had been very brief; within a few days she'd tire of them and stop.

"I so wanted Paula to be happy in college that it was very hard to see signs that she wasn't. Both she and my younger daughter were prone to occasional sullenness. Weren't most teenagers? Paula had always been so sensible. I didn't want to be overprotective or intrusive or annoy her with repeated 'Are you okay' calls. On the other hand, she was barely 18 years old and away at college for the first time. And she certainly wasn't herself. If she'd talked to me, I might not have been quite so worried, but she hadn't, and my uncertainty about her welfare was hard to handle. I'd met Paula's residence adviser at the freshman orientation reception and remembered her warm smile. I let Paula know that I'd be calling the R.A. and then went ahead with it."

Chances are you can relate to this mom's angst as she wrestled with the possibility that her daughter was hurting. Rita's wish not to overreact was totally understandable; many freshmen have difficulty adjusting to college and come through it fine. Though the judgment call that Rita faced was harrowing, her intuition that her daughter needed help was right on target, as was her decision to intervene. Although Rita was aware that interceding would anger Paula and risk further alienation, she put safety first, which was more helpful to her daughter than either of them knew at the time.

"When Mom told me that she was about to call the R.A., one part of me felt defeated and the other wanted to run away," admits Paula. "I told the R.A., Cheryl, about my eating problem but not about my cutting, and she informed me that the college health center operated a confidential telephone hotline for students who were down, frightened, or having negative thoughts and feelings about their bodies. I dialed the hotline once, but the second someone answered, I hung up. When Mom arrived at school, she insisted I go to the health center for a checkup; both she and Cheryl came with me. After the medical exam, another doctor talked with me and then scheduled two follow-up appointments with me for later that week. In the midst of all this, there were phone calls between Mom and the student health center. The doctors recommended that I take a leave of absence from college to get treatment in order to improve my health. I tried to make them think I wanted to stay at school, but that wasn't altogether true.

"With the tumult of leaving college, my feelings were sometimes a jumble and sometimes 'nonexistent.' I sensed that I'd been kicked out, even though I'd been assured that wasn't the case. The dean said my grades were impressive and that I had 'strong potential' but that she was concerned about my health. She promised I could return when I was well. As ashamed as I was about leaving college and returning home, part of me was relieved that certain pressures were off. I'd no longer have to roam the campus feeling homeless or 'camp out' in the library. Furthermore, I'd be free of roommate hassles. And I'd been struggling day and night with my English term paper; now I could let that go.

"But living at home came with its own set of problems. The first night, I lay awake worrying and putting myself down. How would I binge and vomit now that Mom knew about my eating disorder? What kind of wimp was I that I couldn't hack college? I was such a loser! Without my classes, what would I do all day? How would I explain to my sister what had happened? I'd have to be very careful to keep my cutting a secret. It looked like life at home would be different from that at college but equally hard, and if that turned out to be the case, I wasn't sure how long I could keep going. I didn't want to die, but I certainly didn't want the life I'd led over the past few months."

Like Paula, many people with eating disorders feel down, though some suffer more intense, prolonged, or recurrent lows than others. Oppressive moods can make an eating disorder worse and vice versa. Some patients who struggle with both an eating disorder and depression go to school or work, whereas others feel overwhelmed or overburdened to the point where even personal hygiene feels close to impossible. For some people, emotional darkness (or turmoil) precedes their eating disorder; for some, it's the other way around; and for others, both conditions begin at roughly the same time. "That first week home from college, I stayed in my bedroom most of the time, crying, exercising, or staring at the wall," recalls Paula. "I lashed out at Mom a few times and afterward felt guilty. What I didn't realize was that I could, and would, be helped."

## Building on Her Strengths

Paula and most of our patients are talented, hardworking individuals who ache inside. When a patient's problems interfere with various aspects of her life, it becomes all the more difficult for her to recognize her strengths. For many, recovery is a journey of growth and self-discovery in which family members can play an important and rewarding role. Rita and her daughter elaborate here on what went well and not-so-well during treatment.

"The treatment team told me that individuals with eating disorders are very reluctant to give up their behaviors and that the first step in therapy would be to establish an alliance with Paula as a foundation for addressing change," states Rita. "Actually, I'd been hoping that the professionals would have a ready-made solution to her angry outbursts. That expectation was unrealistic, but I was so blinded by my need to restore peace to the household that I tended to lose perspective. Here I was doing my best to help Paula, and all she seemed to do was get mad at me. While I didn't like hearing that her behavior change would take time, receiving that information up front helped me in the difficult months that followed."

Paula raised the subject of privacy. "It was helpful that Mom didn't pressure me to tell her what I talked about during individual therapy. During the first few sessions, I said next to nothing to my therapists. When I finally broke my silence, I told them that it was hard to fall asleep at night and that I wasn't sure what to do with myself now that I'd been 'kicked out' of college. That led to discussions about my way of life on campus and about the diet that had somehow gone awry.

"My doctors explained that restricting one's food intake can result in a binge and that stress and unhealthy beliefs about the body and weight can also serve as triggers. One of my homework projects for therapy was to start a journal for tracking the connections between my thoughts, my feelings, and my binges. Another assignment involved noting what activities I might use instead of eating when feeling angry, nervous, or not good enough. Putting these alternatives into practice was harder than it sounded. An episode of overeating would make me think I'd flunked bulimia treatment and therefore might as well stop trying. That was one of the assumptions I tried to reframe in a positive way; thus, instead of concluding "I've failed," I worked hard at telling myself that goofs are part of the recovery process and that I could now get back on track.

"In therapy, I learned about a tool called a time delay. It meant that when I felt the urge to binge, I'd give myself permission to go ahead with it, but only if I waited 15 minutes. Meanwhile, I was to focus on anything that might distract me from eating. I found crossword puzzles helpful for this purpose. If the urge to gorge was present at the 15-minute mark, I again told myself that I could do it if I waited 15 minutes. The idea was to keep procrastinating until the drive to binge faded. That strategy proved somewhat helpful for cutting as well as for bingeing.

" 'Not good enough' was a topic my therapists and I visited often. Through my eyes, I was so glaringly 'bad' that it was very hard to peek outside that box. Drawing from my personal experiences, I offered one example after another in evidence of my defectiveness, with particular detail to my stupidity. Since I wanted to return to college, one of my hopes was to develop the ability to study for a reasonable length of time instead of to an extreme. That was an ambitious goal, and although I was able to set some limits on my overworking before heading back to college, I continued to push myself hard.

"A few months after I entered therapy, my team suggested that I start an antidepressant medication known as an SSRI [selective serotonin reuptake inhibitor]. I didn't like that idea. Was I really so sick that I had to be on psychiatric medication? Had Mom pressured me to take an antidepressant, I would have refused. I never admitted it at the time, but the medication helped. While it wasn't a magic bullet, it lifted my spirits and helped me move around more freely, without having to exert what felt like a superhuman effort. I didn't have any side effects. The combination of medication and therapy helped me cut back on my bingeing and my cutting, though I didn't overcome the habits completely for quite some time."

## Addressing Her Withdrawal from You

An individual with an eating disorder might be withdrawn for many reasons. Chances are she has isolated herself not only from you, but also from other family members and her friends. Shame about her body size or shape may be one factor that keeps her in hiding. Perhaps she's ashamed of having an eating disorder as well. Oppressive moods, anxiety, painful repetitive thoughts, and inner turmoil add to the tendency to isolate. So do the behaviors that accompany eating disorders, such as cutting, stealing, or substance abuse. Abnormal eating habits often continue well into treatment, leading the individual to feel that she's "failing" therapy or that you think she is.

Recalling the intensity of Paula's first weeks back from college, Rita describes herself as hesitant when the treatment team recommended family therapy. "At first, I feared I'd be blamed for my daughter's disorder. I was very sensitive about that. As it turned out, our family sessions were based on the understanding that no one had caused the disorder. Through meeting together with the therapist, Paula and I explored how we might communicate more effectively with each other. I raised my concern about Paula's reluctance to talk to me. This led to discussion of several subjects over a number of family therapy sessions. We started by talking about how we perceived our own personalities and each other's. As an outgrowth of that dialogue, we addressed the topic of expectations, eventually broaching the question of why it had become so difficult to spend time together."

"In family therapy, I said that I felt under a microscope when I was with Mom," notes Paula. "That was the case well before my eating disorder developed, but it grew worse when I moved home from college. Although she didn't expect me to tell her what I talked about in individual therapy, I always felt that she was critiquing me. If I were to join her for dinner, she'd notice what I did and didn't eat. I refused to go clothes shopping with her because I knew she'd silently pass judgment on my appearance. Summer was coming, and I shuddered to think of her seeing me in shorts, much less a bathing suit. I wanted her to see and value me for who I was as a person, not for what I looked like. And I certainly didn't want her to think of me as an eating disorder. At one point in family therapy, I said that I sensed Mom had a blind spot when it came to who I was inside. I felt she had an image in her mind of how she wanted me to be. The problem was that I didn't fit that picture."

"I disagreed with her about the blind spot," says Rita. "I had to admit, however, that there was a crack in our relationship. Discussion in family therapy turned to whether we wanted to work on mending this rift. Our 'yes' represented a big step forward."

Because every family's situation is different, there is no formula for how to cope with an eating disordered child who is withdrawn. Approaches to the problem must be individualized. Again, let safety be your guide. Is she isolated and not eating? Are her moods dark? Often, withdrawal is complex and multifaceted, with some aspects being easier to address than others. For the teen, the challenge of connecting or reconnecting with parents can be complicated by a thirst for independence that typically emerges during that stage of life.

"Based on input from Paula during family meetings, it seemed that she was grappling with the question of whether and how to chart her own path instead of following the one that she perceived had been planned for her," notes Rita. "It seemed that we had different styles. I'm outgoing; she's introverted. I have a low tolerance for ambiguity; she doubts and questions. We're both achievement-oriented, but our career interests are different. As a small business owner, I consider myself entrepreneurial and competitive. At the time of family therapy, she was unsure what she wanted to do with her life. What she did know was that she didn't want one like mine. For both Paula and me, navigating those waters of identity and independence was a tall order of business. The importance of family therapy was that it taught us to talk about that topic, thereby taking another step forward."

In addition to receiving professional treatment, patients find that having a variety of interests helps them cope. "Some months after beginning the SSRI and family therapy, I became curious about yoga because I'd heard it was calming," recalls Paula. "I observed a group at a community center near my home and decided to sign up. Yoga class served as an incentive for leaving the house and seemed to take the edge off some of my anxieties. I spent a lot of time reading. I found books on eating disorders that shed light on my own situation. Also helpful was keeping a daily journal, which I showed no one. When my mind felt empty, the mechanics of writing by hand—even if the content was nonsense—helped me feel halfway productive. In the process of journaling one day, I began to reflect on the likelihood that many other people felt as

## My Child with an Eating Disorder Barely Speaks to Me. How Might I Help Improve Our Interactions?

There is no one-size-fits-all approach to the eating disordered child who withdraws from her parents. Here are some general guidelines that families we've worked with have found helpful:

- Try to carve out some uninterrupted time with your child—turn off the telephone and television.
- Be clear through your gentle approach that this time is not meant to discuss her eating habits or your concern about her health. It is simply to be together. You can even schedule a regular weekly "appointment" with her that you both can count on.

- When you do spend time with your child, refrain from commenting on her appearance or weight.
- Encourage your child to select an activity. Try to focus on activities that are not related to food or eating. Look for a common interest, something through which you can connect.
- Let your child feel a sense of control. Offer her choices (in activities, in food selection). Giving her even a little choice will go a long way.
- Do not pressure your child to talk with you. If she resists conversation, it may come in time. If your child prefers not to talk, perhaps you can share an activity such as playing a board game, gardening, or watching a movie together. Just sharing space and being together will convey to her that you value your relationship with her, that she is worthwhile and worthy of your time.
- Your efforts at practicing patience and acceptance will communicate to her that you believe in her and that you are in this for the long haul. Make eye contact with her when she does reach out. Convey to her that you know there is a person inside who is much more than a size or a shape. Remind her of her value, her talents, and her gifts. Praise her!
- Don't expect change to happen overnight. It's a process that will take time.

bad as I did—or worse. If that were the case, then they too needed help. That train of thought sparked my growing desire to become a social worker."

## Addressing Her Restricted Social Life

Eating disorder behaviors and patterns conflict with almost any activity involving other people. The disorder can be all-consuming, not only mentally and physically, but also from a practical standpoint. With its relentless thought patterns, rules and rituals, and emotional turbulence, an eating disorder can drain an individual's energy, preventing her from partaking in anything else. Over time, she feels unable to relate to friends or others within her peer group who don't seem to understand or tolerate her disorder. As her illness becomes her way of life, it takes priority over everything. Spending time with friends tends to feel like an intrusion on her single-minded pursuit of thinness and pose a threat to the maintenance of her behaviors. As a result, social activities feel too risky and stress-producing, leaving her no option but to stay away from them.

If your child isolates herself socially, your approach will depend on numerous factors. For instance, you'll need to consider the stage of her illness. The biological process of starvation pulls the individual into her shell, leaving her without enough motivation or stamina to interact socially. When she's in treatment and begins to eat more healthfully, her desire to interact with others can improve or remain hampered by other conditions that occur in tandem with her eating disorder. It's important not to assume from your child's isolation that it's what she ultimately wants. On the contrary, some individuals with eating disorders suffer from a tremendous sense of loneliness, which they are often unable to express.

You will also want to take into account your child's temperament and level of interaction prior to the development of her eating disorder. Was she shy, gregarious, or somewhere in between? What sorts of relationships with other people will she want in the future? Above and beyond the question of basic health, the routines, rituals, and idiosyncrasies associated with eating disorders can put a damper on her ability to attain other goals. For instance, if her inclination to isolate will interfere with her ability to hold a job or pursue her career of choice, she may want to consider working on increasing her capacity to interact. The same holds true if she aims to forge and remain in a relationship with a significant other.

## One Athlete's Struggle to Find Friends

Often, fears about socializing are present before the individual develops the eating disorder. Bruce's anorexia crept up on him the summer before he entered college and escalated during his freshman year. "Although I did well academically in high school, sports were where I made my mark," he recalls. "I was the school's star cross-country runner. As a senior, I won the best student athlete of the year award. All spring, I followed the nutrition regimen recommended by the coach and planned to stay on it after graduation. But that's not what I did. Looking back, my weight loss wasn't a deliberate effort, but it wasn't happenstance either. I was marginally aware that I wasn't eating as much as I had in the past.

"Margo and I met as juniors in high school, and because we shared similar values and thrived on sports, our relationship felt like a good fit. Regarding my eating disorder, she was remarkably compassionate. We were excited about our opportunity to attend the same college. For our first six months on campus, we enjoyed our time together and rarely squabbled. But toward spring, I began to sense her anger at me; unfortunately, she could not or would not tell me what was bothering her. She went out for crew and had to get up at five o'clock every morning to attend rowing practice; when we were out in the evening, she now wanted to be back at nine. Meanwhile, I had my own schedule, which I followed to the letter. For example, I went running at seven o'clock sharp every morning. I lifted weights at four every afternoon, no matter what. I reserved a big block of time every day for studying and would not use those hours for anything else. Ordering my life in this way came naturally to me; that was how my mind worked."

Like Bruce, many people with eating disorders are attached to routine. This often applies not only to their eating regimens, but to their entire way of life. They find it very difficult to depart from their schedules. "My preference for routine started when I was in grade school," says Bruce. "But when my eating disorder struck, I grew more schedule-bound than ever. All deviations from routine were hard, some more so than others. The most manageable were those I knew about well ahead of time, such as appointments for dental checkups. But let's say my roommate had tickets to a ball game and asked me to go; whether I accepted his invitation would depend on how far in advance I received it and what routine it would break. The worst kinds of schedule interruptions were those that struck unexpectedly. It didn't particularly matter whether the change was about something good or bad or whether it required a brief departure from a routine or a longer one. If it happened unpredictably, I'd feel like I was losing my moorings and falling to pieces.

"Once Margo took up rowing, seeing her meant loosening the structure of my evenings, and that proved very difficult. She began to find my routine confining. 'We never do anything new,' she observed. 'Can't you be more spontaneous?' I told her I'd try harder. I hadn't made any other friends at college, and in many ways—though I was unaware of it at the time—I felt dependent on Margo. Nevertheless, our relationship grew stale, and we saw each other less and less. We began to argue about trivial matters, and at the end of our freshman year, we broke up. I took the loss of Margo hard but didn't want anyone to know it.

"When I returned to college for my sophomore year, my hope was to make friends. That was a lot easier said than done. I realized at the time that my thoughts about work were irrational. My daily study periods grew longer and lonelier. Yet I continued to enforce them as if they were jail sentences, because something inside me said that I should always be working, which meant studying or exercising. Taking the time to hang out and chat with other people would make me feel guilty and interfere with my schedule. The unanchored feeling that would come over me when I broke my routines made me cling to them all the harder.

"What's more, I've always been shy and had trouble initiating conversation. I get so nervous about meeting people that I can't follow conversations. If a person is talking to me, I hear her words but not their meaning, and that's really embarrassing. So sometimes I pretend I'm 'with the program' even if I haven't absorbed a word the person has said. For instance, if someone tells a joke, there's no way I can get the punchline because I haven't processed what led up to it. Usually I laugh anyway. That strategy works okay for jokes but backfires in other interactions. If someone is describing an experience and I'm lost in nervousness, I'll nod my head, smile, or make a vague, semiverbal comment now and then to make it seem like I'm listening. If the speaker then asks an open-ended question—such as 'What do you think?'—I'm totally stuck and embarrassed. I've been in that situation more often than I like to think about.

"I decided to try to befriend fellow members of the cross-country team. I figured that the shared interest in athletics would make conversation easier than it otherwise might be. Besides, belonging to a team had always given me pleasure. Unfortunately, I started having trouble with my running times; that, combined with my determination to get good grades, put my friendship goals on the back burner. Though I'd never have admitted it at the time, the reason for my running setback was that I wasn't eating enough. When I was in the grips of anorexia, my motto was 'the lighter the body, the faster the running time.' Upon entering treatment, I was surprised to learn that the saying is false. I had believed it so strongly that it was hard to think any other way. It took me a long time to realize that poor nutrition can contribute to muscle wasting. With better nutrition, my running times would improve.

"Now it's the summer after my sophomore year, and I'm working every day as a landscaper while living at home with my family. My grades for the spring semester were fantastic, and my running speed is back on track. Sometimes I'll have an awesome week, and then—I don't know why—I'll have an eating binge that brings on a bad mood. The problem is that I have no friends. Here at home, there's no social environment, and I'm not eager to return to college in September because friendship groups among my classmates are already made. My thinking often goes like this: 'I'm such a loser. It's Friday night and here I am at home with my parents and not going out.'"

## A Father's Perspective

William, Bruce's dad, feels that his son's journey has been a learning experience for the entire family. "I've always been so proud of his athletic gifts that I probably underestimated the toll that competition was taking on him. He was a champion runner in high school, and I think he felt like a 'little fish in a big pond' when he went off to college. I was aware of his 'the lighter, the faster' philosophy, but I never imagined that it would reach such an extreme. His eating disorder took me by surprise—I couldn't understand how someone so thin could possibly see himself as overweight. Bruce's primary care physician informed me that his weight loss was not about food per se but rather about how he felt inside. That was a real eye-opener for me.

"As for Bruce's shyness, that's where he takes after me. When I was his age, I had trouble making friends because I always thought that I was being judged. I'm still shy to some extent. So I can definitely see where Bruce is coming from, and I continue to work on communicating that compassion to him. Ways to meet other kids are something he and I have been able to discuss to a point. My wife and I encourage him to go out with others, but sometimes there's a fine line between encouraging and pressuring, and I'd rather stick to the former. He is trying very hard to lead a more balanced life, and little by little, he is heading toward his friendship goals."

William's candor about his own apprehensions was highly valuable. It is not unusual for family members of an eating disordered individual to experience anguish in social situations, self-doubt, obsessive ways of thinking, or oppressive moods. The possibility that eating disorders are tied genetically to anxiety, depression, or both is now under investigation.

## Everyone with an Eating Disorder Is Unique

When discussing the conditions that travel with eating disorders, it is important not to overgeneralize. Most people with anorexia, bulimia, or binge eating disorder suffer from the theory that they are not good enough. But while some experience dark moods, others don't. A number of individuals with eating disorders struggle with anxieties. But there are different kinds of anxieties. Some patients, like Bruce, become trapped in routines (in addition to those involving food) that are hard to live with and hard to live without. Angst about making friends is not uncommon among individuals with eating disorders. Furthermore, depression and anxiety occur along a continuum, with people experiencing different degrees of these emotions. Although some patients with bulimia are restrained, others are on the impulsive side and engage in cutting, as Paula did, or in other self-defeating behaviors. The individuality and dimensionality of every patient cannot be emphasized enough.

With all the challenges you are facing in caring for a child with an eating disorder, it can be hard to keep sight of those parts of her that are healthy and positive. Despite their problems in the way they experience their bodies and despite the additional emotional hardships they face, many individuals with anorexia, bulimia, or binge eating disorder have inner resources and capabilities of which they aren't yet aware. While your child is in treatment, your empathy and encouragement are likely to be instrumental as she discovers her strengths and taps into them.

You are probably wondering how your child will fare as a result of treatment. Will she get better? How much better? And if she does regain her health, will she maintain it? Chapter 8 will address those questions.

## CHAPTER 8

# Managing and Preventing Relapses

What is recovery? Although there is still much to learn about the journey from eating disorder to health, recent research and the expertise of many clinicians in the field have provided important knowledge about how patients do in treatment. The word *recovery* is used in a variety of ways, sometimes referring to the process of recovering, other times denoting an endpoint or destination. Complicating the situation further is the expression *in recovery*. This is not to say that one use of the term is right and the others wrong. In fact, all of them are valid.

Most patients who receive professional treatment improve over time. As your child works with her team to restore her nutritional balance, reduce her unhealthy behaviors, and discuss her thoughts and emotions, her illness will often recede gradually. The road to wellness, however, is not easy. For some, it takes months; for others, years. Along the way, most patients slip occasionally, falling back temporarily into old behaviors. Some people reach their treatment goals fully; some do so partially (for example, experiencing weight increases but continued body dissatisfaction); a smaller number continue to struggle. Janet first came to see our group eight years ago about her then-15-year-old daughter Courtney, who had developed an eating disorder. Their stories will help give you an appreciation of the amount of territory covered by the term *recovery*.

## Janet's Perspective

"When Courtney was a toddler, she was quite the mischievous one," recalls her mother. "Her independence and resourcefulness have proven invaluable in helping her cope with her eating disorder. The youngest of my three children, Courtney took a lot of ribbing from her brothers and seemed remarkably capable of holding her own. She used to respond to their teasing so cleverly that they'd pause in their tracks, baffled by her ingenuity, yet at the same time, proud of her. Her quick wit combined with her sensitivity earned her a special respect, not only from her brothers, but also from kids at school and in our neighborhood. People couldn't help but like her.

"During the summer after eighth grade, Courtney joined a community acting group and seemed to thrive on it; at first, she showed more interest in friendship with the other students than in the plays themselves. But in August, she won a role in a musical, which would mean learning dance skills and practicing one evening a week throughout the fall and winter. Stan and I were pleased that our daughter was committed to such an interesting and worthwhile goal. My only hesitation was that she was undertaking the dance project at the same time as she was transitioning into high school, and I talked with her about whether the combined demands might prove taxing. Given her enthusiasm about participating in the musical, I saw no reason to hold her back.

"I wasn't the first to catch wind of Courtney's eating disorder. One not-so-productive afternoon at work, I answered the phone and was taken aback when the caller introduced himself as her ninth-grade English teacher. Unlike her brothers, Courtney was a top student, and so her teacher was just about the last person I'd expected to hear from. But he wasn't calling about her grades. His concern was a blog [a Web log, which may take the form of a diary or journal] she had recently created. Courtney had a relatively thin, athletic frame, but in her blog, she described herself as 'a useless tub o' lard,' 'fat stuff,' 'fatter than fat,' and 'getting fatter all the time.' Those expressions, he said, sent chills down his spine. And that wasn't all. Although the blog didn't say so directly, it had given him the hunch that she may have developed disordered eating behaviors. He suggested that I take Courtney to her primary care physician or pediatrician for evaluation. So began our journey."

## On the Road to Health

"In reflecting on Courtney's professional care," continues Janet, "many memories stand out in my mind. The first was our initial visit to Courtney's pediatrician. On the way to his office, she urged me to turn the car around, claiming that she felt fine and that my worries about her health were 'ridiculous.' The stop-and-go traffic made every minute of that drive feel like hours. At one point, my daughter was madder at me than I'd ever seen her. Such outbursts weren't like her at all. With sweat trickling down my neck and the noise of an ambulance siren coming from behind us, I had all I could do to keep my eyes on the road, much less try to reason with her. She was so riled up that I was afraid she'd open the car door and dash out. She'd never been prone to that type of impulse, but she'd changed so much lately that I didn't know what to expect.

"I don't want to give you the impression that the earliest phase of Courtney's treatment was laced with drama. On the contrary, our home was ruled by unspoken words. Although this atmosphere was nothing new, it became much more pronounced once Courtney's bulimia gained momentum. From the minute she returned from school until she left the next morning, she stayed away from Stan and me. Even though we never saw her binge, we were acutely aware that she did it. But because none of us knew how to approach the topic of the eating disorder, we swept it under the rug. The silence grew so emotionally charged that we were all afraid to break it.

"Meanwhile, our pediatrician stayed in contact with me to explain the multifaceted nature of bulimia and to help me set the wheels of treatment in motion. He reported that her weight was a bit low and that her binge-purge habit was occupying a great deal of her time and energy, making her vulnerable to medical problems. He offered to monitor Courtney medically, keeping a close watch on her electrolytes. The therapist role was to encourage her to regulate her eating habits and to rethink her beliefs about food and body weight that had contributed to the disorder. In addition, therapy would help her to like herself better and to feel more comfortable in her relationships with others. The pediatrician recommended that Courtney see her dentist, explaining that vomiting brings up stomach acids that can erode tooth enamel and increase the risk of cavities. He also suggested that Courtney see a nutritionist to learn about healthy eating and clear up misunderstandings she might have about her need for food. Although I felt that nutrition counseling was a good idea, I seriously doubted that she would accept it, so we decided to hold off on that and focus instead on motivating Courtney to engage in therapy.

"The treatment team kept me updated on Courtney's progress and talked with me about starting her on an antidepressant medication known as an SSRI [selective serotonin reuptake inhibitor] that turned out to be a big help. A few weeks after she began the medicine, she seemed a bit more comfortable around us, even sitting with us some evenings at the dinner table. She didn't always eat with us, but just having her there was encouraging. In addition, she seemed to have a slightly better handle on her moods and was less apt to snap at me. The doctor suggested that the SSRI might also help to ease some of her anxiety about weight and reduce the frequency of her binge-purge episodes.

"While I knew that the matters of binge eating and purging would be covered in therapy, I had no idea what sorts of comments my child would make about me. One part of me figured that such details were none of my business, but an insecure, irrational part worried that the disorder was my fault and left me wondering whether Courtney and other family members were blaming me as well. Sometimes I wished I could be a fly on the wall of the therapy office. When I communicated this angst to the treatment team, they scheduled an appointment for Stan and me to discuss the possibilities of family therapy.

"For our first two sessions, Stan and I met with the family therapist alone, without Courtney, to air our concerns and think about potential goals for continued work. One of the first topics I raised involved the tension in the household regarding Courtney's bulimia. Stan and I were often at odds about how to handle her food-related behaviors. While I favored setting rules aimed at regulating her eating patterns, Stan was more permissive. Thus, there were a number of practical matters to settle. Should I keep cookies and other sweets out of the house? That would mean these foods wouldn't be available for my sons. If I didn't stock the cupboards, might she resort to unacceptable means of getting food? Often, I'd open the refrigerator to discover that large quantities of food had disappeared. In addition, she'd taken to eating in her bedroom, mostly at night, and I didn't like that."

Janet's use of family therapy to discuss food management was right on target. The behaviors associated with eating disorders are often disruptive to family life, and it is only natural for patience to falter. It is not unusual for one parent to disagree with the other regarding how to address food issues. If you're facing challenges similar to Janet's, your fear, anger, hurt, and disappointment are understandable and expected. Because every family is different, there is no stock answer to the food management question. As Janet's family therapist explained, the most viable approach is often to focus on how everyone in the household can work together toward the common goal of helping the eating disordered child. A unified family effort requires an appreciation on everyone's part that they are not failures and are likely to experience frustration along the way. For the family teamwork to be effective, it needs to take place in an atmosphere of mutual respect and caring, conveying to the child, "We appreciate how hard this is for you, and we're going to do all we can to support you." You'll want to offer her choices and elicit her input. Questions such as "What will help you feel supported?" will give your child an opportunity to play an active role in her treatment program.

Janet remembers the obstacles her family faced in working together. "Given that my daughter wouldn't talk about her eating habits, I wasn't sure if I could help her mend them. Our therapist explained that an illness experienced by one member of a family inevitably impacts all the others. Including Courtney in our sessions would give us an opportunity to share our concerns with her, to learn more about what she was going through, and to work on improving our relationships with her. Among my most vivid memories of family sessions with Courtney was her account of how disgusting she felt, not only for being 'too fat,' but also for having bulimia. We devoted a number of sessions to the question of how Courtney interpreted some of our comments that were meant to help her. She claimed I'd been critical of her eating habits. 'Don't you think I'd stop doing this if I could?' she asked.

"While one part of me felt like saying, 'I know you can't stop your eating behaviors,' another part wanted to answer, 'But I think you can.' I silently wondered how much of her eating problem, if any, was under her conscious control. Was her binge-purge cycle driven by some kind of biochemical abnormality, or was it a matter of teaching her to take responsibility? I was nervous about bringing up this question in family therapy. When I did raise the issue, I felt relieved that the therapist guided the discussion, seeking input from Stan and Courtney and supporting our conclusion that whether or not she could currently control her behaviors, we would work together to help her feel better.

"I'm not saying that family therapy was a cure-all for Courtney. The value of these sessions was that they opened a window into sides of my daughter I'd never seen and offered me ideas as to how to talk to her. In family therapy, we eventually turned our discussion from how to help her with her eating disorder to topics that did not involve food. From day one, Courtney had been our high-achieving, outgoing child, the one teachers and coaches characterized as 'exceptional,' 'a leader among her peers,' and 'a joy to work with.' Yet one day in family therapy, Courtney announced, 'I'm not half as good as people think I am.' It astonished me that she didn't feel worthy of the praise she'd earned. Through her eyes, her numerous accomplishments meant that she had to 'keep up the good work'; that is, something inside her told her that she had to perform as well, if not better, next time and forever."

Like Courtney, many people with eating disorders are talented and high-achieving but struggle with intense feelings of "I'm not good enough." Some describe a belief that they are undeserving of the praise and rewards they receive from the outside world. These individuals sense that what they are able to project to others does not reflect their true selves. They argue that people who get to know them will eventually discover their "real," defective selves. Hence, the world can feel like a stage where the individual must constantly exert herself to act out a role in order to maintain her facade and avoid being "found out."

## Courtney's Perspective

Courtney, now 23 and a college graduate, speaks of the progress she's made over the last eight years: "I entered treatment convinced that modifying my eating habits would make me feel worse, and I clung to that notion well into the therapy process. I was slowly able to change my thinking due to a combination of things.

"First, I had to trust. This may sound easy, but for me, it was a huge challenge. In order to tell my therapists about my eating problem, I had to be confident that they wouldn't consider me a freak. At the beginning of therapy, I talked about school and about my blog but not about my eating habits. It helped that my therapists seemed to like me and to see me as a person instead of a disorder. They brought out the parts of me that were good-natured and people-liking. Tentatively at first, I began to poke my head outside my shell to see what—if anything—might lie beyond the realm of my eating disorder. Was it safe out there? Was there anything good? Then, as if on reflex, I'd get scared and go back inside myself. As treatment continued, I found I could be outside myself and involved with others for longer and longer.

"When I was ready to discuss my eating in therapy, it was much less scary than I'd anticipated. If my therapists had asked, 'Why do you binge?' I'd have turned beet red and wished I could fall through the floor. I would've shrugged the question off, changed the subject, or said 'I haven't binged lately,' even if I'd done so that very morning. I'm glad my therapists never put me on the spot with those harsher kinds of questions. They were more interested in getting to know me than in passing judgment on my eating habits. When I first started therapy, I didn't know why I binged. It was a puzzle my therapists and I worked on together. They phrased their questions in ways that never embarrassed me, and that made it a whole lot easier to talk.

"I was terrified that I'd gain weight and that changing my eating habits would make that happen. So starting to do things differently meant a leap of faith on my part; I gradually came to believe that my therapists were on my side and had my best interests at heart. If, for example, they said that trying such-and-such a food would not make me fat, I slowly learned I could take their word for it. When they first suggested that eating planned meals and snacks would help prevent the urge to binge, I was frightened and skeptical but willing to try it—just as an experiment. Testing the waters in this way often helped me feel secure enough to move forward, bit by bit, toward a healthier lifestyle.

"Just as I learned—albeit slowly—in therapy to try a wider variety of foods, so too did I inch my way out of isolation. In October of the ninth grade, when I started feeling fat and bad, I tended to keep to myself. Being with other people simply required more mental and physical energy than I could muster. I attended school and rehearsed for the musical in body but not in spirit. Everything played second fiddle to keeping my bingeing and purging going. I couldn't appreciate how they tried to help me till I began to feel better, but throughout treatment, my parents, therapists, and especially my brothers quietly encouraged me to stay in touch with my friends. Even in my darkest weeks, I tried to make a point of calling kids during the evening, just to chat and make plans to get together that didn't involve food. I didn't know it then, but friendships resulting from those efforts would be key to my journey."

## Slips Along the Road

Temporary lapses into old behaviors are common, and one goal of professional care is to prepare patients to cope with them. "Though I became better at controlling my bingeing, there were plenty of times when I slipped, not only during treatment, but also during follow-up," says Courtney. "One such lapse involved a play rehearsal. As the only newcomer to dance, I found it hard to keep pace. One evening, the instructor reviewed a couple of steps, then—as an exercise in creativity—asked each of us to put these together into a very brief solo routine. I was part frantic, part awed as I watched the other cast members, all good dancers, at work. One invented movements resembling a flower opening. Another became a cat awakening from a nap. I liked the idea of rippling water but was afraid the instructor wouldn't. Some kids volunteered to perform their dances for the rest of us. To make sure it would never be my turn, I snuck off and hid in an empty classroom until it was time to go home. Later that night, after everyone at home was asleep, I binged and vomited."

Courtney is one of many eating disordered individuals who have high self-expectations and harbor great concern about how others judge them. For some, the need to please becomes paramount, overriding their own opinions and inhibiting their self-expression. The creativity exercise would have been challenging, if not daunting, to most new dancers. For Courtney, who was particularly sensitive to what teachers thought of her, the difficult assignment was understandably overwhelming. "I didn't mention the slip to my family," she admits. "But they knew about it anyway. I figured they'd raise the issue in family therapy and was sort of okay with that."

Courtney goes on to describe her later teens and early 20s: "Midway through the 11th grade, I thought I'd overcome the binge problem. But I was wrong. Sometimes I'd have a single-episode slip, but more often, I'd binge and purge more than once over a period of several days before regaining control. In college, I'd practically fall apart the week before exams. Anticipating that I might binge, I'd cut back on my food intake and lose a few pounds. But just as I'd learned in treatment, food restriction can help trigger bingeing, and that's exactly what happened. After reregulating my eating, for which I sometimes needed the help of a counselor at the college health service, I'd realize that it had been a mistake to diet, but in the intensity of the moment, my fear of getting fat and my urges to binge-purge had been very real and forceful.

"After college graduation, I took a job in sales and haven't binged or purged for 10 months. Have I 'recovered' from bulimia nervosa? Some people I've met who have broken the binge-purge habit feel beyond the point where it will return; that perspective is valid. My own situation, I feel, is more like that of the alcoholic who stops drinking. I do sense that my eating disorder has the potential to return. I used to have two mind-sets: either I was 'ill' or 'all better,' with nothing in between. Even the most minor departure from my healthy lifestyle would rattle me into thinking that the illness was back in full force. But that assumption was false. So far, I've been able to make comebacks from my goofs by calling on the skills I learned in therapy. These tools include asking for help from my closest friends, from family members, and from professionals. It's important for me to hold on to the belief that if I slip, I can get back on track. Just as managing alcoholism may grow easier with continued sobriety, I look forward to more peace of mind and increasing freedom from bulimia."

## What Is a Relapse?

There is a difference between brief, transitory behavior (slips) and relapse (resurgence of the illness). In theory, relapse requires outside help whereas brief slips do not. The glitch in this approach is that the two categories are not always neat; that is, there's no definitive cutoff point where slipping ends and illness begins. Relapse is common among individuals recovering from eating disorders. Some people relapse after they have been free of their disordered eating for some time, but many tumble back into the illness when they have made some progress but are not yet well. Some relapses happen rapidly and others gradually. A number of individuals with a history of food restriction and weight loss develop the binge-purge habit. It is not unusual for a person with an eating disorder to suffer more than one relapse during the course of her journey toward wellness.

Patients experience considerable shame regarding their relapse behaviors and frequently fear harsh judgment, blame, or rejection. Your child may be afraid that she has failed, disappointed, or hurt you by returning to her behaviors. Furthermore, when someone descends back into her eating disorder, she does not necessarily see herself as having a problem. Thus, there's a chance that your child will not tell you when her illness returns. To bridge this possible communication gap, try to introduce the topic of relapse to her when she is doing well. After conveying to her that you under-stand and admire how hard she's worked to improve her health, explain that it is common for patients to slip occasionally and that you won't be angry with her if it happens. Reassure her that you're on this journey with her for the duration.

Relapse prevention is often an integral part of treatment, and you'll want to talk about this topic with your child's team of pro-fessionals. In therapy, older adolescent and adult patients often formulate a plan to implement when they slip or sense that their disorder is worsening. This can consist of strategies an individual has found helpful in the past. Depending on her age and family communication styles, try to gently reinforce one or more ele-ments of the plan. For example, you could encourage her to moni-tor her moods and meals, structure her time, stick to three planned meals and two planned snacks a day, remind herself that one slip need not turn into a cascade, think about what triggered the slip, and talk about her problem with those she trusts. Younger patients often benefit from having parents take gentle charge of the plan under a therapist's guidance.

A patient who has undergone treatment for bulimia or anorexia is vulnerable to relapse during periods of stress. Of course, people vary greatly in what they perceive as stress; there are, however, some situations that are commonly experienced as difficult. As we've discussed, the message "I'm not good enough" often fuels the development of unhealthy eating habits. Encounters with bullies frequently exert a powerful impact on how younger children and adolescents feel about themselves. Interpersonal relationships can generate intense emotions that sometimes reopen the door to eating problems. Real or perceived rejections, betrayals, disputes, and misunderstandings are all potential triggers. A child typically experiences problems between her mom and dad or the success of a sibling as stressful. Losses, such as the death of a loved one, and family health issues can precipitate lapses, as can pregnancy or having an abortion. Yet a relationship issue needn't be a bad one to contribute to an eating problem. Although a first romance is wonderful in many ways, it can, at the same time, tap into fears of intimacy, insecurities about body size and shape, or angst related to sex. Successes, such as meeting a scholastic or athletic challenge, can also set the stage for inner turmoil. As in Courtney's case, tension over final exams or other tests sometimes results in slips. Transitions, such as entering high school or college or moving to a new town, are challenging enough to throw many young people off-kilter. As children grow up, the experiences that cause difficulties tend to shift, so sources of stress for an 11-year-old (such as not fitting in with peers) differ from those of a 17-year-old (such as writing her college application essay).

Patients who have been hospitalized for the treatment of an eating disorder are at particular risk of relapse. Some of them have gained weight in the hospital just to get out; they have not made the emotional changes necessary for recovery and soon slide back into illness. A number of individuals who have improved nutritionally in the hospital are ambivalent about following their eating programs after discharge; some of them continue to move forward despite occasional slips, whereas others do well for a while but relapse when pressures mount. Perhaps your adolescent with anorexia will reach a point in her recovery where she feels healthy even though her weight is still lower than her doctor wants it. Pointing to her schoolwork, energy level, and overall sense of responsibility, she may ask, "See how well I'm doing? What's the purpose of gaining more weight if I'm functioning so well at this one?"

Just as eating disorders are multidimensional, so is the road to recovery. An individual's ability to function—to pursue educational, career, athletic, and social goals—is a key part of getting better. We also like to see that she has cut down on her abnormal eating behaviors, that she has reached more than 90 percent of the average weight for her age and height, and that she is menstruating. But weight gain alone, without emotional growth, is unlikely to sustain recovery; we also look for an improvement in the patient's overall sense of well-being. Is she more at peace with herself than she was when her eating disorder ruled her life? Each of these components contributes to the patient's improving health.

If your child relapses, her treatment team will help you determine the next step based on her medical and emotional condition, the severity of her abnormal eating behaviors, her level of motivation, and health insurer decisions. Often, the best course of action in helping a patient overcome a relapse depends on how ready she is to change. School personnel—nurses and guidance counselors—can be enormously helpful, not only in providing fresh insights into the at-risk student's situation, but also in contributing to her daily care. For example, the school nurse may offer your child support and understanding at lunchtime.

Ironically, a relapse sometimes serves as a motivator for getting well. As harrowing as it is, a medical scare related to the eating disorder can give the individual the push she needs to get better. When discussing recovery, there's always the question of permanence. Rather than apply the literal meaning of *cured* to a person who has regained some weight after relapse into anorexia, it may be more realistic to envision her as continuing to improve and moving toward the ability to lead a productive, gratifying life despite a vulnerability to eating problems.

# What Is a Pro-Ana Website?

"Pro-anorexia" websites are part of an ongoing online effort to promote anorexia as a viable way of life instead of as the serious illness it is. Although these groups purport to offer individuals with eating disorders support and a sense of community, their offerings are misleading and potentially harmful. Photographs and videos of skeletal females and quotations lauding thinness are meant to encourage weight loss. Also prominent is information about unhealthy reducing methods, with some sites including extreme food restriction, diet pills, and substances marketed as metabolism boosters. Focus on calories is standard fare, and it is not unusual to find suggestions regarding how to maintain one's self-discipline and pursuit of thinness when faced with the temptation to eat.

We feel that the ideas presented on such sites are distorted. For example, a number of these groups claim that the achievement of weight loss is a way to take charge of one's life; this is a false premise. Some sites try to convey that weight loss is a barometer of a person's strength and success; this notion is potentially dangerous. A third theme touts anorexia as consistent with America's thin-is-in ideal; this rationale is horrific because our mainstream culture's glorification of thinness is highly problematic.

With these various images, pro-ana websites help viewers justify their eating disorders. By championing weight loss, the pro-ana philosophy overlooks the medical problems that can arise from these conditions, such as abnormal heart rhythms or osteoporosis. People with eating disorders often suffer from a sense of not fitting in, making them prime targets for pro-ana groups. The result may be a firmer commitment to the illness. Although these sites are very worrisome, they continue to thrive on the Internet, and we hope that you will encourage your children to steer clear of them.

## Creative Approaches to Healing

As an adjunct to your child's professional treatment program, a number of other potentially healing interventions are available. Although scientific research on these treatments is minimal, many individuals with eating disorders use them and report positive effects.

### Arts-Based Therapies

An integral part of many residential and hospital treatment programs, arts-based therapy groups provide instruction and encouragement in music, dance-movement, drawing, painting, sculpture, or drama. For individuals who have difficulty verbalizing their feelings, these services, which are run by registered art therapists, offer an alternative form of self-expression. The idea is to help patients understand that, as compared to food restriction, binge eating, and purging, undertaking a creative project is a far healthier way to cope with personal problems. As an example of an art group, the therapist may ask participants to use design and color to show how they are feeling or to explore a theme such as loss or friendship. A music exercise can be chosen not only for its relaxation potential, but also for its life-affirming lyrics. Dance-movement therapy aims at helping patients experience their bodies in positive ways; interventions include relaxation methods and mirror work. Drama therapy affords the individual the opportunity to explore her feelings and styles of self-expression by acting the part of a fictional character.

### Mindfulness Training

Derived from Buddhist meditation practices, this training helps individuals develop an awareness of the here and now. Mindfulness exercises teach people to experience thoughts and feelings without acting on them or passing judgment. For instance, it is not unusual for a person with an eating disorder to struggle with the impulse to binge when she faces uncomfortable emotions.

By keeping her mind in the present moment, she may be able to simply experience her feelings rather than act on her urge. As an example of a mindfulness meditation, the individual takes slow, deep breaths while repeating the phrase "Just this moment." Ultimately, as these moments are strung together, she is better able to accept the notion that feelings are just feelings and that eventually all feelings subside and become more manageable.

## Yoga

Dating back to ancient times in India, yoga aims at creating harmony between mind, body, and spirit. Although there are different kinds of yoga, the branch most widely practiced in the West includes physical postures (poses), breathing techniques, and perhaps meditation. Individuals with eating disorders often appreciate this discipline for its calming influence. Practicing yoga encourages the individual to attune to body sensations, which can, over time, play a role in helping her recognize and respond appropriately to perceptions of hunger and satiety. The person with anorexia or bulimia tends to compare her body to that of others and may become distraught if she perceives someone as thinner than she. Yoga may help counter this mind-set, given that one of its primary teachings is that no human being is better than another. Yoga classes are widely available in health clubs and community education programs. A variety of videos and books on the subject are also helpful.

## Journaling

Many patients with eating disorders find that keeping a personal journal or diary helps them explore their inner selves and reflect on their relationships with important people in their lives. Confiding in a journal can be an effective outlet for anxieties and other uncomfortable feelings. Entries often include visual images as well as narrative. Our patient Fran, now doing well after a long struggle with bulimia, speaks candidly about the far-reaching impact of the written page: "I kept a journal throughout some of my dark years. Now, when I feel 'not good enough,' rereading those entries reminds me how far I've come and helps motivate me to get back on track." Of course, what's helpful to one person may be less so to another. For those who enjoy writing, however, journaling can be a fine mode of self-expression and a means to improved self-understanding.

## Community Support Groups

In Chapter 5, we pointed out that support and self-help groups can help patients connect with others who are suffering from eating disorders. These discussion groups are offered by some college health services and many community outreach organizations. Members share their experiences, giving and receiving support. Examples of the myriad topics that arise at such meetings are coping with the holidays, interactions with friends and family, how to deal with unstructured time, and the use of prescribed medication for eating disorders. Do you know about the 12-step addiction recovery model? In the tradition of the well-known Alcoholics Anonymous, 12-step programs for eating disorders offer meetings, sponsors, and free membership. If your child expresses an interest in a particular program, you will want to consult with her treatment team to evaluate its suitability to her specific needs.

## Self-Help Workbooks

For older adolescents and adults who suffer from eating disorders, professionally authored self-help workbooks focus on cognitive behavioral therapy. They help patients convert the negative thoughts and feelings (such as "I'm defined by my weight" or "I'm fat and bad") that may have contributed to their disordered behaviors into positive ones. Some of these workbook programs are designed for the individual to study independently, while others are intended for use under a therapist's guidance. In some cases, learning from a workbook encourages the patient to enter "face-to-face" psychotherapy. You'll find the titles of specific workbooks in the Resources section at the back of this book. For literature evaluating the effectiveness of self-help cognitive behavioral therapy for eating disorders, consult the References section.

## Self-Help on the Internet

Over the past several years, a number of self-help and support communities for eating disorders have appeared online. You will want
to screen sites for or with your adolescent, selecting those that
encourage recovery and growth and avoiding those that promote
disordered eating patterns and glamorize thinness (pro-ana). Many
people with eating disorders feel lonely but shun social activities,
particularly those involving food. Online support systems—such
as positive, recovery-focused chat rooms, bulletin boards, and discussion groups—offer these individuals an anonymous, nonthreat-
ening, and geographically friendly way to connect with others in
their situation.

In addition to support groups, there are online self-help recovery programs that offer patients tools for reducing their disordered
behavior patterns. If you have questions about whether a specific
online program will be beneficial to your child, don't hesitate to
ask your treatment team.

## Guided Imagery

Many people with eating disorders find it difficult to comfort
themselves when they are upset. Some describe binge-purge
behaviors as efforts to deal with intolerable emotions. Treatment
often involves providing the individual with healthier ways to calm
herself. Guided imagery is a potential healing technique whereby
the patient learns to focus her mind on soothing scenarios. The
word *guided* stems from the practice of performing the exercise
while listening to a description of the comforting image.

To introduce this technique, the therapist begins by asking the
individual what scenes she might find soothing. Perhaps the patient
draws from the natural environment (such as a pine forest, a field of
wildflowers, or the seashore) or selects a cozy indoor setting (such
as reading in front of a fire on a wintry day). Next, the individual
settles in a comfortable position, takes slow deep breaths, and listens
to her therapist synthesize the chosen images into a smooth-flowing
narration. The patient is transported out of her current mind-set
into her soothing environment. As the therapist guides the jour-

ney, she may audiotape it for the patient to take home and listen to on a day-to-day basis. A number of guided imagery audiotapes are available commercially. Or your child may wish to create and record her own. With practice, it may become easier and easier for her to travel to her favorite places when under stress.

### Pet Therapy

The human-animal bond is a timeless and celebrated theme that resonates with people far and wide. Art and literature abound with images—some of them famous—of animals helping people. Many eating disordered patients describe themselves as lonely but leery about letting others get to know them. Dogs, cats, and other animals often encourage such individuals to accept love and offer it. Pets don't care a whit about what their humans look like or have accomplished. Instead of having complicated expectations of their owners, they simply want to be with them, to give and receive love.

In an effort to counter inner turmoil, many people with eating disorders lead very structured, scheduled lives that are incompatible with social activities. Caring for a pet can challenge these daily routines and encourage the individual to become more flexible. Taking a dog for a walk, for a romp in a park, or even to obedience school can become a way of meeting people and allowing relationships to form. In addition to offering unconditional love, animals tend to help their humans express their playful, more spontaneous sides and feel more relaxed.

## The Role of Professional Monitoring

Because setbacks are common, it is important for your child to have contact with a physician or therapist after formal treatment ends. Sometimes a patient in follow-up is reluctant to confide relapse behavior to her therapists. She may be afraid she has let them down or worry that they'll give up on her if they learn of her relapse. If you suspect your adolescent is returning to her old ways, apprise her doctors of the situation and consult with them about what will motivate her to accept their help. Meanwhile, it is possible that your empathy will encourage her to talk to her doctors and maybe to you about her slips and about the factors that may be contributing to them. Try statements such as "The work of getting better can be so hard" or "I imagine the slip feels scary [or disappointing, frustrating, or embarrassing] to you, and I'm sorry you have to go through it."

As we discussed in Chapter 7, it is not unusual for individuals with eating disorders to also suffer from other mental health challenges, such as anxiety disorders and depression. These conditions can play a role in relapse, warranting a reassessment of the medications the patient is taking; perhaps she will need a dosage adjustment or a different kind of medicine. An individual with anorexia or bulimia who suffers from perfectionism, persistent worries, or low moods often continues to have these tendencies to some degree once she has recovered from her abnormal eating behaviors. Sometimes a person who corrects her unhealthy eating patterns develops other extreme forms of behavior, such as overwork or overexercise. Thus, the importance of professional monitoring and follow-up cannot be overemphasized.

Once your child is maintaining her health successfully, she may continue to see her treatment team, though appointments will not be as frequent as when she was ill. The intensity and duration of follow-up care differ based on many factors, including the individual's overall degree of stability, short- or long-term stressors that have the potential to impact her health, the wishes of the patient and family, and the decisions of insurance companies.

## Recognizing Signs of Progress

To explore the territory of recovery, it is helpful to think in terms of the three major components of eating disorders: thoughts, feelings, and behaviors. Chances are your child will improve in all three of these areas. In treatment, the first priority is the patient's safety. As long as her weight and binge-purge cycles are not resulting in medical complications, you will need to be patient, as substantial changes in her eating don't happen right away. Often, other signs will come first. Perhaps she'll show increasing willingness to stay in treatment; venture out of isolation to see a friend; try a new food; or agree to talk to a nutritionist, not to discuss weight gain, but to see what else she can learn. Has her sense of humor started to return? Does she seem more self-confident or assertive? Has she begun to explore how "I'm not good enough" or perfectionism plays a role in her illness? These are all positive steps that deserve your recognition and praise. The weight gain may follow.

During the course of everyday conversation, listen for hints that your child is starting to consider her eating disorder a burden. Does she want the good times she used to have with friends? Has she begun to sense that attaining a particular weight requires more sacrifice than it's worth? When school's out for the summer, suppose she wants to go swimming; knowing that she'll feel cold in the water, she may perceive her eating disorder as getting in the way. Last year, we received a letter from an athletic 15-year-old who had recently improved following a long struggle with anorexia. She and her family were vacationing in Vermont for a week, just as they had every July. She described how much fun it had been to swim in the lake, an activity she hadn't been able to enjoy for the past two summers due to undernutrition. We saw the sense of well-being expressed in her letter as reflective of the inner growth process that is so important to recovery.

As you strive to stay supportive toward your child, it will be important for you to assess your own limits and take time for yourself. In the next chapter, we will take a closer look at the potential impact of your child's eating disorder on you, other family members, and friends.

## CHAPTER 9

# Handling the Effects on Family and Friends

"Greg has worked very hard to recover from anorexia," says Mona. "Our challenge was to convince him that he had an illness and that he could get better. His eating disorder has been hard for the whole family."

Mona and Kurt first came to see us about a year ago when their son, then 15, was suffering from anorexia. As we discussed in Chapter 8, an illness suffered by one family member has an impact on the others. Furthermore, the vast set of issues involved in eating disorders can complicate relationships between parents as well as those between siblings. Yet all families are different, so when we talk about stress imposed by an eating disorder, we are referring to a wide range of experiences. In addition to managing your own emotions, day-to-day intensity on the home front, and career pressures, it is possible that you are facing ongoing dilemmas regarding how your child relates to the world beyond her family. In this chapter, we will address these challenges and offer strategies to help you cope. The perspectives of Mona and Kurt illustrate how complex and multilayered the effects of an eating disorder can be.

"Greg loves sports," says his mother. "As an eighth grader, he was number one on his school's squash and lacrosse teams. He earned a B average with little effort, coming across as easygoing and happy-go-lucky. That year, his height shot up, his voice changed, and he developed facial and body hair. Coping with puberty is hard for kids under most circumstances; for Greg, these normal changes took place quickly, making it all the more difficult to adjust. In just a few short months, he moved onto girls' radar screens. During the summer before ninth grade, he and Melissa started seeing a lot of each other. Looking back, I'd say that the unfamiliar physical sensations and emotions of this first romance were, understandably, a bit scary for him."

Kurt sheds further light on the changes Greg experienced that summer. "While attending tennis camp, he mentioned a desire to be thinner. The couple of comments he made were just in passing, and I didn't give them much thought at the time. He'd always been chubby, and I figured he had simply reached an age when looks take on greater importance. Given our culture's focus on physical appearance, how can kids grow up without such concerns?

"In the fall, Greg faced mounting academic pressure. His school ended with the ninth grade, and this would be his final year. From the time he was very young, one of his dreams had been to attend boarding school, and that was his plan for grades 10 through 12. In order to get accepted by his schools of choice, however, he needed to boost his academic performance into the A range, and he had a narrow window of time in which to do this. It was a task he did not take lightly. Greg, like his mom, is very social, and I think his drive to be with other kids was one reason he chose boarding school. Another was that going away to school was a tradition in my family and in Mona's, and Greg was eager to follow suit."

Mona recalls that Greg's disorder seemed to start suddenly. "Although it is possible that academic pressures, girlfriend concerns, and other factors helped trigger Greg's anorexia, I feel that the final straw was the death of Kurt's father," she notes. "Given that his grandpa had always been one of his biggest fans and vice versa, Greg took the loss particularly hard. Kurt needed to catch an immediate flight to join his mother, so I set out to drive him to the airport. Since Greg did not feel up to school, he accompanied us in the car. On the way back, when he asked me to drop him off at school, I suddenly realized that he hadn't eaten breakfast. I parked outside a convenience store while Greg ran in, returning to the car with a bagel. That's when I noticed the change in his eating behavior. After finishing a third of the bagel, he meticulously wrapped the remainder. Soon he unfolded the paper, took one bite of the bagel, and carefully rewrapped it. He went through this routine six times. That afternoon, Greg—for the first time I could remember—skipped his after-school snack. I felt like I'd been hit over the head with a baseball bat.

"If I'd known that my son wouldn't be eating healthy again for months, I'd have completely lost it. My sense of urgency was so overwhelming that I was on the phone that very night seeking help for Greg and, within 24 hours, had found a professional through a friend of a friend. The health provider was a dietitian, who informed me that most of her clients with eating disorders were girls but that she'd be happy to work with us. Her caveat didn't surprise me. It wasn't the first time I'd heard it, and it wouldn't be the last. I appreciated the dietitian's honesty and found her as knowledgeable as she was compassionate. Unfortunately, she excluded me from the treatment process, and I didn't like that. Meanwhile, Greg showed no signs of improvement and, in fact, continued to lose weight."

"That certainly was a bleak stretch of time," agrees Kurt. "I felt bombarded by bad news. Within a day after my dad died, my son showed signs of a serious problem, and my wife was more upset than I'd ever seen her. Greg was clearly not making progress in nutrition counseling, so we started him in psychotherapy. In addition, he, Mona, and I attended family sessions. Because Greg was extremely skinny, we also brought in a physician. The treatment team explained that anorexia can have an addictive quality. That is, Greg's initial weight loss may have offered him a sense of accomplishment and discipline that led him to continue his pursuit of thinness, only to find that he couldn't stop. The therapists helped me view his illness through a realistic lens, to understand on more of a gut level what I was up against."

Like Mona and Kurt, many parents look back on the onset of their child's eating disorder and realize that hearing about the potential severity of the condition—albeit very hard in the moment—was ultimately beneficial. To help families understand the seriousness of the illness and the nature of treatment, we often draw an analogy between an eating disorder and cancer. The sooner it gets treated, the less likely it is to spread. For the individual with anorexia, increasing calories and more frequent feedings create discomfort; chemotherapy also has side effects. If you were to find out that your child had cancer and that the treatment would require surgery, chemotherapy, radiation, or some combination thereof, chances are you'd go through with it. It is useful to think of anorexia in a similar manner. Although restoration of nutritional health is far from pleasant, it's necessary, and one of the goals of therapy is to help your child cope with and move beyond her weight gain–related discomforts. Individuals recovering from bulimia often describe a sensation of fullness that is close to unbearable. To help them anticipate and strategize for this, we often compare it to the tension that accompanies stretching exercises. Though generally not painful, the feeling is uncomfortable; in order to get better, your child must learn how to manage it, and therapy can help with this. In fact, the sensation of tension is itself a sign of progress. As your child sticks with her program and advances in recovery, the discomfort is likely to diminish.

Seeing your child starve when food is readily available may feel more harrowing than you ever thought possible. Will he live? Will the illness cause long-term disability? Did I cause his eating disorder? Mona remembers those fears all too well. "When Greg's illness gained momentum, he had four to five doctors' appointments each week. At the time, I was working as a freelance graphic designer and serving as a member of three boards. I called an emergency meeting and put all these responsibilities on hold so that I could devote my time to taking care of my son. I'd pick him up after school and drive him directly to his doctors' appointments in the midst of his nonstop protests. During these drives, Greg would sometimes yell, 'I hate you.' That's when my own anger would flare. 'Don't you dare talk to me like that. It's you who won't eat! If you would just eat, you wouldn't have these appointments.' Since that response always made matters worse, I asked my treatment team how to handle Greg's outbursts. The idea was to express sympathy for what my son was going through and then to remind him that it wasn't me he hated but rather the eating disorder. I tried to follow that advice, but in the heat of the moment, it wasn't easy, and it's something I continue to work on.

"One of my most vivid memories involves Greg's study of the Holocaust as part of his ninth-grade curriculum. One evening, I found him looking at textbook photographs of concentration camp survivors. 'Can you see my ribs?' he asked, pulling up his T-shirt. Sadness ripped through me as I gently explained to him that he looked as thin as the victims in the pictures. His eyes filled with puzzlement. 'When I look in the mirror,' he replied, 'I see big rolls of fat.' Horrified, I realized that something was very wrong with the way my son saw his body.

"During the scariest part of our journey, Greg was losing three to four pounds each week, and his doctors recommended hospitalization. Though Kurt and I thought this would probably be necessary, we wanted to give Greg a bit more time to begin the road to health as an outpatient. Meanwhile, I felt like a basket case. One day, I was in the middle of the supermarket when I found myself in a state of panic, struggling to think rationally about what Greg might eat. Should I prepare chicken and rice? He used to like that before his eating disorder struck. The panic gave way to sadness as it occurred to me that it didn't matter what groceries I bought or what I served Greg for dinner; his illness wouldn't let him eat.

## Shifting Gears

As you know, there are different approaches to the treatment of eating disorders, and when your child's doctors formulate her individualized care plan, they will—with your input—make a concerted effort to evaluate which option best meets her needs. During treatment, you and the members of her team will monitor your child's progress on an ongoing basis and perhaps make adjustments in how to address her thought patterns or behaviors. Since no treatment consistently brings about permanent recovery for individuals with anorexia or bulimia, it is sometimes necessary to try more than one avenue to move forward. Being open to different strategies will stand you in good stead as you accompany your child on his journey.

Mona and Kurt know firsthand about changing gears. "I read everything I could get my hands on about eating disorders and highlighted text for Kurt to look at after work," recalls Mona. "Most advice was consistent with what our therapists had recommended. That is, we were to remove ourselves from our son's day-to-day decisions about eating. That's exactly what we'd been doing. We'd given Greg the freedom to prepare his own meals. What and when he ate was up to him. Unfortunately, he'd continued to lose weight. I'll never forget the night I asked him, 'But why can't you eat? What is it that's bothering you?' 'You,' he answered. 'Why can't you just leave me alone?'

"One day, I was browsing in a bookstore when a publication on the Maudsley treatment model caught my eye. Unlike the majority of books I'd read, this one supported an approach to anorexia whereby the parents take charge of the adolescent's meals and snacks until he is well enough to reclaim this responsibility for himself. The Maudsley method appealed to me on several counts. First, studies suggested it had worked for a number of families. Second, staying out of food management had left me on the sidelines of Greg's treatment. I welcomed direct involvement in his care."

Mona's resourcefulness was commendable. The approach that attracted her attention is the best-studied and thus far the most promising treatment for adolescents with anorexia nervosa. Developed at the Maudsley Hospital in London, it is a specific kind of outpatient family therapy that calls on parents to become key players in their child's return to health. For the severely ill patient whose safety is at risk, Maudsley treatment does not substitute for hospitalization but may be undertaken once she is medically stable and well enough to go home. Although data on the Maudsley model are impressive, the question of what family approach is appropriate when and for which patients remains under investigation and is a topic to discuss with your child's health providers. If your treatment team prescribes the Maudsley method, your therapist will teach you important skills as you work with your adolescent to help restore her nutritional balance (phase one). Once she is eating well under your direction, you will be guided in encouraging her to manage her own meals and snacks (phase two). The third phase of therapy will branch out into the challenges of adolescence that do not involve food.

Mona remembers how her family-based therapist (a family therapist who uses the Maudsley method) prepared her and Kurt to try the Maudsley approach. "She suggested that we think of the anorexia as a loud voice in Greg's mind that instructed him to lose weight and restrict his eating. The idea was to lower the volume of anorexia's message, which was now blasting, and to amplify the voice of health. At dinner, I'd give Greg the same portions as his sister, Kurt, and myself. Placing Greg's meal in front of him, I'd say, 'I know this looks like a lot to you and that you are feeling bad about eating it. Try to have faith in what your doctors, Dad, and I are telling you—eating what we ask will help you get better.' Gently, Kurt and I would remind him that the voice blaring 'eat less, lose weight' is not to be trusted. I'd stay with him until he ate everything on his plate, praising him afterward and suggesting that he turn to something relaxing, such as listening to music, immediately following the meal. Greg began to make progress.

"This is not to say that everything ran smoothly. On the contrary, there were times when my son had such a look of defeat about him that I'd have to excuse myself from the room before I burst into tears. I desperately missed the fun-loving, low-key Greg I'd known a few months back. Terrified of gaining weight, yet urged by us to eat, he perceived himself in a no-win situation, as if he'd always feel as miserable as he did currently. Sometimes I was too upset myself to try to comfort him. Other times, I'd give it my best shot: 'Greg, I can see how hard you're trying and that it's taking a lot of courage to get better. I'm sorry you have to go through this. Try thinking of it like this—the turmoil you're going through now, as hard as it is, might turn out to be the worst part of your life. I doubt you believe this right now, but stick with your program and things can get much better.' Looking back, it seems like this pep talk was as much for me as it was for Greg, but I like to think that it helped both of us.

"Of the challenges raised in family therapy, the one that stands out most in my mind involved who expected what of whom," continues Mona. "Did I want my son to grow up to be successful? Of course. What parent doesn't? Was it important to me and Kurt that he attend boarding school? I tried to reassure Greg that he needn't go to boarding school unless he truly wanted to, adding that I'd been under the impression that he'd been looking forward to going. I reiterated what I thought I'd been conveying since he was very young—that boarding school was an opportunity, not an expectation. Had he misinterpreted that message all these years? It was hard to know. That's because so many factors were involved. For instance, when it came to boarding school, Kurt and I weren't exactly on the same page. It was one thing to agree on a meal plan for our son. It was quite another to discuss some of these less tangible issues. Family-based therapy helped because it brought the topic of expectations out of silence. But these questions weren't the kind that could be answered right there on the spot. They required a lot of thinking time. In fact, a year after Greg became ill, they still feel unresolved."

## Helping Him Choose Health

Although correcting malnutrition and reducing the binge-purge habit are key, they do not, by themselves, constitute recovery. As we explained in Chapter 8, internal changes are also necessary. Over time, an individual may reach a point where his single-minded pursuit of thinness interferes with his ability to reach other goals. Gradually, his eating disorder becomes more trouble than it's worth. Kurt describes how he tried to help his son make positive decisions about his health: "Greg experienced disappointments as a result of his eating disorder. I tried to convince him that anorexia would not get him what he wanted out of life. Because of his malnutrition, his doctors wanted him to skip sports. This was a temporary measure, not meant to punish him, but rather to conserve his energy and prevent injury. Nearly every afternoon while his teammates were on the playing field, Greg was at doctors' appointments. Lacrosse had become important to him, not only because he excelled at and enjoyed it, but also because playing on the team allowed him to see friends and make new ones. When his doctors recommended time out from sports, he took it really hard, and I felt so bad for him. I'd point out, as gently as I could, that improving his eating habits would mean a return to lacrosse and a lot fewer doctors' appointments. In response, he'd shrug, making it hard for me to know how much of that message he'd taken in.

"In addition, Greg's eating disorder put a damper on his freedom. Because he needed mealtime and snack-time supervision, an adult—a parent, teacher, or school nurse—was checking in with him every couple of hours. On a number of occasions, I gently reminded him that he needed to be healthy in order to gain admission to boarding school. Acknowledging how hard it was for him to change his eating habits, I frequently reassured him that I was on his side and that I would be there for him as he traveled the road to recovery.

"I wanted to impress on Greg the seriousness of his condition, so I took time off from work. My son knew this was very unlike me. As much as I love my job and as unsettling as it was to leave projects hanging, having a sick child pushed everything else way down in priority. Alarms went off in my mind, yet it was unclear how to respond to them. I'll never forget Greg's hollow cheeks, sallow skin, and tired eyes that seemed to send two simultaneous messages: 'Help' and 'Leave me alone.' The times when he was willing to talk to me about his feelings were few and far between. But when he did discuss them, he was articulate—much more so than I am now or was as a boy.

"Certain dialogues I had with Greg during that time were particularly hard for me, and looking back, I can see why. First, his anorexia blocked his ability to see how serious his condition was. Second, when I tried to tell him about the potential consequences of anorexia, I wasn't sure whether he believed me. Kids his age tend to think they're invulnerable; they don't scare easily. Besides, I'd never imagined the remote possibility of losing either Greg or my daughter as teenagers, and now that danger pressed on me. In order to have a fighting chance of getting through to Greg, I had to make direct statements such as 'You could die,' or 'Your anorexia could have a permanent impact on all our lives.' I'll never forget those interactions. To say that I felt all choked up is an understatement.

"At one point, Greg said that he felt guilty for keeping me home from work and for inconveniencing the family. Intellectually, I knew that he hadn't consciously chosen to get anorexia and that it isn't something one can turn on and off. But sometimes, especially when I was overtired, I'd lose sight of that and come out with comments I later regretted. Most nights, the four of us had dinner together. I'll never forget this one evening when Greg hemmed and hawed more than usual about eating. In my frustration, I blurted out, 'Greg, can't you see what you're doing to yourself? Can't you see what you're doing to all of us? Snap out of it!' He stood up and yelled, 'No, Dad, I can't snap out of it,' and stomped out of the room. After an awkward silence, Mona looked me straight in the eye and asked, 'Kurt, can't you be more patient with him?' I wasted no time in reminding her that there had been plenty of occasions when she had gotten mad at Greg. It was unfair to throw that in Mona's face, but I was so overwrought that the words just came out. That was a hard evening."

When they're frustrated or scared, most parents make comments they don't necessarily mean. So do siblings, athletic coaches, friends, and everyone who is concerned. Chances are you too will have outbursts. Given the strain of caring for an ill child, it would be unrealistic to expect yourself to be a paragon of patience and kindness. Stress can cause tempers to rise, and as a result, a child's parents might blame each other for the illness. It is not unusual for a mother and father to have different parenting styles. Perhaps one is more lenient, even giving in to the child's demands, while the other doesn't believe in backing down. Sometimes there is disagreement between parents regarding how to manage eating disorder behaviors, in addition to conflicts that don't involve food. Rifts can form between the parents, making it difficult for the eating disordered child to make progress. If you are facing these obstacles, it's even more important for you to have emotional support, and your child's treatment team will help you evaluate the best way to get it.

## Taking Care of Your Other Children

Caring for your child with an eating disorder is likely to require a great deal of your time and energy. If you have other children, spending time with them while ensuring that your affected child is well cared for can take an enormous toll. Chances are you feel pulled in many directions at the same time. Perhaps you feel guilty for focusing so much attention on your ill child. Mona experienced both of these emotions. "As dedicated as I was to helping Greg," she says, "I also wanted to be there for my bright and very athletic daughter, Ella, then almost 13. But between his doctors' appointments, meal management, and communication with his school, I had all I could do to make it to Ella's soccer playoffs; luckily, I arrived in time to see her winning goal.

"I was unsure how to approach her about her brother's condition. To address this question, I took inspiration from Kurt, who had a long history of mild depression and had suffered a particularly difficult bout six years ago. Though Kurt says he's awkward about expressing his feelings, he has been open with both our children about his condition, particularly in regard to his seasonal affective disorder [depression during the shorter days of winter]. Over the years, he'd described his mood issues to Greg and Ella in straightforward, down-to-earth terms that gave them a realistic yet positive outlook on the condition. It was in that same spirit of gentleness and directness that I talked to Ella about Greg, reassuring her of my steadfast love for her, explaining the seriousness of her brother's illness, and leveling with her about the need for me to spend extra time with him. 'There may be times,' I added, 'when you'll feel mad at me and Dad and your brother because of all the attention he's getting. It's only natural for kids to get upset under these circumstances. If you get mad at me, or if you get sad or frightened, I want us to be able to talk about those feelings so that I can help you through them.' At that point, Ella asked, 'What do I tell people when they ask what's wrong with my brother?' I advised her to say she didn't know, a plausible, kid-friendly standby that I hoped would take the pressure off her."

Kurt feels that it's too early to know precisely how Greg's eating disorder affected Ella. "If Mona or I were arguing with Greg, she'd give us her 'This is so stupid' look and leave the room. We invited her to participate in family therapy, and at first she wanted nothing to do with it, but with some encouragement, she agreed to attend sessions with the rest of us. Ella has a lot of inner strength, and thus far, she seems to have weathered the storm well. I have to assume, however, that the impact of Greg's illness on her was huge. I imagine she was worried about her brother on several levels and that she was jealous of the time and care we gave him. Sure, she acted up occasionally when Greg was ill, staying out with friends later than she was allowed and neglecting to call to tell us where she was. Were these episodes a reaction to the extra attention we focused on her brother? Possibly. Were they typical of 12- to 13-year-olds? Absolutely. I hope Ella realizes that, if she were in Greg's shoes, we'd be there for her, just as we were for him."

The vigilance that Kurt and Mona showed on behalf of their daughter was right on the mark. Every family is different, and the impact of an eating disorder on a sibling depends upon a host of factors including her age, her relationship with the affected child, her day-to-day challenges and habits, and her genetic tendencies. For a sibling in her late teens or early adulthood, understanding the nature of anorexia or bulimia is hard enough; for the preteen or early adolescent to comprehend the complexities inherent in an eating disorder ("My brother says he's fat, but he's really skinny") is unrealistic. This doesn't mean that young ones aren't upset or worried about the afflicted member. They tend to see her as unavailable and remote. Sometimes a child with anorexia or bulimia will request that her siblings not be told about her disorder because she is afraid that they will look down on her or "keep an eye on" her behaviors. We do not favor secrets. Chances are, your decision to give information about your child's illness to his siblings will allow him to be seen as more real and to receive increased support.

A brother or sister of any age often will resent the child with the eating disorder or experience a mix of emotions that is unsettling and difficult to tolerate. In addition to envying the extra attention he is getting, she may feel frustrated that he won't eat, afraid he'll get "sicker," guilty about past interactions, or sad that she has "lost" the brother she once knew.

How siblings express such feelings varies. At mealtimes, while your son or daughter with the eating disorder pushes food around on the plate or cuts it up into tiny pieces, how do your other children react? Do they excuse themselves from the table or spend dinnertime elsewhere? Do they withdraw from the family? Some children "take advantage" of their parents' busyness with the ill child by testing or breaking household rules. Some confront the eating disordered child directly, perhaps—out of anger—teasing him or making comments that interfere with his ability to stick to his treatment program. Others fall back into more childlike behaviors in an effort to get the same level of care and concern as the ill youngster. In some cases, a brother or sister takes on behaviors that are characteristic of anorexia or bulimia. A sibling who has a competitive relationship with the affected child can develop body image problems herself. If you have any questions about how your child's eating disorder is affecting your other children, don't hesitate to consult your health care providers. They recognize the strain your family is under and are there to help you.

## Coping Day-to-Day

As Kurt and Mona have described, taking charge of the meals and snacks of an eating disordered individual is an emotionally charged and potentially draining experience. Because the process of recovering from a disorder takes time, your caregiving tasks are likely to continue for weeks, if not months. If you are using the Maudsley approach, managing your child's food involves interacting with her every couple of hours about what she needs to eat versus what she wants to eat (or not eat). A child who suffers from anorexia may be at a stage where she cannot see that she has an illness, a mind-set that can understandably generate parent-child friction. On the one hand, you want a good rapport with her; on the other, the potential severity and urgency of her condition are driving you to help her get well—and this means persuading her to do what she dreads. For you and other parents, this is a tall order.

If your child engages in the binge-purge cycle, your treatment team will help you work together as a family to discourage this habit. For example, if she tends to induce vomiting, try to plan joint after-meal activities, such as washing dishes, playing Scrabble, taking a walk, or watching TV to distract her from her powerful urge to get rid of what she eats. At times, you may find yourself exasperated, especially if weeks pass with minimal improvement or if she engages in more than one purging method (laxative and diuretic abuse). Perhaps you will find statements such as the following rolling off your tongue: "If I take my eyes off you for two minutes after a meal, you'll head straight for the bathroom. I've had enough." In fact, you'll probably experience a host of powerful emotions while taking care of your ill child—sadness, fear, helplessness, anger, or various combinations. All of these feelings are valid.

## Riding the Emotional Wave

Once you are aware that frustration and other forceful emotions come with the territory of taking care of an adolescent with an eating disorder, the next question becomes how to cope with these feelings. All along, we have emphasized how important it is to separate the child from the illness. Thus, when you feel angry about your son's or daughter's behavior, you should blame the illness, not the child. We have also advised you to hone your empathy skills with the goal of understanding rather than judging your child.

Here is another tool that will help you stay on an even keel as you interact daily with your child. Let's say that you and your daughter are having a hard time and you're angry. Rather than criticize her in the heat of the moment, the key is to cool off and allow yourself to think about the situation rationally; you'll want to identify your feeling, ponder its possible source(s), formulate a plan to address it, and finally put your strategy into action. To give yourself the time and space to step back from the anger and do this problem solving, we suggest that you visualize your feeling as an ocean wave that rises, peaks, and falls. Try to recognize the points at which your anger is moving through each of these stages of activity. Can you detect your wave when it first develops? Notice what it feels like as it starts to gain momentum. Is it about to crest? After it peaks, it will gradually subside. The secret to coping with these intense feelings lies, in part, in your timing. The best point to do your problem solving is not when the wave is rising and certainly not while it's cresting, but rather after it has subsided.

Remember that, like any new skill, riding the emotional wave requires practice, so be patient with yourself. The advantage of this tool is that, once you learn to use it effectively, it can model a healthy way to cope with difficult emotions for your child.

## Finding Time for Yourself

When is the last time you took time off? You're probably wondering whether we are referring to your parenting and caregiving responsibilities, to your paid job, or to the various other roles you play. Actually, we're talking about taking a breather from all of your tasks and giving yourself some sorely needed downtime to use any way you'd like. Read a novel, go to a ball game or museum, confide in a friend, watch a movie, take a walk in the woods or along the seashore—the possibilities are numerous. The key is to use the time to meet your needs, not somebody else's. Looking back, Mona describes how much it has meant to her to set aside time for herself. "When Greg first developed anorexia, I was so afraid he'd suffer medical complications that I pushed myself very hard—perhaps too hard—in my efforts to help him. All along, our family therapist had been advising me to take breaks from the intensity of the home front, but I hadn't really taken those suggestions in. The words *day off* just weren't in my vocabulary back then. And I felt so jittery that it was hard to sit still.

"I didn't realize how important it was to take breaks until I came close to burning out. The bottom line was that I needed to give myself permission to spend time on myself. At first, it wasn't easy. Kurt was great about supervising Greg's meals on weekends, but after working a full week at the office, he needed downtime too. Orchestrating our schedules was quite an undertaking. I'm trying to become more aware of and realistic about my limits; I want to be there for Greg but be better able to recognize when I need time to myself. If, for example, my frustration is rising toward the peak of its wave, that can be my signal that I need a break. I'm hoping that teaching myself to slow down will set a good example for Greg. He takes after me in that we both push ourselves too hard. It would be great if he could learn to be kind to himself."

## Max, the Pup

Don't underestimate your intuition about what will help you and your family. Mona's voice turns exuberant, her expression vibrant, as she talks about an idea she brought to fruition when her son was in the throes of anorexia. "It's our tradition to host holiday celebrations for our relatives. Our household was so tense and horrible last winter that I knew I had to do something to perk it up. On Christmas Eve, Kurt and I brought home a new puppy, Max. We purposely chose a lap breed so he could be cuddled. Greg loves dogs, and the pup provided him with hours of distraction from his weight worries. But Max was the runt of his litter, and when he arrived, he weighed only one and a half pounds and needed a lot of TLC. In a sense, Max's issues paralleled Greg's. We explained to our son that the puppy needed to eat to avoid having health problems. We had to sit with Max while he ate to make sure that he finished his food and that our other dog didn't snatch it. Our son would dip his finger into Max's food and encourage the pup to lick it. In evaluating what brought Greg back to health, I wouldn't say Max was the tipping point, but the pup certainly brought a lot of fun and happiness into our home. He still does."

## How Do You Feel About Sharing Information with Others?

As we discussed in Chapter 4, parents' privacy preferences vary greatly based on the patient's age and on relationships and communication styles among family members. It's not just a question of whom to tell. It's also how, what, and when to tell them. There are no cookie-cutter solutions here. What works for one family can be untenable for another. When describing the factors that saw them through the most difficult six months of their lives, Mona and Kurt agreed that being open about their situation was key. Mona details how she reached out for support from friends, family members, and the community. "When people asked me what was wrong with Greg, I told them the truth. Once I opened up about his disorder, I didn't feel so alone. The staff at his school were really helpful. I'll never forget how one teacher came forward and told me about her own experience with an eating disorder. So did acquaintances, cousins, and friends of friends. Many of them said, 'I'm so sorry. Is there anything I can do to help?' I did tons of reading about eating disorders, and in an effort to process the new information, I'd parrot it back to friends and then ramble on about it. They deserve medals for listening and for offering input on what might be helpful for Greg. Their generosity meant the world to me."

As Mona and Kurt would be the first to admit, advice about sharing information cannot be reduced to the maxim "Be open." When you reach out for support, it's not a question of whether you are doing it "right" or "wrong." It's more a matter of who is comfortable revealing what kinds of information. Try to read the person with whom you're interacting to gauge what level of disclosure to pursue; choose your confidantes judiciously. Mismatches sometimes happen, even to the most emotionally intelligent individuals. For example, you may give someone minimal information who can handle more or vice versa. Be patient with yourself. Though the garnering of emotional support is challenging, it's a project worth pursuing, not only for your own well-being but also to set an example for your child. Close friends and relatives can be invaluable sources of support. And if you are able to express your feelings in family therapy sessions, your child may learn to do the same.

Many parents find it beneficial to communicate with other moms and dads whose children struggle with eating disorders. Talking about the shared experiences of fear, frustration, or guilt with people who are in your situation can give you fresh insights and help you feel connected. Contact national advocacy organizations (listed in the Resources section) and ask them to put you in touch with other parents. There are also group programs that offer parents tools for taking care of adolescents with eating disorders (again, consult the Resources section).

## How Does Your Child Feel About Sharing Information with Others?

In addition to having an initial discussion about disclosure with your immediate family, you'll want to revisit the issue now and then during the course of treatment, because feelings about whether or how to tell relatives and friends tend to shift or fluctuate. Kurt recalls, "When Greg first entered treatment, he raised no objections to adults knowing about his disorder, as long as they kept it confidential. At that point, he preferred not to let his peers in on his situation, and we certainly respected his wishes. About six weeks later, however, he changed his mind, claiming that 'everyone knew anyway.' Aware that kids can be hard on those with eating disorders, I wasn't sure opening up would be a good idea for Greg. But I needn't have worried. As it turned out, his classmates and his buddies outside of school were enormously helpful to his recovery."

Like Greg, some eating disordered individuals tell their friends and romantic partners about their illness. But a number of aspects of the problem are not easy to talk about. It is not unusual for a person with anorexia or bulimia to feel flawed, perceiving that the relationship is uneven, that she's the inferior one, and that she's fortunate to be involved with her partner. She fears that any information suggesting fragility will tip the balance of the relationship over the limit, with the result that she'll be rejected. For a while, perhaps she is able to hide her behaviors and hang on to the relationship. But gradually, her rigid eating habits and rituals will restrict her ability to engage in give-and-take communication. For example, if she repeatedly avoids social eating, she is likely to leave her partner puzzled and eventually alienated. Her shame related to her body ("I don't want anyone to see or touch my fat") and her strict adherence to routines may send her significant other the message that she is not interested in closeness.

A number of people with eating disorders have difficulty making friends. As we discussed in Chapter 7, some are so isolated in their illnesses that they lack the energy for social activities. It is not unusual for a person with an eating disorder and anxiety to have a hard time reading interpersonal cues that say, "I like you," and to react by finding flaws in others. Some with anorexia or bulimia are so convinced they are defective that they can't conceive of anyone enjoying their company. Others are under the impression that being liked is about achievement and performance rather than about who they are inside.

For eating disordered individuals who would like to gain insight into their interactions with key people in their lives, interpersonal therapy should be a part of the treatment program. In this kind of talk therapy, patients examine how their eating problems affect their current relationships and vice versa. Examples of topics that are often explored include grieving over the death of a family member or friend, adjusting to transitions (such as college, a new job, marriage, or divorce), and unraveling friction between two people in a relationship. Interpersonal therapy can also be beneficial to those who are socially isolated and have difficulty making and keeping friends.

## Moving Forward

In reflecting on the road to recovery, parents often report that their overall perceptions of eating disorders have changed. Mona describes how her perspective has shifted during the course of helping her son. "Before my journey, I used to look at girls with eating disorders in a not-so-favorable light. I'd assume they were ditsy individuals who focused far too much on their appearance. If I saw a magazine article about a girl with an eating disorder, I'd feel like saying, 'Get over yourself.' Based on my son's experience, I've learned how shortsighted that attitude was. There's a lot more to eating disorders than I imagined before the problem hit home. For Greg, as for most people with these conditions, improving his health has been a struggle. Our road to recovery continues, and in the long run, I hope that Kurt, Greg, Ella, and I will be stronger, more sympathetic people for it."

Mona's candor about her change in attitude is extremely helpful. Over the years, myths and misconceptions have evolved about eating disorders. Unfortunately, some people think that individuals with anorexia are to blame for their eating problem. Some perceive kids with this illness as brats who engage in their behaviors primarily for the purpose of drawing attention; that, too, is wrong. Others are under the false impression that patients with eating disorders can "turn off" their behavior at will. And although research supports the idea that biology plays a role in the development of these disorders, some people refuse to believe it. These popular but misguided notions make it even harder for individuals with eating disorders to seek help and confide in others about their condition. Later in the book, we will talk about a national advocacy movement that strives to combat stigma by raising public awareness of eating disorders and improving access to professional treatment. But first, you are probably wondering what causes eating disorders, a topic we will address in Chapter 10.

# PART III

# Preventing Eating Disorders and Raising Awareness

## CHAPTER 10

# Examining Risk Factors and Causes

"Why does my child have an eating disorder? Why did this happen? Is it my fault?" Although scientists have found clues as to why eating disorders arise, there are no definitive answers. What we do know is that no single influence is responsible for the development of these conditions. In all likelihood, a number of determinants play a role. As shown in Figure 10.1, the challenge facing researchers is to examine the pieces of the puzzle to discover how they fit together.

In their efforts to find the causes of eating disorders, scientists search for risk factors; that is, they identify what increases the likelihood that an individual will develop an illness. Who is vulnerable? What characteristics do individuals with eating disorders share that set them apart from those who don't develop these conditions? Learning about the possible roots of eating disorders will help you in a couple of ways. First, by appreciating how complex these illnesses are, you can begin to see that no one is to blame. Second, knowing that eating disorders stem from many factors will give you an increased understanding of your child's treatment program and help you support her on her road to recovery.

**FIGURE 10.1** What Causes Eating Disorders?

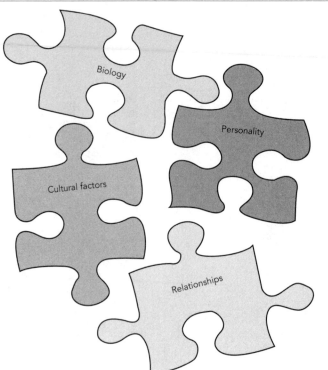

## Culture and Eating Disorders

Mainstream American culture exerts relentless pressure on girls to be thin. Billboards, subway ads, magazines, films, TV, and the Internet promise that thinness leads to romance, success, and a lifetime of happiness. The notion that body size produces these rewards is an illusion—a powerful one—that exploits girls from a very early age and strikes them with full force during the years when they are insecure about growing up and therefore vulnerable to believing harmful definitions of womanhood (such as "You are what you weigh," or "Thinness equals fulfillment"). Sophisticated advertising strategies lead many viewers to feel negatively about their bodies and to think that changing themselves to look a certain way—which inevitably means buying a certain product—will solve their problems and allow them to live happily ever after.

Though dieting is not synonymous with an eating disorder, it can increase a person's chance of developing one. The ultrathin body ideal espoused by Western culture is unattainable for the vast majority of girls. Yet young women are a captive audience for the supermodels who fill the pages of fashion and beauty magazines. As girls approach puberty, they naturally and appropriately gain weight and take an increased interest in their looks—for some, looking at fashion magazines is a way to express this interest and find people to model themselves after. These sylphlike images are *not* real; they're created, largely through the use of technology, to convince girls that thinness confers a perfect life. In comparison to such figures, a young person tends to experience her own body as "not thin enough," a perception that can help fuel her development of unhealthy weight-loss practices (food restriction, binge eating, and purging). Often, a girl who is dissatisfied with her body will also dislike herself in other ways; perhaps, for example, she senses that she is less intelligent, less likable, or less athletic than she wants to be. Research has found that up to half of middle and high school girls associated their desire to lose weight with magazine images; the large majority of these girls said that pictures of models inform their idea of a perfect body.

## Abnormal Eating Practices and Diverse Populations

One of the myths surrounding eating disorders is that they are a "white kid's problem." The truth is that body angst and unhealthy eating practices beleaguer people of all races and ethnicities. There are increasing data that body dissatisfaction is equally common among Asian American, Hispanic, and Caucasian women and somewhat less common among African American women. The latter group is less inclined to idolize thinness or to restrict food intake, even with the weight gain that accompanies puberty. The difference in body satisfaction between African American and Caucasian women seems greatest for those in their 20s, disappearing at around age 40.

Fitting in, being one's own person, making and keeping friends—these everyday trials and tribulations of adolescence are hard enough. But when changes such as moving to a new home or entering a new school occur, even the most resilient young person can feel off-kilter. Immigrant families face these stressors on a mammoth scale as they encounter values, norms, and even a language that may be very different from their own. For a young person to enter a classroom worlds away from her former one and see a host of unfamiliar faces requires enormous courage and fortitude. Longing for acceptance by her new schoolmates, she may adopt their codes of behavior; for example, she might dress like them, listen to the music they enjoy, read their favorite magazines, view their preferred TV shows and movies, and use their popular expressions as well as their instant messaging vocabulary. If they diet, she may too.

As a parent, you may feel ambivalent about whether (and to what degree) to adopt the culture of your new land or adhere to tradition. Perhaps you grapple with decisions regarding which set of norms (the old, the new, or some combination) to encourage in your children. Then there is the question of what to do if your child insists on dieting or on other peer- and media-driven aspects of society that are unlikely to be in her best interest. Torn between two cultures, a person might turn to disordered eating behaviors as an attempt to escape inner conflicts. Yet one doesn't have to be an immigrant or the child of an immigrant to face these challenges; the need for acceptance combined with the pressures of mainstream culture can lead to turmoil for many young people and contribute to the development of disordered eating.

## Teaching Your Child About Teasing and Bullies

Although not all demographic groups ascribe to the same body ideal, weight bias is a problem in our society. Many individuals erroneously associate a large body size with laziness, ineptitude, emotional insecurity, friendlessness, and an unsatisfying dead-end job. In contrast, thinness conjures up images of perfection, high achievement, loving relationships, initiative, and leadership. Teasing about body weight can have a negative effect on how a child or teen feels about herself and may play a role in her development of abnormal eating patterns. Girls who reach puberty earlier than their peers may be particularly vulnerable to cruel body comments. Yet they are not the only ones who are teased. Many girls recall the overwhelming hurt or anger they felt when they were called names related to the size or shape of their bodies. Cultural mandates for slenderness can be so demanding that individuals sometimes consider themselves or others overweight when, by objective standards, that is not the case.

Do you remember incidents from your own childhood when you made or received unkind body comments? Perhaps you will want to share some of those memories with your child; by doing so, you can lead in to a discussion about her peer relationships, including any body-teasing incidents she has experienced. It is not unusual for someone who is obese or who has obese parents to develop an eating disorder, making it all the more necessary to impress on young people the importance of respecting all body sizes and shapes, including their own. We suggest building an ongoing dialogue with your child about her interactions with peers, conveying that you are receptive to hearing not only about the good times but also about the bad. When she describes her day, try to tune in to the feelings behind what she says (or doesn't say). Is she feeling comfortable and safe in her friendships?

If your child reveals that she has been teased, listen closely as she tells you what happened and accept her report of the incident as the truth. Your understanding can make a huge difference in how she perceives herself and copes with the teasing. You will want to offer statements such as "I'm sorry those girls were mean to you. It sounds like you had a hard afternoon," or "I imagine you felt very alone and helpless," or "It's understandable you feel angry after being called those names."

She will need a strategy for disarming bullies, and you can help her devise one by asking her to recall approaches that worked successfully for her friends who have been teased. Once your child has hatched a plan that sounds promising, try to boost her confidence with some role-playing. One of you can act the part of the bully while the other puts the new strategy into action, then switch roles. Learning to be assertive doesn't happen all at once, so you need to give your child ongoing emotional support while allowing her some space to process what you have taught her. With each step she takes toward freedom from a bully, your praise (for her initiatives as well as for her courage) will mean the world to her.

For the most part, it is not helpful to call the teaser's parents. If your child's safety is at risk or if the bullying escalates, you should contact her school. Does she have positive friendships to help counter the negative impact of the teasing? Is she involved in enjoyable hobbies or after-school programs that are outside the bully's reign of influence? Such activities can give your child the opportunity to make new friends in a safe environment and learn that she is not too this or too that simply because a bully said she is.

## Coping with Cliques

Adolescent girls tend to form exclusive groups called cliques, complete with leaders and specific codes of behavior regarding what is acceptable. A given middle or high school may include many cliques, each with its own distinct subculture. For example, when members greet each other, a specific phrase (as in "Wha's up?" or "Yo"), gesture, and voice inflection may be required. Often, there are certain expectations regarding clothes and physical appearance; perhaps members all ascribe to multiple ear piercings, streak their hair, sport the same style bracelet, or worship thinness.

When a girl aspires to join a particular clique, her day-to-day progress (or perceived lack of progress) toward that goal are of dire importance to her; any remark, however casual, from a popular clique member can either make her day or consign her to the doldrums. However, life inside a clique is not as rosy as wannabe members assume; although these groups may offer a sense of belonging, they sometimes exert intense pressure to conform and become hotbeds of subtle or not-so-subtle aggression. A girl who is "in" one month can be "out" the next. Holly knows about that firsthand. A year ago, she developed anorexia shortly after a falling-out with her girlfriends. Now 13, she and her parents have kindly offered to tell their story.

"My daughter's outgoing personality draws people to her," states Jordan, Holly's father. "She's always been very popular, a leader among her classmates. Her seventh-grade teacher described her as an extraordinary girl not only because she is an enthusiastic learner and has a strong work ethic, but also because the other kids looked up to her. Never timid, she gets a great deal of satisfaction from her friendships."

Holly describes how her social life took a turn for the worse: "It started as a little fight and blew up way out of proportion. Melanie was my best friend in seventh grade, and there were four other girls in our group. In the winter, Melanie started feeling left out. And she was right; the others weren't including her like they had in the past. She wanted to know why they were down on her, so she tried to talk about it with them, but they got mad at her for making a big deal about it. When they were mean to Melanie, I stood up for her, and then they turned against me as well. If I'd given in and taken their side in their fight with Melanie, they would have liked me again. But I never gave an inch. I'd pass them standing in their usual spot in the hallway, and they'd get closer together and sort of whisper. One of them, Christie, used to say, 'Bitch,' just loud enough for me to hear it. I tried to keep on walking, pretending that I didn't care. But one day, I must have blushed or looked upset because I paused for a second. So Christie turned to me and said, 'I was just joking around. Can't you take it?' I'd never been so embarrassed in my life.

"After a while, I stayed away from their hallway get-togethers. But sometimes we'd all be in class and one of them would look over at me and mouth, 'Bitch.' I'd feel like mouthing that same name, or a worse one, back at her. But I didn't because they just would've hated me more. It was hard to get away from their mean looks, especially when they rolled their eyes as if I was from another planet. Before all this started, I'd shared all their inside jokes. Now they had new ones. These girls had been friends with me since kindergarten. They knew which buttons to push to upset me. Mostly, they acted like I didn't exist. It went on like that for months."

The kind of bullying Holly experienced is all too common. Mainstream American culture places girls in a bind regarding how to cope with anger and other emotions. Females tend to place special value on their friendships and go to great lengths to preserve them, sometimes at substantial personal cost. Resolving a dispute in a healthy way generally requires opposing parties to talk about their feelings. Yet many women have grown up unprepared for this. Raised to be nice at all times, girls typically avoid voicing anger face-to-face. Instead, they tend to express it quietly and indirectly. Like Christie, the girl who is annoyed at a friend may engage in name-calling, claiming to be kidding when she isn't. Maybe she passes nasty notes in class, spreads rumors about her perceived rival, or stops talking to her, encouraging others in their social circle to do the same. Perhaps she finds safety in numbers. Recruiting peers as allies often affords her the opportunity to bully under the protective blanket of a group; if she's one of many aggressors, no one is likely to blame her directly. In fact, with access to e-mail, girls can gang up on an opponent without saying a single word to her face.

"By sticking up for her best friend," says Holly's mother, Marianne," Holly did what was strong and noble. It bothered me that she had to pay such a high price for being a true friend. She took the aggression of these girls hard, and I sympathized with how she felt. For the first time in her life, kids weren't knocking the door down to be her friend. Ostracized from her group, she became withdrawn, slept much later than usual on weekends, and spent a lot of time moping. Another change was that she complained of headaches and stomachaches prior to her hip-hop ballet rehearsals. I wondered whether these were the result of social pressure. Or maybe she was stressed about the new dance routine she was learning; she tends to come down hard on herself when she doesn't catch on to something as quickly as she wishes or if she flubs a step that she feels she should have mastered. When I discovered how skinny she'd become and how little she was eating, I realized that her headaches and stomachaches were probably hunger signals.

"I clung to every last hope that Holly didn't have an eating disorder. She'd always been average in weight for her age and height. I reminded myself that she'd never before been obsessed with the size or shape of her body. Why now? What's more, she'd just turned 12 the previous month. Wasn't she too young to have an eating disorder? My pediatrician explained that although these illnesses commonly begin between the ages of 13 and 25, they have, over the past decade, started to afflict children at increasingly young ages. While no one knows exactly why this is happening, he said that improved awareness of parents is likely allowing more kids to receive help."

Holly remembers the turmoil that marked her descent into anorexia. "I was on a diet before the fight with my friends, but afterward, I cut way back on my eating. Lots of girls dieted, so I never thought anything was wrong with it. I just wanted to look thin. At lunchtime in school, girls always talk about what they should or shouldn't eat. Someone might say, 'I can't have that. It's too fattening,' or 'I ate too much yesterday, so today I have to be good.' When I first lost weight, everyone said how great I looked. Then the diet kept going. My doctors said I had an eating disorder, but I didn't feel sick. At the time, I thought losing weight would help me. That's why I fought against gaining it back."

Jordan's memories of that time period are vivid. "Treatment was a team effort," he says. "Holly started out seeing the pediatrician every week to have her weight and vital signs checked and to learn why it was important for her to eat more. She also had individual therapy every week, as well as an appointment with a nutritionist. At first, she was all smoke and mirrors around food. If Marianne or I hadn't been right there with her at every meal, she might not have eaten. She also put up a fuss about going to individual therapy. But over time, that changed. One day, I was driving her home from an appointment when she mentioned the possibility of using the same level of control to gain weight as she had to lose it. I liked that line of thinking, which, I figured, had come from therapy. Granted, she wasn't yet ready to put that theory into practice, but she was processing it, and that was a good sign."

Marianne adds, "Throughout every stage of treatment, Holly's professional caregivers have made it clear to Jordan and me that we did not cause our daughter's eating disorder. Given that I tended to blame myself for the illness, the reassurance was more than welcome. The thought that Holly was caught up in physical appearance at such a young age struck a sensitive chord in me. When I was growing up, I too had idolized the sleek models in magazines. Even now, I have to think twice about buying in to the advertisements that connect happiness with skinniness. And my own mother had dieted. Maybe I'd absorbed some thin-is-in thinking from her.

"I'd always made a point of serving my children balanced meals, including lean meats, salads, veggies, and starches. Sometimes, however, I'd be watching my carbs, and that might have had an effect on Holly. It's not that I broadcast my intention to lose weight to my children. On the contrary, I barely mentioned it. Still, Holly was at an age where she may have picked up on my personal weight concerns and developed similar ones about her own body."

In talking about what has helped her improve her health, Holly focuses on her friendships. "Some of the girls from that group acted so mean to me that I wasn't sure I wanted their friendship back," she admits. "But there were a couple I still liked. My therapists were on my side, and we discussed how to go about ending the fight. One day, I sort of cornered one girl, Alexa, and spoke my mind. I told her how a fight I'd never wanted in the first place had gone on far too long, how we'd both been in tough spots, and how I wanted us to like each other again. To my surprise, she felt badly about everything that had happened too. So we ended up hugging and staying friends. It was scary to approach Alexa, but it was worth it."

During treatment, Holly's parents and therapists helped her modify the extreme stand she took in response to her girlfriend crisis. They guided her as she changed approaches to the problem from those that didn't work (locking horns with the aggressors) and were actually harmful (starving herself) to those that proved productive (reevaluating the friendships, talking to Alexa). Now doing well in recovery, Holly acknowledges the pain of last year's girlfriend crisis and feels good about the steps she took to resolve it. Of her stoicism, she says, "I wouldn't do the same thing again."

Marianne and Jordan are heartened that Holly has gained some weight and that her natural vibrancy and sociability—which waned with the illness—are starting to return. Between dance rehearsals, academic requirements, and social activities, Holly's days are busy, and, like many individuals in recovery from anorexia, she continues to demand a lot of herself. In addition, she sometimes has trouble going with the flow. Switching gears—moving from one train of thought or plan of action to another—comes more naturally to some people than to others. For many individuals with past or present anorexia, adjusting to unexpected changes—going from one mind-set to another—is not always easy. On the bright side, Holly is gradually realizing that she doesn't have to do everything to the max. In addition to learning less extreme ways to cope with problems, she is trying to be kinder to herself, a skill that will help her throughout adolescence and long after.

## Is She a Perfectionist?

As we mentioned in Chapter 3, perfectionism often occurs with an eating disorder, sometimes predating the illness. Although compliance is commendable, some children take it too far. These are children who obey everything requested of them to the nth degree and make painstaking efforts to stay out of trouble. Eager for approval, they aim to be model children, sometimes at the expense of their own needs. If they mostly operate based on what others tell them to do, it may become hard for them to chart their own course. Rather than making every decision for your child or expecting her to make them in isolation, work with her, allowing her to make the final choices.

Perfectionists typically expect themselves to perform flawlessly—in school, in extracurricular activities, on the athletic field, and on the job—in order to earn and keep approval. In addition to setting high standards for everything they do, these individuals have difficulty bending their self-imposed rules to take their personal needs into account. For example, a pupil who continually overstudies in her quest for the perfect A is not necessarily doing herself a favor. Suppose she insists on doing homework until midnight Monday through Friday. Some nights she's sleepy by 10:30 or 11:00. Her drowsiness is a signal that it's time to quit working. But that's not what happens. Instead, she strains to stay awake until the stroke of midnight. As the semester progresses, sleep deprivation prevents her from performing as well as she'd like. In addition, working many hours every evening keeps her from participating in other activities. Yet she resists reevaluating and possibly modifying her study habits.

## Does She See and Believe That She Is Special?

Conscientiousness and a drive to excel are positive qualities through which a person can make great strides. But not everyone who works hard in school is an A student. Not everyone who aspires to the lead role in the school play gets the part. Not every qualified applicant to a given college gets admitted. In your child's quest to excel, how can you and she manage the disappointments that may occur along the way?

As you talk to your youngster about competition, there are many factors to consider: What does "the best" mean and who determines this? Are the terms *winner* and *best* synonymous? How do you and your child define success?

To help your child weather her disappointments, offer her a balanced perspective. Let's say, for example, that she is a college student who has earned a B instead of an A in a certain course. She might erroneously conclude that she does not belong in such an advanced curriculum or, even more unfairly, that she is "stupid." Actually, there are any number of possible reasons why she has received a B, some of them having little to do with her intellect or with her potential for success. Like most people, she is probably stronger in some areas than in others, and she might look on her grades as one of many clues that show where her true talents lie.

It is wise to reinforce your child not only for her progress in learning a skill but also for her inner qualities. Observe and point out her positive characteristics on a regular basis. Here are just a few examples of praiseworthy behaviors: offering her opinion, standing up for herself, accepting a compliment, taking a break from baseball practice when she feels tired, prioritizing, and rationing her energy instead of approaching everything at breakneck speed.

## Does She View You as Perfect?

It is not unusual for a young person to perceive her parents as more perfect than they are. If your child is under the impression that accomplishments come very easily to you, she may feel that she must be perfect in order to be valued. Although she can come to understand that you are flawed like everyone else, this is a process of parent-child development and takes time.

One way to convey to your children that you are human and fallible is to describe your own life experiences, referring not only to your successes but also to your struggles and failings. Try to send the message that perfectionism is not just a motor that keeps running; it comes with its own set of fears and distresses such as, "Will I really be the best? What will happen if I'm not?" Revealing these and other costs of your perfectionism can pave the way for dialogue between you and your child. Some parents find discussing their pasts viable while others don't, so if it doesn't work well for you, don't hold it against yourself but instead realize that there is more than one approach to communicating your experiences.

As an alternative or addition to disclosure, try engaging your child in a joint activity that will allow each of you to see various aspects of the other. This is not about competing, but rather about learning to play, about building that sandcastle with imperfections; in fact, your mistakes may ease her fears of making her own. Focus on enjoying each other in the *process* of the activity. Your efforts to spend time with her in this manner can be effective whether she is a child, a teenager, or an adult. It is a good idea to suggest an activity that will appeal to her even if it is not your first choice. Tennis, gardening, a home-improvement project, visiting a museum—the possibilities are many. (See Figure 10.2.) Remember to keep your goals realistic; instead of expecting your joint activity to repair your relationship with your child, try to think of it as a stepping-stone.

**FIGURE 10.2** Enjoy Positive Activities Together

## Is She a Future Olympiad?

The ability of a serious athlete to push herself to the limit can be a unique gift. Over the past 30 years, more athletic opportunities have opened up to women than ever before; now that sports play an important role in the development of young women, many aspire to be champions and opt to "go for it." Thus, the question becomes how to encourage your child in her athletic pursuit without letting it get overly consuming or destructive to her. Encourage her to strive for excellence, not perfection. What's the difference? Excellence is achievable; perfection isn't. The athlete who shoots for excellence sets high but realistic standards, appreciates her progress, enjoys the sport for its own sake, and understands that mistakes are an inevitable—and valuable—part of the learning process. The athlete who seeks perfection, on the other hand, may drive herself to do whatever it takes to be the best, sometimes at the expense of her physical and emotional health.

To support your athlete in her quest for first place, it helps to be aware of the challenges that may lie ahead. As we discussed in Chapter 3, participants in competitive physical activities that link body size to performance—such as gymnastics, figure skating, ballet, and long-distance running—are particularly vulnerable to developing an eating disorder. The thinness ideal promoted by these sports cultures can pose a nutritional risk or play a role in the development of binge eating and purging. Some athletes find it upsetting that the musculature needed for optimal performance increases their weight. Injuries happen even to the best athletes, but those who are undernourished are at higher risk.

In thinking about the emotional health of your athletically talented child, remember that competing will bring her not only the joy of winning, but also the disappointment of losing. Her undertaking requires enormous dedication. Will the benefits of vying for a championship outweigh the potential personal costs? Is she willing to give up other desirable activities in order to practice? Athletes in perfectionistic, competitive environments focus intensely on beating everybody, a style that challenges the trust necessary to make friendships work. How will this impact your child? Try to establish an ongoing dialogue with her about these issues so you can address them proactively and effectively.

While some athletes achieve immeasurable stardom, others reach various degrees of success. There may come a time when your child is no longer willing to do all that is necessary to make it to the top, even if she's almost there. How will you feel and respond? Regardless of whether she wins the gold medal, encourage her to enjoy her accomplishments and keep the costs to the other aspects of her life as low as possible. Reassure her that she has options and there is a way out. Discuss the value of learning to accept one's limitations and cope with losses. In addition, she should devote some attention to her emotional and social growth, which will also help shape her future.

## Eating Disorders Run in Families: Yvette's Story

Yvette, 47, an acclaimed long-distance runner, relates her eating disorder, which struck as a college senior and lasted 10 years, to her determination to run the perfect marathon. Coached to discipline herself and train hard, she achieved running times most athletes only dream of. Yet her success came at a huge cost. "I grew up in a close-knit family where I was eager to please my parents and to do everything right," she explains. "As the oldest of six children, I helped care for the younger ones, did housework, participated in sports, and managed to pull off top grades in school. I didn't go out much with other kids. I was shy and too caught up in everyday situations at home to devote the time and energy to dates. I defined myself based on how I perceived others were judging me. I had a lot of insecurities, often feeling like I was teetering between 'good enough' and 'not good enough.'

"In college, I developed a passion for running. Nothing beat the freedom of soaring down the track, the wind at my heels.

To my surprise, I made the college track team. The joy of winning was seductive; it brought out my competitive streak. I figured that dieting would improve my running speed. Now I realize that trimming down can increase the likelihood of developing an eating disorder, but back then, I hadn't a clue. To me, dieting seemed like part of womanhood. One day, in reaction to an offhanded body size comment from the coach, I promised myself I'd solve my chubbiness problem once and for all. I became hell-bent on losing weight, cutting way back on my eating and running extra miles in practice. Restricting my intake made me so hungry that I'd splurge on sweets and pastries. There were a few weeks when all I did from morning till night was binge, purge, and run.

"When the problem reached its worst, I was like an automaton. I used to run by myself at 6:30 A.M. every day, no matter what. I'll never forget this one morning when I woke up chilled and achy. The reasonable decision would have been to rest. But true to form, I forced myself out of bed, threw on my sweatsuit, and headed for the track, as if the run were a life-and-death necessity. It wasn't that I wanted to run that morning; it was rainy and raw, and the very thought of getting drenched made me shiver. It was all a question of getting the exercise over and done with so that I wouldn't feel guilty or have to run double the distance the next day. Something inside me enslaved me to my training schedule. Less than four months shy of college graduation, I functioned almost mechanically. I was a stranger to myself, out of touch with where my life was going and who I wanted to be."

Despite her ruthless diets, bingeing, and purging, Yvette insisted for months that she did not need mental health services. "I grew up thinking I had to stay strong for everyone else," she admits. "Asking for help wasn't in my nature. But when I finally entered psychotherapy, I became aware that my perfectionism contributed to the disorder, and in the earliest years of my marriage, especially during my first pregnancy, I took much better care of myself.

"With the birth of my first daughter, Felice, my joy knew no bounds. As a toddler, she showed remarkable self-sufficiency, preferring to accomplish tasks herself rather than letting me help. She pushed herself hard from an early age, never giving less than 100 percent. Given her drive to be the best, I focused on freeing her as much as possible from performance pressure and helping her to feel good about herself. At age six, when Felice asked to participate in athletics, I took care in selecting upbeat, praise-based programs; observing her reactions to the classes; and communicating with the coaches. The idea was to afford her healthy sports environments."

The precautions Yvette took to protect her daughter from anorexia and bulimia were right on target. Genes contribute to the development of these disorders. The likelihood is that the heriditary component of eating disorders stems not from one gene, but from the combined effects of many. Although scientists have not yet pinpointed the contributing genes, they are making headway on this subject. In addition, there may be a genetic tie-in between eating disorders and perfectionism, a quality that Yvette knew she and her daughter had in common.

When Felice was 13, Yvette—still healthy and now a mother of three—faced a challenge she had done everything in her power to prevent. "At first, Felice's weight loss was minimal," she recalls. "But when a teacher reported purging, I felt devastated. That phone call instantly awakened the horrors of my illness. The news was so painful that I had the urge to binge and purge to tune out the world. But my child needed me, and she needed me to be strong."

Making the situation even harder was the special bond Yvette enjoyed with her firstborn. As she elaborated on this theme, the pain she experienced when her daughter fell ill was practically palpable. "I had a history of fertility problems," she explains, "and I often thought of Felice as my 'miracle child.' My recovery from anorexia and bulimia took hold when I was pregnant with Felice. Now she had an eating disorder, and I couldn't save her. I knew her as a sweet, generous, and open-minded child with a lively sense of humor and a zest for life. But once she became ill, I felt like I could no longer reach her or connect with her. It felt like she was gone."

Despite these excruciating moments, Yvette wasted no time in seeking treatment for Felice, first in an outpatient program and eventually as an inpatient. Now, about a year after her discharge from the hospital, Felice—a superb student and athlete—is progressing well in treatment, and Yvette, who has remained healthy, is gaining perspective on all that has happened. "During the darkest weeks of Felice's illness, I was bereaved and guilt-ridden," she says. "The thought that I could have passed a genetic predisposition to eating disorders on to my daughter was difficult enough. Even harder to bear was my hunch that—even though I'd never verbally pressured Felice—I may have unwittingly modeled a weight consciousness that gradually rubbed off on her. I eat well, but I'm a competitive athlete, and my leanness sent a message."

While children who perceive weight as important to their mothers are prone to dieting, fathers also exert an influence. Dads can go a long way toward helping their daughters feel good about themselves and their bodies. Felice's father (Yvette's ex-husband) cared a great deal about his children; due in part to his cultural background, he found it hard to communicate with his daughters and let them know that their inner qualities are more important than their physical appearance. The divorce and 50-50 child custody arrangements were understandably tumultuous for Felice. Even as she longed to spend more time with her mom, she continued to try to be perfect, pushing her feelings inward, a problem that—in conjunction with a perceived rejection from a boyfriend—made her return to health even harder.

Yvette's story has inspired hope and courage in other individuals and families who struggle with eating disorders. Over time, she has realized that Felice's eating disorder is no one's fault. Infinitely more valuable than laying blame is finding help for a high-risk child. She believes it is also important for parents to take good care of themselves so they can accompany their children down the road to recovery. We couldn't agree with her more.

## Risk Factors in a Nutshell

What increases the likelihood of developing an eating disorder?

- Female gender
- Body dissatisfaction
- Dieting; eating in secret
- Neurochemical changes, particularly around the onset of puberty
- Participation at the top levels of sports that tie body weight to performance
- Obsessive thoughts and behavior
- Difficulty moving from one train of thought or plan of action to the next
- Perfectionist tendencies; avoidance of risks
- Perception that thinness is important to mother
- Media images and fashion magazines
- Personal or family history of eating disorder, obesity, substance abuse, and/or depression
- Personal history of teasing or harassment
- Childhood physical or sexual abuse
- Personal history of anxiety problems, particularly an intense fear of engaging in social activities
- Relocation to a culture that worships thinness from one that doesn't

## Puzzles Within the Puzzle

At the beginning of this chapter, we referred to the possible causes of eating disorders (biology, culture, personality, and relationships) as pieces of a jigsaw puzzle that need to be put together. In Western societies, almost all girls are exposed to the thin body ideal, but relatively few get eating disorders. What accounts for this discrepancy? The likelihood is that genetic predisposition to eating disorders helps set the stage for the individual to succumb to cultural pressures. But there is probably a lot more to it.

It turns out that each of the four major puzzle parts is complex in itself. For example, the biology piece includes not only genetics, but also neurochemical changes that take place around the onset of puberty. In Chapter 6, we introduced the chemical serotonin as one of a number of neurotransmitters that transport messages from one brain cell to another. Serotonin helps regulate mood, anxiety, and eating behavior. Research suggests that imbalances in serotonin contribute to the long-term mood issues, obsessions (repetitive, unwelcome thoughts), and perfectionism that characterize eating disorders. Evidence that selective serotonin reuptake inhibitors can be helpful to patients with eating disorders provides an additional clue that serotonin may be involved in the development of these illnesses.

The personality piece of the puzzle is also multifaceted. A number of people with eating disorders are inhibited, others are impulsive, and some fall between these two poles. While Holly is gregarious and Yvette is slightly shy, it is not unusual for people who develop these conditions to have a history of extreme anxiety in social situations, a problem that can continue after a return to healthy eating. Many questions remain. Is intense fear of socializing linked to genetics? Do the obsessions (repeated thoughts) and compulsions (driven behaviors) that characterize eating disorders have genetic roots? Like Holly, some individuals with current or past anorexia have trouble changing gears to accommodate change. Is this a genetics issue, a serotonin problem, or both? Why is dieting a risk factor for some people and not for others? Research on these issues is ongoing.

The good news is that while the exact causes of eating disorders remain unknown, the clues that researchers have uncovered can help inform strategies for preventing these illnesses and treating them in their earliest stages. In Chapter 11, we will detail what you can do to send your child a healthy message and help prevent illness.

## CHAPTER 11

# Sending Your Child a Healthy Message

Although this book is written for the parents of individuals with eating disorders, many moms and dads have confided to us that they worry about their children developing this type of illness. Perhaps you have a friend whose son or daughter is suffering from anorexia or bulimia. Or maybe your child is starting to watch her weight and you're afraid that she might take it to an extreme. This chapter describes what you can do to prevent your child from developing an eating disorder.

A few months ago, Loretta and Rob sought our advice about their daughter, Quinlan. "At 11, she's getting concerned about her looks and would do just about anything to be popular," said Loretta. "She's been choosing more low-calorie foods lately, even though there is no need for her to lose weight. Some of her classmates diet, and I'm worried their 'I'm fat' talk is having an effect on her. And I wouldn't want her to pick up unhealthy attitudes from me. How can we teach her positive attitudes and eating habits?"

Before we answered Loretta's question, we explained that some degree of body dissatisfaction is common among women; whether or not a mom has trouble accepting her own weight, there's a lot she can do to send positive messages to her child. Then we asked Loretta and Rob to tell us more about their family. What were their interests, likes, dislikes, hopes, and dreams? Was Quinlan self-confident? Did she feel good about herself and her body? At that, Loretta looked puzzled. "Every time I pick up a women's magazine, I see the term *body image*," she noted. "That's so vague. What does it mean?" This was an astute observation on her part.

The term *body image* has become popular over the past decade and often refers to how an individual perceives her body. Does she like and respect it, or does she think it isn't good enough? Does she seem preoccupied with her weight? An individual's body image is subject to change. Some people like themselves fine until they experience the physical and emotional growth of puberty. Or a person can feel reasonably good about herself when she gets up in the morning only to find herself grumbling, "I hate my thighs," a few hours later. Loretta and Rob's story addresses some of the challenges you are likely to encounter as you try hard to give healthy messages to your children.

Loretta, 36, reflected on her attitudes toward food and her body. "I didn't think much about whether I was pretty until I was in my early teens," she began. "I was average in weight and very self-conscious, often feeling that I took up more space than I deserved. I wasn't out to win any beauty pageants, but I longed to be popular and envied the girls who were perky and outgoing. It's not that I didn't have friends. It's just that I was quiet, and it took kids a while to get to know me. In middle school, lots of girls dieted or at least talked as if they did. Outer beauty, especially body size and shape, served as a yardstick that determined how good I was. Was my future bright? Hidden somewhere in my mind, beyond what I was capable of comprehending in middle school, was one stipulation. It said, 'You'll be happy, but only if you are thin.'

"My body image—how I liked my body—didn't change much between high school and college. I continued to feel too large and to diet off and on. Between labs, lectures, and hands-on training, my college days were full. I was a real stickler for detail and used to check my school projects over and over before I'd feel confident enough to turn them in. When I felt nervous, particularly before exams, I'd overeat; a few days later, I'd decide that I was too fat and start a diet. It seemed like there was always one reason or another why I should be dieting. In high school, it was because I wanted to be popular. In college, it was because I overate when I was nervous. Once I met Rob, it was because I wanted to look good so he would continue to like me. While in college, I talked in my usual offhanded way about eating this or not eating that. Rob picked up on my inhibitions about food. He'd try to reassure me by saying, 'Loretta, you don't have to worry about what you eat.' No matter what he or anyone else told me though, I couldn't shake the sense that I was fat and should do something about it. The discomfort of 'I'm too big; I weigh too much' followed me everywhere."

Rob, 38, took Loretta's attitude about dieting for granted. "Having grown up with two weight-conscious sisters, comments about calories and fat seemed like everyday girl-talk," he said. "For as long as I've known Loretta, she has occasionally mentioned needing to lose a couple pounds or cheating on her diet. To be honest, I've never paid much attention to these comments. I assumed just about all women watch their weight. When Loretta says, 'That's too fattening,' 'That will go straight to my thighs,' or 'If I so much as look at food I gain weight,' her tone of voice sometimes suggests that she wants a response. But frankly, it's hard to know what to say. When I reassure her that she looks terrific just as she is, she doesn't necessarily believe me. If I take a lighthearted approach, she thinks I don't take her seriously. Listening to Loretta now, I'm starting to realize that diet talk is more than idle chatter. It's emotionally charged, and the messages behind it are hard for me to figure out."

"Rob isn't the only one who finds my diet talk puzzling," said Loretta. "I have trouble understanding it myself. I've not talked with Rob or with my women friends about the emotions underlying my food comments. That's partly because I'm not sure how to describe these feelings and partly because they're embarrassing. I think dieting carries different meanings for different people. For me, the topic of weight loss offered a way to communicate. Starting in my teen years, being labeled 'stuck up' was a fast track to losing friends, so criticizing my body was an effort to convey that I wasn't conceited. Sometimes, talking about calories with my friends helped me feel close to them. At least dieting was something we had in common. Other times, there was the undercurrent of competition that I described earlier. The result was that I sometimes wondered who my true friends were.

"On the whole, I feel more confident than I did in high school and in college. I have two great children and a job in the emergency room of the local hospital, and I get in touch with my artistic ability and childhood passion by creating gift cards on the side. No matter how many lives I help save and no matter how well my cartoon cards sell in the gift shop, I still criticize my body. I've never been prone to heaviness and have always been active. I had a routine physical recently, and my primary care physician gave me a clean bill of health. Intellectually I realize that there's no need to diet. Yet I still do it. In the hospital cafeteria, I still choose a salad when I want a sandwich. On the days they serve pizza slices, my all-time favorite, I still force myself to walk past them, and I'm not sure why. Something inside tells me to avoid certain foods. It could be that self-restraint is so ingrained in me that it's hard to break free. Maybe I diet as a way of saying, 'I shouldn't have needs,' or 'I feel guilty for being successful.' It wouldn't surprise me if I'm still trying to prove to myself and others that I'm good enough. Media influences loom large as well. Whether it's on TV or in the magazines I flip through when I'm in the grocery checkout line, I see images that emphasize thinness. Chances are I watch my weight for a combination of many reasons. I'm trying to sort it all out."

Loretta's self-reflection will serve her well in her efforts to send her daughter healthy messages. As we explained to her and Rob, thin-is-in culture misleads women into assuming that the best way to improve their lives is by controlling the size and shape of their bodies. A huge flaw in the "manage your weight, manage your life" mind-set lies in the fact that body size and shape are not readily changeable. That's because a healthy adult weight range and body type are genetically predetermined. Eating habits and physical activity can impact size and shape, but only to a small extent. Since your weight is healthiest in its genetically programmed range (also called your set-point weight), your body will try its best to stay at that level. Let's say you shed pounds due to severe food restriction; in order to safeguard its health and return to its set-point weight, your body will slow the rate at which it burns fuel. Thus, when you stop your diet, you will probably regain the weight you lost. Loretta was impressed with the idea that healthy weight is genetically predetermined. "It's a compelling reason not to diet," she said, "and a key piece of information to impress upon my daughter."

In thinking about other aspects of body image to discuss with her daughter, Loretta said, "One of my concerns is that my fear of being fat—irrational though it is—has colored my view of what constitutes good nutrition. Given my determination to protect Quinlan from developing an eating disorder, now would be a good time to brush up on nutrition guidelines. It's been years since I was in nursing school, and I imagine there have been modifications, if only minor ones, in professional recommendations regarding the various food groups. I'm the meal planner in the household, but Rob does a lot of the cooking. Although he has great common sense about child care, he would also benefit from some education."

## Eating for Health and Vitality: Setting a Good Example for Your Child

As we explained to Loretta and Rob, parental attitudes and behaviors play a key role in determining how children perceive themselves and their bodies. As important as it is to talk about good nutrition with your child, the everyday examples you set may influence her even more. It is a good idea to approach food as a source of energy and health and to keep your focus off weight and physical appearance. Healthy eating pyramids can assist in planning meals. (See Figure 11.1.) One of the cornerstones of good nutrition is balance. Since no single food group offers all the nutri-

**FIGURE 11.1** Healthy Eating Pyramid for Adults

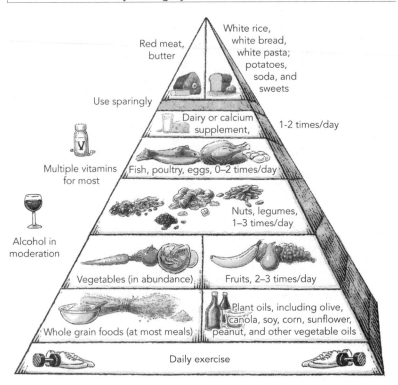

ents the body requires, the pyramid consists of a number of categories: grain products, fruits and vegetables, dairy foods, meats (or beans, eggs, and soy products), and fats. Aiming for balance in your meal plan means that you choose foods from each of the groups. It is also important to select a variety of foods from within each category. Consider vegetables, for example. Although many provide vitamins, they don't all provide the same ones. Selecting different veggies as part of a balanced menu will help ensure that your body gets the vitamins it needs.

Try to avoid rules that involve extremes. For example, it is unwise to ban treats from your household or to offer your child sweets as an incentive or reward for good behavior. Spread your food intake throughout the day rather than delaying it all for the evening meal. Eating at regular intervals will help prevent you from becoming irritable and will keep your energy level away from extreme highs and lows. Terrified of acquiring body fat, those with eating disorders often divide foods into "safe" versus "unsafe" or "good" versus "bad" categories. This notion, which has no basis in fact, is an example of the all-or-nothing thinking style that characterizes these illnesses. Yet the mind-set that some foods are fattening and therefore off-limits is widespread, not only among people with anorexia or bulimia, but also among dieters who do not have full-blown eating disorders. Continually avoiding a food group (such as fats or carbs) for the purpose of losing weight can backfire, because deprivation and subsequent craving sometimes lead to overeating. Although some foods are healthier than others, the bottom line is that all foods may contribute to balanced eating.

Because the food groups work together to keep your body well, dietary fats are more than allowable—they're necessary. So are proteins and carbohydrates. If you picture your dietary fat as heading straight for your hips, thighs, or any other part of your body, please understand that this is not what happens. The extra energy that the body stores as fat comes from fatty foods as well as from other kinds. The healthiest dietary fats are obtainable from vegetable oils, seeds, nuts, whole grains, tuna, and salmon. Fat makes food taste good, but it also does much more. It helps prevent you from overeating by initiating signals to your brain that trigger your sense of being full. The outer, protective lining (membrane) of every cell in the body contains fat. So does the outer sheath that protects your nerves. The fats you ingest contribute to your reservoir of energy, help keep your skin and hair healthy, enhance your absorption of certain vitamins, serve as raw materials for the production of some hormones, and play a role in the growth and maintenance of your bones. Fat tissue helps regulate your body temperature and serves as padding to protect your heart, lungs, and other vital organs from injury in the event of a high-impact accident such as a car crash. As we discussed in Chapter 6, a girl's body requires a healthy amount of fat in order to achieve menarche (first menses). For individuals with anorexia, semistarvation and loss of body fat are key factors that cause menstrual periods to stop, increasing the risk of bone loss and fracture.

While some dieters take an extreme stand on fats, others have a tendency to severely restrict their carbs. Loretta knew that carbohydrates are the body's chief providers of fuel and are present in a wide range of foods, from nutritious whole-grain cereals to the candy and soft drinks that have come to be known as junk food. What she didn't realize was that if a person overrestricts carb intake and precipitates a serious energy shortage, her body will draw on muscle tissue for fuel, thereby opening the door to potential medical problems. Give some attention to choosing nutritious carbs (such as whole-wheat bread, brown rice, or oatmeal) but not to the extreme of depriving yourself of others that you enjoy. If there comes a time when you eat more junk food than you'd planned, realize that this occasionally happens to just about everyone, try not to give yourself a hard time about it, and try to choose healthier foods the next day. See Figure 11.2 for examples of portable snacks that often appeal to adolescents. It's balance that counts!

As an exercise in flexibility, you may want to introduce yourself and your family to a new food every so often. Consider reacquainting yourself with a food that you like but have avoided because of weight concerns. If you have been eating according to strict rules, however, relaxing them won't happen overnight. We were delighted when Loretta told us that she planned to resurrect pizza as an option. As we explained to her, it is important to keep food-related goals realistic and to expect ups and downs along the road to healthy eating. You will want to think of learning to eat more flexibly as a process that you can tackle in small, manageable steps. Though the journey won't be easy, it is likely to be rewarding in the end, not only for your own well-being but also for your child's.

## Deciding How Much to Eat

If you have difficulty determining the right amount to eat, you are not alone. As you know, individuals with eating disorders struggle

**FIGURE 11.2** Backpack Snacks for Teens

**Protein**
*Builds muscle*
Nuts
Peanut butter
Protein energy bar
Soy nuts
Sunflower seeds

**Grains**
*Provides energy for muscles and brain*
Bagels
Baked chips
Cereal
Crackers
Graham crackers or animal crackers
Granola bars
Popcorn
Pretzels
Trail mix

**Milk and dairy**
*Builds strong bones*
Yogurt
Milk
Pudding
String cheese
Soy milk

**Fats, oils, and sweets**
*Satisfies sweet tooth (okay once in a while)*
Candy
Chips
Cookies

**Vegetables**
*Vitamins and minerals for healthy skin, hair, nails, and immune system*
Carrot sticks
Celery sticks
Cherry tomatoes
Cut up broccoli, cauliflower, or peppers
Vegetable juice

**Fruit**
*Vitamins and minerals for healthy skin, hair, nails, and immune system*
Apples
Bananas
Berries
Grapes
Oranges
Pears
Dried fruit, raisins
Light fruit cups

profoundly with this question, but they are not the only ones. Many people who do not suffer from full-fledged anorexia or bulimia experience similar problems on a less intense level. Some severely restrict their food intake, binge, or purge more frequently or for longer stretches of time than others. Like Loretta, many individuals harbor nagging doubts about whether they and their bodies are good enough, and these worries can have an effect on their children. From a health standpoint, Loretta had no need to lose weight, yet she dieted off and on because she thought she should. As we pointed out to her and Rob, there is no one-size-fits-all solution regarding how much food to eat. Metabolisms and activity levels vary from one person to another. Also, an individual's need for fuel fluctuates based on a number of factors, including her amount of exercise, hormone cycles, stress, and what she has eaten during the day.

The best approach to gauging how much to eat may be to listen to your body's cues that say, "I'm hungry," or "I'm full," and respond to them in a positive way. Sensations of hunger are different for everyone. Does your stomach rumble or feel empty? Do you become lightheaded or slightly nauseous? Do you feel grouchy or irritable? Do you get a headache? There are all different expressions of hunger. The idea is to become aware of your hunger signals and their patterns with the goal of learning to eat when you're hungry (but before you are overly hungry). In addition, you'll want to teach yourself to stop eating when you are full (but not overly full). Most people overeat on occasion, just as sometimes they don't eat enough. What matters most is not what you choose at any one meal, but rather whether your overall pattern is balanced.

For many individuals, becoming aware of hunger and fullness signals is much more easily said than done. It is all too common to eat on the run; while working, watching TV, or surfing the Internet; or in the midst of other activities. These multitasking situations make it very difficult, if not impossible, to pay attention to internal sensations that arise during a meal to let you know how full you are getting.

Eating while engaged in other activities is one obstacle to identifying body signals. Dieting is another. When an individual counters her appetite by restricting her food intake, her body's signals can become harder and harder to recognize. That is, if she bases her food amounts on rules (such as "I eat the same number of calories every day") instead of on her body signals ("I feel hungrier than usual today, so I'll have a little more"), she may gradually lose touch with the sensations that indicate hunger or fullness. The good news is you can take steps to increase your awareness of these sensations. Building such skills requires time, so be patient with yourself.

One tool that is often helpful involves learning to appreciate the sensory quality of eating. This means paying close attention to what food feels like in your mind and body. To get started, try the following exercise: Choose a snack to eat or something to drink at a time when you are unlikely to be distracted. Ingest it slowly, a little at a time, while noticing its taste, texture, temperature, and other qualities. If your mind wanders, gently bring it back to your eating or drinking experience. As an example, suppose you've returned home from a walk on a snowy day. Your legs are tired, and there is a slight but nagging hollow sensation in your stomach. You hunker down with a cup of hot chocolate. All is quiet. Wrapping your chilly hands around the mug, you take in the cocoa's rich, sweet aroma as a wisp of steam rises toward your face. Maybe you blow on the surface a few times to cool it. When you take your first sip, the temperature of the beverage is just right, and its flavor brings you immediate pleasure. What's more, you can feel the cocoa's warmth and comfort all the way down to your stomach. You pause frequently to savor the taste and smoothness of the drink, and when most of it is finished, you feel content and cozy. You say to yourself, "Mmm, that cocoa really hit the spot." The hollowness in your stomach that you noticed when you first arrived home has faded. Over time, awareness exercises such as this one are likely to help you recognize when you are hungry and when you have had enough.

Just as the body signals you for food, it generates sensations representing other needs. For example, "butterflies" in the stomach tell you that you need calming, so you try to reassure yourself or talk the situation over with a friend. Have you ever eaten in response to stress? Although there are times when just about everyone does this, some people take it to an extreme, often eating not because their bodies are asking for food, but rather as an effort to soothe themselves, numb difficult emotions, or fill an emotional void. These individuals run the risk of losing touch with their hunger signals as well as with their sensations (such as stomach butterflies) that convey emotional needs.

Loretta's openness about her food habits was refreshing. "My use of food to steady my nerves started in college and continues on and off to this day," she explained. "I sometimes overeat to unwind after a stressful day at the hospital or to postpone decisions that I don't know how to make. I eat when I'm lonely as well." We explained to Loretta that tuning in to her body sensations can help her differentiate between signals that ask for food and those that call for something else, such as comfort, friendship, self-expression, intellectual stimulation, or peace and quiet. Over time, her awareness of her body signals and ability to respond to them will help set a valuable example for her daughter.

## Helping Her Build a Positive Relationship with Her Body

As you know, individuals with anorexia or bulimia tend to evaluate their worth based on weight and physique, overlooking the value of their inner qualities and placing undue emphasis on physical beauty. What's more, those who suffer from these illnesses dislike their bodies and try to control them through dangerous eating habits. For a child in the throes of an eating disorder, the topic of physical appearance is emotionally loaded. Even for children who have never had an eating disorder, it's important to keep your focus off looks. That is a lot to ask because, let's face it, looks do count. There is a place—albeit a limited one—for them in day-to-day interactions and lifestyle. The question is not whether looks matter, but rather how much they matter. For adolescents to pay attention to external appearance is normal and inevitable. It's when focus on outer beauty becomes a way of approaching the world that body image problems are apt to arise. The idea is to keep physical appearance in perspective so that it is appreciably lower in priority than health, safety, and personality.

Loretta described her relationship with Quinlan as becoming more complicated than it had been in the past: "I've always thought of her as a spunky and adventurous child, a bit of a 'tomboy.' When I picture the true Quinlan, I envision a spirited girl running through the woods feeling comfortable in her body and good about who she is. She also has a highly sensitive side. She can intuit when her best friend, Fran, is just a little under the weather or when something is a bit 'off' at home. Unlike myself when I was her age, she keeps her room neat and orderly. In fact, she's meticulous about how she arranges her belongings, especially the items she keeps on her dresser; everything has to be just so. When she was eight and nine, she had a lot of self-confidence. I wish I could have saved some in a jar to be returned to her as needed, particularly during her teen years, which are bound to be hard. Not that being 11 is a breeze. She takes her schoolwork very seriously, often finishing her projects well before they are due. Her sixth-grade class is full of cliques, and I think she's conflicted about joining one. While she's very eager to be popular, she's convinced that she doesn't fit into any of the current groups and feels discouraged about that. I don't like the thought of peer or media pressures inhibiting her or molding her into someone she doesn't necessarily want to be. I want her to look forward to womanhood."

Loretta wanted to know whether it was okay to tell Quinlan about the troubles she had experienced in the area of healthy eating. This was an excellent question. Very few people have a perfect attitude toward food and weight at all times. If you have body image worries of your own that you would like to share with your child, the timing of your self-disclosure will depend on her age and readiness to engage in the subject matter, as well as on your family's communication style. Pondering her relationship with her daughter, Loretta said, "Quinlan is an astute observer of everything around her. If I don't level with her about my diet issue, she'll only sense it. I make a point of not putting myself or my body down in her presence, but she sees me taking smaller portions of food than everyone else and declining pizza when the rest of the family is eating it. One reason I don't want Quinlan to diet is that whenever she's takes on a project—such as the solar system model she made in science class—she throws herself into it completely and doesn't let up until she gets it 'right.' I'd imagine that my dieting sends Quinlan confusing messages. A part of me is surprised that she hasn't asked, 'Mom, why do you eat so little?' But another part tells me that she is probably hesitant to raise a topic that she considers personal. I have to wonder, if she were to pose that question, how would I answer it? Rather than feeling tongue-tied or being caught off guard, I feel I'm better off giving Quinlan some personal information, not as a one-time discussion, but more in the interest of initiating ongoing dialogue."

Loretta's insights were right on target. It is often better for parents to tell their child about their body angst than to keep it secret. Talking to your child about your own struggles can be a helpful way of showing her that you understand and care about what she is going through. Besides, your candor about your personal difficulties help encourage her to discuss her own. The key to disclosing your body image concerns to your child is to do it in moderation. Give her some information, but don't flood her with it. Share your feelings without dwelling on them, without putting her in the position of solving your problems, and without taking your frustration out on her.

"But how can I model body confidence for my daughter if I don't have much myself?" asked Loretta. We explained to her that it is important that she not be so hard on herself. First, through her self-awareness and the efforts she was making to curb her dieting, Loretta was setting a good example of how to approach the challenge of something inside that says, "I have to do it," whether "it" is food restriction, overexercising, overworking, or any other unhealthy habit. Second, many aspects of Loretta's current life-style were very healthy, including her enjoyment of sports, her respect for people of all different shapes and sizes, and her intuitive understanding of how crucial it is not to tease or criticize her children about their body shape or size. It's important to note that body acceptance isn't something absolute that one either has or doesn't have. It's much more fluid than that. As we explained to Loretta, it often helps to think of one's degree of body satisfaction as a spectrum, with far more people between the two poles than at either one of them. The idea here is that increasing your awareness of your own food and weight issues can play a role in helping your daughter develop a healthy body image.

Just as you try to acknowledge your inner strengths, encourage your child to appreciate hers. Note the personality traits, values, and talents that help make her unique, and praise her for them. You can also compliment her for progress and effort. Although you'll be proud of her achievements, bear in mind that some children who are at risk for eating disorders are perfectionists who think they must be flawless in order to please their parents. If your child is overly careful to do no wrong, try to convey that mistakes are allowable and inevitable—not only for her, but for everyone. Check in with yourself every now and then to see if your expectations of your child are realistic, and understand that even if they are, she may think they aren't. If she perceives your expectations as too high, try to maintain confidence in your ability to deal with the situation. Reassure your child that, in the event that you are disappointed in something she does or doesn't achieve, you'll both get through it. Point out to her that letting you down occasionally is a far cry from always being the ultimate disappointment, then remind her of the many qualities that make her special.

## A Father's Perspective

As difficult as it is for girls and boys to tolerate the sense of not being good enough, it can be harder for them to put a name to it and talk about it. To feel this way is embarrassing enough without having to admit it to others. The experience of body insecurities covers a wide range of territory and varies in intensity and quality from one person to another.

Feeling too large, out of bounds, self-conscious, or exposed is not exclusive to women. Rob can speak to that. "Starting in middle school, I liked basketball and spent a lot of time shooting hoops in the park near my house. I was a chubby kid and didn't much like that. But then again, I didn't give it a lot of thought. Looking back, it just seemed that the lean, muscular guys commanded a lot of respect. My height seemed to shoot up all at once when I was in ninth grade. I had no objections to getting taller—in fact, it suited me fine once I got used to it. But for a while, I felt like the biggest, clumsiest thing on two feet. Although many of my basketball memories have merged, one incident stands out in my mind as if it were yesterday. It happened when I was almost 15, just at the peak of my awkward stage. I was younger than many of the guys on the school basketball team and very eager to prove myself. One day during practice, I sensed that I was in good position to receive the ball and tried to signal my teammate, who was dribbling, to pass it to me. He didn't throw it my way, but at the moment, that didn't faze me; as far as I was concerned, it was all part of the game.

"At the end of practice, however, the assistant coach gave us input on our performances. Recalling my efforts to communicate that I was open and ready for a pass, he said something to the effect that I'd been moving my arms and legs every which way and taking up a lot of space but accomplishing nothing. I didn't say anything in response. For some reason that I've never understood, his comment blew up in my mind over the course of the next couple of hours, wreaking havoc with my self-confidence. Looking back, I'd probably describe my feelings as a murky blend of 'I'm bad' and 'I'm too much of nothing.' But at the time, there was no way I could have articulated those reactions to his comment. I could only imagine how stupid I'd looked gyrating like a wild man on the court. When I was a little older, I took up weight lifting. For me, that turned out to be a positive step, because it allowed me to feel strong and good about my body. I know that about 10 percent of those with anorexia and bulimia are male and that some men become obsessed with building muscle. I'm hoping that Loretta and I can help our son, Eric, now nine, steer clear of all those problems."

The emotional isolation that Rob felt after the incident with his coach was not unusual. Boys in mainstream American culture are brought up to hide their feelings and to appear "cool" or invulnerable at all times. This relentless pressure to conceal emotions can take its toll if the individual is afflicted with negative body thoughts and embarrassed to talk about them. The popular perception that eating disorders are girls' problems makes it even harder for boys to let anyone in on their body image concerns. That's why it's a good idea to work toward establishing an ongoing dialogue with your son to reassure him that having feelings is not a sign of weakness, offer him empathy, convey that many kids have body insecurities, and bolster his self-confidence by reminding him of his talents and strengths. (See Figure 11.3.)

**FIGURE 11.3** Positive Activity Can Help Build Self-Esteem

## What Is a Healthy Sports Environment?

Rob described Quinlan as an avid baseball fan. "At age 10, she was one of the only two girls on her Little League team, and she really held her own. She wants to participate again this spring, and I have no objections. Eric plays on a neighborhood soccer team. The coach likes to give each child a chance to play a variety of positions. Eric balked when it was his turn to try being goalie, and I'm glad the coach didn't push him." Rob's approach to sports was flexible and upbeat. We share his view that healthy physical activity includes opportunities for both organized and less structured activities. In addition to benefiting long-term physical health, participation in sports often leads to emotional and social gains, such as improved self-confidence and a sense of belonging that helps build team spirit. The experience of working as part of a team is invaluable. So are the opportunities to learn how to handle the joy of winning, the disappointment of defeat, and the practice of good sportsmanship. All of these skills transfer to adult life. What's more, research suggests that participation in sports can help protect an individual from developing an eating disorder.

It is advisable for children to experience sports as fun, so you should explore with your child what kinds of physical activity appeal to her and help her find a confidence-enhancing setting and level of involvement. When you talk about your own physical exercise, avoid linking it to looks and focus instead on enjoyment and health. Remember the importance of balance. Although sports have a lot to offer, they are part of a healthy lifestyle, not the be-all and end-all.

Young people generally look up to their athletic coaches and often go to great lengths to earn their approval. This presents an opportunity for coaches to join parents as frontline players in preventing eating disorders. It is paramount for physical education instructors to avoid teasing or criticizing students about body size. As Rob's basketball incident points out, however, even comments that are well-intended are sometimes not as sensitively worded as they could be, and some negative comments are made inadvertently. When your child expresses interest in a sports program, you'll want to evaluate whether it will be a good fit for her temperament and preferences. Major characteristics of a healthy sports environment include the following:

- The coach is aware of the dangers and warning signs of eating disorders.
- The program does not subject players to weigh-ins.
- The coach avoids commenting on students' weight, body size, and shape.
- The core of the training program is praise.
- The emphasis is on balanced nutrition as necessary for top athletic performance.
- The coach communicates to students that overtraining can be harmful to performance.
- Students are encouraged to share their body image worries with a trusted adult instead of suffering in silence.

As the athletic program continues, you'll want to monitor your child's self-confidence and maintain a dialogue with her regarding how she feels about the training.

## Countering Negative Media Messages

The immensely wealthy fashion and beauty industry cashes in on the insecurity of young women by drilling into their hearts and minds the message "You are what you look like." One way to help protect your child from believing this falsehood is to teach her media literacy skills. The term *media literacy* means looking objectively at messages as business enterprises' calculated attempts to promote their own interests, usually by convincing you to buy something. Many schools are offering media literacy programs, which are adaptable to students of all ages. In these classes, children learn to recognize and see through media messages that may lead them to dislike their bodies. To give students a healthy perspective on the fashion industry, for example, media literacy programs emphasize that the beautiful—and extremely thin—supermodels who grace magazine covers do not represent real bodies. Most models sit for hours while professionals apply their makeup, give them manicures, and coif their hair. Many models undergo plastic surgery to achieve the "perfect" look, and well before a fashion magazine hits the newsstand, its photographs undergo sophisticated processing techniques and computer enhancement in order to create a desired effect, such as the message that thinness equals beauty, and beauty equals happiness. A recent example of this involves acclaimed journalist Katie Couric, whose image was touched up to appear 20 pounds thinner in the promotional photograph for her debut as TV evening news anchor.

Media literacy programs are interactive and thought-provoking, and children tend to enjoy them. Many young people seem to have built-in radar for identifying what is phony, and once they are taught that the fashion industry tries to con people, they become adept at applying this knowledge. Whether or not your child's school system has implemented such a program, you can enhance her critical-thinking skills by looking at magazine and TV images with her and discussing how they make her feel, as well as how they were probably designed to instill negative self-image and body thoughts in viewers. She is likely to catch on quickly, and in the process of debunking the commercial agendas behind specific thin-is-in pictures, you will both gain an appreciation of the many potentially harmful messages that target young girls.

Once your daughter is confidently pointing to unrealistic portraits of women, you can introduce her to the contradictions inherent in many media presentations. When it comes to women's bodies, messages are so topsy-turvy that it's no wonder girls and women have difficulty regulating their food intake. Open just about any fashion or beauty magazine, and you are likely to find some articles touting weight loss and others—perhaps only a few pages away—promoting food indulgence. A recent issue of a popular women's magazine is a case in point. On the contents page is a picture of a smiling young figure skater whose legs are so thin that one wonders how they hold her up, much less propel her across the ice. Midway through the issue is advice on how to accelerate one's metabolism "without dieting." One of the last features is a colorful smorgasbord of holiday sweets; one side of this two-page spread groups the treats according to caloric content. Implicit in the name of each calorie category are two edicts: one implies, "Eat all you want," and the other cautions, "Don't ruin your diet"—a contradiction that is also evident in the article's subtitle, "Give In to Your Urge to Splurge with These Diet Delights." This hodge-podge of images that tell women to diet one minute and not to diet the next is standard fare, not only in print media but also on TV. Such mixed messages can make it very hard for children to know whether it is okay to eat, what foods to select, and what portion sizes are appropriate.

Over the past half-century, our mainstream culture's body ideal for males has become increasingly muscular. Today's media images often portray greater muscle mass than is attainable for the vast majority of men without dedicated weight training and the use of anabolic steroids. While the advertising industry's representation of women has been under scrutiny for about 15 years, it is only more recently that public awareness of negative male images has begun to grow. Television, movies, the print media, and the Internet associate the "perfect" (tall, muscular) male body with power, romance, and career success. As a typical example, consider the following: a current sports magazine features a photograph of a muscular, lean, 30-something father standing on the beach against a blue sky and surf; in one hand, he is balancing an adorable toddler. The message—that a muscular body means a perfect life—preys on the insecurities of adolescent boys and may have a negative impact on girls as well. Thus, whether you are teaching media literacy to a son or a daughter, it is wise to talk about the fallacies generated about both genders.

## Curricula for Preventing Eating Disorders

In the past decade, professionals in the field of eating disorders have developed a number of programs aimed at reducing the risk of developing these illnesses. Such programs range in format from workshops (hosted by mental health professionals or educators) to multisession, school-based curricula to CD-ROM programs and Internet-based interventions. Research studies have shown these types of programs to be effective with adolescents and college students. The curricula cover topics such as developing media literacy, appreciating oneself, challenging weight bias, recognizing hunger and fullness signals, and countering negative self-thoughts with positive ones. Some prevention curricula are designed for those who have not exhibited signs or symptoms. Others are meant for individuals who are engaging in behaviors like dieting but have not reached the extreme of suffering from full-fledged anorexia or bulimia. More and more schools, community counseling centers, and youth groups are embracing prevention programs. For information on specific curricula, please see the Resources section.

## In a Nutshell

What you can do to send your child healthy messages:

- Model healthy eating and involvement in physical activity.
- Keep your emphasis off physical appearance and praise her for her inner qualities, skills, and values.
- Help her understand that weight gain during puberty is natural and healthy.
- Encourage her to see sports as a way to have fun and stay healthy.
- Teach her about media literacy.
- Teach her that people come in different sizes and shapes. No one size or shape is better or worse than another.
- Find out about eating disorder prevention programs in your community.

Throughout this book, we have focused primarily on adolescents and young adults because these age groups are at the highest risk for developing eating disorders. But people in their 30s, 40s, and beyond also suffer from these illnesses. They include individuals who were treated as adolescents but either didn't recover completely or did very well only to relapse one or more times later. Some individuals actually develop anorexia or bulimia for the first time in adulthood. In Chapter 12, we will discuss how you can help an adult child who suffers from anorexia or bulimia.

# 12

# Eating Disorders Throughout Life

"My daughter is about to turn 35," says Claudia. "A decade ago, her eating disorder was getting the best of her, and I was terrified that I'd lose her. She's doing well now, and I hope she can keep the health she's worked so hard to gain." Perhaps you, like Claudia, have an adult child who suffers from an eating disorder. We've talked at length about the hardships faced by parents whose adolescents are afflicted with anorexia and bulimia, and we've pointed out that these illnesses strike children at increasingly early ages. But not everyone who struggles with an eating disorder is young. In fact, many of those who visit doctors' offices and clinics for help are in their 30s, 40s, or older. Is your adult child experiencing food and weight obsession for the first time? Maybe she developed anorexia or bulimia in high school or college and recovered, either fully or partially, but relapsed later in life. Perhaps she has experimented with extreme weight control measures (food restriction, binge eating, purging) in the past or suffered a steady but relatively low level of obsession that escalated into full-blown illness when stress increased. Every stage of life comes with a wide array of challenges regarding body image, self-esteem, and relationships. How successfully a person copes with the trials and tribulations of any one stage can influence her ability to cope with the next.

The story of Claudia and her daughter will shed light on questions we are frequently asked by adults with eating disorders and their families.

"Sybil is hardworking," says her mom, "but she also has a spunky, lighthearted, and generous side that allows her to make friends easily. As a child, she was sturdy and strong, and her weight was about average. Although she wasn't overweight in her teens, she seemed to think she was. Occasionally she'd say, 'I wish I were thinner,' or 'I'm going on a diet,' but a week or so later, she'd be back to her usual way of eating. To be honest, I didn't try to stop her from skimping on meals, and if I had, she only would have said, 'But Mom, you watch your weight'—and she would have been right. Though I wasn't as serious about dieting as some women I knew, I wanted to keep my youthful figure. Back then, I took dieting for granted as something that came with the territory of being female.

"During her school years, Sybil set high standards for herself. I never had to remind her to do her homework; in fact, I often encouraged her to close her books at night so that she would get enough sleep. She was always eager to prove herself, not only academically, but also in sports. The pictures I took of her dribbling the ball down the soccer field are so precious. But when I look at them now, my memories are bittersweet. That's because Sybil developed anorexia and bulimia, not during high school or college, but when she was first married and making plans to attend graduate school. Her husband, Darren, went through a lot with her; we all did. When I first found out she was 'sick,' I thought there had to be some mistake. Sybil had always been so sensible. Why, just when she seemed to be doing so well, did she start to starve herself?"

"I've asked myself that question throughout my recovery," notes Sybil, "and I'm still not sure I have an answer. I had supportive parents, a loving husband, all that anyone could dream of. Yet something was wrong—something about me that I couldn't quite put my finger on was 'bad.' This feeling was familiar but at the same time indefinable. Maybe other people had it, maybe they didn't—I often wondered about that. Now that I've had therapy, I can look back on that feeling-without-a-name and describe it as a sense of being nothing. I viewed myself as having no personality, no particular interests, and definitely no skills. Of all my perceived defects, my stupidity was the most embarrassing, so I bent over backward to keep others from discovering it. When I went away to college, I chose the easiest courses I could to improve my chances of getting good grades. Within my first few weeks in the dorm, I heard my roommates talking about the 'freshman 15.' That was the first time I'd heard that expression, which seemed to imply that it's inevitable for women to gain 15 pounds during their first year in college. Looking back, I wish I'd had the wisdom to take that saying for what it was—a myth. But at 18, I took it literally and began to think of weight gain as something scary that I had to guard against; otherwise, it might creep up on me gradually, without my realizing what was happening. Throughout college, I studied a lot longer than other students and held myself to a strict schedule. I also set dietary rules for myself like no bread and no snacks, but I had a hard time sticking to such limits, and I'd gradually drift back to eating what I wanted, only to start a new diet weeks or months later.

"After college, I had three good years working in a children's day-care center. During that time, one of my coworkers introduced me to Darren. He and I hit it off immediately. Our family and friends often commented on how Darren and I were meant for each other. In those early years, he and I just enjoyed being together—it didn't matter where we went or what we did. We were silly, head over heels in love. We talked about building our futures together and eventually becoming parents. We would even chat about our favorite girl names and boy names and joke about what our children might be like. Would they have my quirky sense of humor or what I called Darren's 'special laugh'?

"I enjoyed my work at the day-care center and was interested in advancing my career. I'd always wanted to be a teacher, so I set my sights on graduate school. But when the time came to fill out applications, a familiar sense of 'I'm not good enough' returned full force. I've never been good with uncertainty. I wouldn't say I'm a control freak, but I like knowing what my next move will be well before I make it. When applying to grad schools, I felt the weight of the world on top of me. What if I didn't get accepted anywhere? What would others think of me? Would they realize that I was a fake, that I wasn't as capable as they'd believed? If I were accepted to more than one grad school, which one would I choose? And once I was enrolled, would I be smart enough to do graduate-level work? Without realizing it, I began to channel these insecurities into weight loss. While I continued to worry about grad school, I became very sensitive to the way clothes felt on my body, especially after eating. I wore the baggiest clothes I could find because the sensation of fabric against my arms, legs, or waist gave me the unbearable perception that I'd gained weight. I experienced my body as thinner and 'better' if my clothes were loose.

"I did not choose to get an eating disorder. In fact, the notion of starving myself to death wasn't even on my radar. If I had any forethought at all about what I was doing, it was a vague hope that practicing some self-discipline and losing a little weight would make me feel better. But as my diet grew stricter, I began to feel frantic most of the time—panicked about my body size and annoyed with anything or anyone who interfered with my routines. The slightest suspicion that I might have accidentally disobeyed a food rule and increased my risk of weight gain would inflate in my mind and take on dire importance. An example of that involved the half a banana I routinely allowed myself after my strenuous 6:00 A.M. run. Hours later, I'd be watching TV or tidying up the apartment when all of a sudden it would occur to me that maybe the banana I'd halved that morning had been longer than average; if that had been the case, I reasoned, I had eaten more than my allotment. My panic level would rise as I'd replay the dividing of the banana over and over in my head to detect whether I'd in fact committed the 'crime' [overeating]. A couple of times, I even examined the evidence by going to the kitchen trash and picking out the peel of the half I'd eaten. I held it end-to-end with the uneaten half to check their combined length, which I then compared to the size of each of the bananas I'd scheduled for the next few days. Part of me felt desperate to prove that I'd done nothing wrong, because I knew that I'd have a high price to pay for my mistake. Inevitably, however, the verdict was 'guilty.' After badgering myself about my carelessness and stupidity for a while longer, I'd impose a penalty, such as no fruit for a week. But within an hour or so of my sentencing, I'd decide that my punishment was too lenient. So I'd make it harsher, perhaps forcing myself to run extra miles. And the 'you're bad, exercise harder' tyrant inside me wouldn't stop until I'd completed every last lap. Once I met that requirement, I might feel some relief. But it wouldn't be long before my mind would grind out another food or exercise demand, and the harangue would start again, often driving me to tears. These obsessions, which I now believe stemmed—at least in part—from intense hunger, greatly interfered with my ability to connect with other people.

"As my weight was slipping away, so was my relationship with Darren. One of my dilemmas was how to avoid eating with him. In the earliest phase of the disorder, we'd sit down to dinner together, and he'd eat while I'd fake it, pushing food around my plate and concentrating more on whether Darren was detecting my abstinence than on our conversation. Pretending to eat was hard, not only because it required a lot of finesse, but also because the food was tempting, and one part of me begged for it while another—more forceful—part said, 'Leave it.' I had no idea that I had an illness and was oblivious to the evidence that my self-discipline and weight loss were doing me more harm than good. It seemed easier to stay out of the apartment, especially at mealtimes, so I extended my workouts at the gym well into the evening. There were days when Darren would call me from work to ask if I wanted to go to my favorite restaurant for dinner, and I'd say that I didn't feel well or that I'd eaten a late lunch and wasn't hungry. I felt guilty making up these excuses but would have done anything to stick to my routines and to keep Darren from knowing about my eating habits. A few times, he said that I seemed distant and preoccupied. 'Are you okay?' he'd ask. I'd reassure him that I loved him and that I was fine, just a bit stressed out about whether I'd get into grad school.

"I dreaded intimacy with Darren and tried to avoid it at all cost. I no longer dressed or undressed in front of him. I became so self-conscious about my body and how fat I felt that I was unable to relax when Darren tried to make love with me. I sensed that he felt hurt and rejected by my emotional and physical distance, and I hated myself for making his life miserable. Was I afraid that Darren would leave me or end the marriage? Vaguely. But I never talked about these fears—or any other emotions for that matter—in part, because I was only marginally aware that I had them. I'm ashamed to admit this, but had Darren given me a choice between keeping the relationship or keeping my eating behaviors, there was a point in the darkest hours of my illness when I would have selected the latter.

"Luckily, he made no such ultimatum. That is not to say he never got mad at me. Sometimes he'd ask, 'Why can't you just eat?' And when I'd start to become defensive, he'd get exasperated and leave the room. Other times, he begged me to eat, and when I refused, he'd grow impatient and blurt out, 'Sybil, I'm sick and tired of your food problems. I just want to go back to the life we used to have together.' On numerous occasions, Darren expressed concern about my health and urged me to seek professional help. I wasn't sure what treatment involved, but I assumed that it would make me fat, so I wanted nothing to do with it. What I didn't understand was that professional care would help me feel better. Darren was so worried about me that he called my parents. I was furious about that. Between the three of them, they convinced me to see my primary care doctor.

"The weeks immediately after my discharge from the hospital were, I think, particularly hard for Darren. At least part of him had expected me to come home 'cured,' and when he realized that I still had eating problems, he was understandably upset. Since I had very little to say to him, he started leaving me handwritten notes. At first, he'd write just a few sentences, highlighting that he loved me and that he was there for me. He didn't know it at the time, but those quiet reassurances meant the world to me and touched me in a way that his attempts to 'talk reason' to me had not. Later, when I continued to struggle with my food problem, he wrote me two letters that revealed some of his private thoughts about our relationship. The second one had a particularly powerful effect on me:

Dear Sybil,

I write this with some hesitation. On the one hand, I don't want to upset you—the last thing I'd ever want to do is set off another bout of starving or purging. On the other hand, you and I both know that things between us are not the same as they once were. I'd like us to mend the gulf, and I'm hoping that airing my feelings in this letter will be a first step in the right direction.

When you are under the power of your eating disorder, I sometimes feel that I am irrelevant or even a nuisance to you. It seems like you care more about whether you can get to the gym by 5:00 than about spending evenings with me; I hope that isn't true. I miss the days when you and I were equal partners, when you were stronger and fun to be with. I don't know how to say this exactly, so please excuse me if it comes out wrong, but sometimes I've felt that your eating disorder changes you from the vibrant woman I married into a sick person who needs to be taken care of. There are also times when I feel that maybe our relationship, or maybe something I've done, has contributed to your eating disorder. Will you help me sort these questions out so that we can both be happier?

Love,
Darren

"I wish I could say that Darren's letter turned my life around. But the truth is far more complicated. At that point, I'd regained some of the weight I'd lost after I was discharged from the hospital, but I was binge eating and vomiting, and my recovery from my eating disorder was still a ways off. I didn't know it at the time, but sorting out our marital difficulties would take a lot of hard work. Looking back, I can understand why Darren wrote that letter; he felt that my eating disorder had changed my personality, taken over my life, and pushed him away. Since I was barely talking to him, he wasn't sure what was left of our relationship, and his letter was an attempt to find out. But when I first read the letter, I wasn't able to see his point of view. Instead, I felt like I'd been hit by a tidal wave of criticism. I sensed 'I'm bad' coming from so many different directions that I could barely keep my head above water. That's where individual therapy helped. I was afraid that my therapists were mad at me for starting to binge, so I didn't want to tell them much about what was going on. But as it turned out, they were not angry and just seemed to want to get to know me better as a person. I liked that. Soon, my treatment team adjusted the dose of my antidepressant medication [a selective serotonin reuptake inhibitor], which began to take the edge off my dark thoughts, making it easier to get through the day.

"When I mentioned the tension between me and Darren to my therapists, they viewed my recognition of this problem as a sign of progress and encouraged me to elaborate. A few weeks later, they suggested that Darren and I consider couples counseling, which would offer us an opportunity to work on our relationship together under the guidance of a therapist. At first, I didn't like the idea because I was afraid the couples sessions would focus on how I was ruining our marriage. But when I told Darren about the recommendation, he was surprisingly receptive, even mentioning that our problems were no one's fault and that he couldn't imagine how we could fix our marriage without professional help. Deep inside, I sensed Darren's openness to couples counseling was right, so we signed on, attending sessions every week for more than a year. This work proved invaluable in a number of ways. First, we hadn't shared our feelings openly for so long that we'd almost forgotten how. The counseling helped us break the ice so that we could communicate more effectively. In addition, the joint sessions helped each of us see where the other was coming from and—as Darren had requested in his letter—explore how my eating disorder had affected our relationship and vice versa."

In discussing the impact of an illness on a marriage, it is important not to overgeneralize or oversimplify. Every interpersonal relationship is different and complex. Like Sybil, many people with eating disorders are so engrossed in their food and exercise routines that they cannot communicate in ways that are necessary to develop and sustain healthy relationships. Darren began to feel angry at Sybil, rejected by her, and sad to have lost the woman he had loved. Such feelings are not unusual among the significant others of people who suffer from eating disorders. Under such circumstances, couples therapy can prove very productive.

Looking back, Sybil tried to put couples counseling in perspective. "It wasn't a magic bullet," she explains. "It couldn't undo the pain of the last several years or get back the idealism and bliss that we enjoyed during our first year of marriage. But couples sessions did make a positive difference in our lives, not only by addressing the past but also by helping us look ahead. I was 29 years old. Four long years after my eating disorder had developed, my nutrition had improved, and my body was healthy. Darren and I began to think about starting a family.

## Pregnancy and Childbirth

Will she be able to have children? If your daughter developed an eating disorder as a teen or young adult, that question may have gnawed at you before she was ready to address it. Chances are your relationship with your daughter is complex. Your emotions pertaining to her health and future tend to run deep; add to that the prospect of change—of her becoming a mother and your becoming a grandparent—and it's only natural that you are experiencing a whole spectrum of intense feelings (excitement, joy, fear, anger, sadness), many of them mixed. Understandably, you have many questions. Can she get pregnant? Will the pregnancy make her eating problem worse? Will her baby be healthy?

When a woman does not take in enough nourishment, her body tries to protect itself against starvation by making some changes, one of which is to channel fuel that was formerly available for the reproductive system to the life-sustaining heart and lungs. Under these circumstances, the hormone system that perpetuates the menstrual cycle slows down and the woman's periods stop. The absence of periods (amenorrhea), a defining feature of anorexia nervosa, results from a combination of factors, including undereating, overexercise, low weight, and particularly insufficient body fat. Infertility can occur as a complication of anorexia nervosa. In order to reactivate her hormones and resume her periods, the patient needs to regain the weight and fat tissue that her treatment team recommends. If she continues to maintain adequate nutrition, her overall health will be better, increasing the likelihood that she will be able to get pregnant.

As you might expect, pregnancy can be challenging to an individual who struggles with or has recovered from an eating disorder. Although some moms with a history of this type of illness recall pregnancy as a positive experience, others report troubling thoughts and feelings. "For the entire nine months and beyond, I continued to see my treatment team," states Sybil. "Without therapy, I'm not sure I would have been able to accept the changing shape of my body. Even with professional help, it was hard to hold my abnormal eating habits in check. On one level, I knew that I had to eat right and gain weight, and I took these responsibilities very seriously, even posting handwritten reminders such as 'I can and will eat healthy,' and 'I can be proud of my progress,' around the kitchen. On another level, the tyrant in my mind was never quiet. My perception that my belly and breasts were puffing up made me more irritable than ever at the sensation of clothes against my skin. Early in the pregnancy, I was constantly tired, and that bothered me because I'd always pushed myself hard, and napping during the day made me feel lazy, spoiled, and good for nothing.

"Intellectually, I was aware that it is normal and necessary for a woman's appetite to increase during pregnancy. When I'd get a hankering for a snack, the rational part of me said, 'That's good. Listen to your body.' But no sooner would I down the snack than the dark side of me would yell, *'Bad!'* My mind would tell me that my snacks were supposed to be bigger than those I'd taken in before my pregnancy, but my feelings would tell me that what I'd just eaten was much more than I deserved. I'd scold myself for being 'a pig.' Then my old, excruciating urge to make myself vomit would come over me. I'm not saying that I purged every time I sensed that I'd overeaten. I'd induced vomiting enough in the past to know that it can lead to dehydration, and I was so nervous that my disordered eating would somehow harm the growing baby that I couldn't afford to take any chances. My therapists explained that if negative thoughts about my body arose, I should talk about them instead of acting on them. While pregnant, I was mostly able to follow that advice and managed to keep my vomiting to a minimum.

"Preventing myself from vomiting was one problem. Getting myself to eat enough was another. For the most part, I stuck to the meal plan advised by my nutritionist, but there were times I slipped. Darren and I decided that, until I was three months along, we'd keep the news about my pregnancy a secret from everyone except our parents and health care providers. The downside of our privacy policy was that I began gaining weight before most people knew I was having a baby. I was sure that when friends saw me, they'd deem me 'bad' for eating more than I should have and ruining my looks. This wasn't just a passing worry. It grew so intense that I avoided neighbors and friends and became almost as self-conscious about eating in social situations as I had been when my eating disorder had ruled my life. One evening, when I was

225

10 or 11 weeks pregnant, Darren and I went to a holiday party at the home of a couple we'd known for years. There was a relaxed buffet dinner that I ordinarily might have enjoyed. But when Darren and I walked up to the center table to get our food, I selected tiny portions because something inside me insisted that if I helped myself to what I really wanted, the other guests would look at my plate and conclude, 'No wonder she's getting fat.'

"Luckily, the body image troubles in my first few months of pregnancy gave way to a quieter stretch of time. Though I continued to have 'I'm fat and bad' thoughts, they now seemed fainter and less disruptive to my everyday life. When I felt the baby moving inside me and my pregnancy started to show, the challenges I was facing as a new mother became more real. In the past, I'd often considered myself a 'nothing.' Now that I was having a baby, I felt more like I was becoming a 'something.' Having a healthy baby and being a responsible mom gave me a purpose in life and, along with it, a stronger determination to take care of myself.

"This isn't to say that all was fine and dandy; in fact, at about seven months, my negative body thoughts came back worse than ever. I had gained weight in keeping with my obstetrician's recommendations, and I felt disgusted by my size. To me, my belly looked like a huge mountain jutting out from the rest of my body. I spent a lot of time trying to figure out how I could lose weight fast after the baby was born. Darren came with me to childbirth classes and tried to comfort me when I complained about being fat. He would reassure me that he loved me as I was and would love me at any size. The birth of my healthy baby, Suzanne, was a joy unlike any I'd experienced before."

It was important that Sybil had made significant progress in treatment prior to getting pregnant. Women with eating disorders who recover prior to conception and maintain adequate nutrition throughout pregnancy are not at substantially higher risk of obstetrical problems than those who have never had an eating disorder. Actively engaging in abnormal weight control practices during pregnancy can increase vulnerability to complications, such as miscarriage, premature delivery, Cesarean delivery, and low-birth-weight babies. To prevent such problems, obstetricians monitor each patient based on her individual needs.

Yet women who have had anorexia or bulimia do not necessarily share this information with their obstetricians. Many are embarrassed about their past eating behavior and go to great lengths to keep it secret. Pregnancy can aggravate this sense of shame. Perhaps your daughter is afraid that if she tells her obstetrician about her past or present abnormal eating behaviors, he will pass judgment on her or lose respect for her. Let her know that even if she feels that she is beyond the point where her disorder will return, it is best for her to reveal her history to her doctor(s). On occasion, the illness gets worse during pregnancy; for many women, however, pregnancy is a time when abnormal eating behaviors improve. If your daughter has been on medication prior to becoming pregnant, she needs to talk with her prescribing physician about continuing to take it. Being able to discuss her past and present problems with a therapist can provide her with an important safety net and help ensure that she receives the professional monitoring she needs while she is pregnant.

## New Beginnings

The months immediately after childbirth (which are known as the postpartum period) can pose quite a challenge to new moms who have recovered from anorexia or bulimia. Heightened concerns about food and weight are not uncommon during this time. Sybil took care of herself and stayed healthy. So do the large majority of other new moms with histories of eating disorders.

This doesn't mean it's easy. Sybil describes the turmoil she experienced during her first months of motherhood: "After Suzanne was born, my belly and thighs seemed flabby. Looking in the mirror made me feel that I did not deserve to exist. As far as I was concerned, I needed to lose weight quickly. At first, I aimed for my prepregnancy weight, or at least that's the impression I tried to give Darren, my parents, and even my doctors. 'After all,' I asked them, 'don't most women want to lose the pounds they gained during pregnancy?' I signed up for an exercise class for new moms, but it only met once a week, and I figured that I had to be much more active than that if I hoped to get rid of my flab. I tried to calculate the amount of physical activity I'd have to get each day to make the pounds melt away.

"With taking care of Suzanne, finding the time and energy for my exercise regime was easier said than done. And there was another problem. I'd always structured my days carefully so that I knew ahead of time what I'd be doing when. I had a set time each week for doing laundry and a block of time every day for working on grad school assignments. I'd been particularly strict about my exercise schedule, allowing no interruptions whatsoever. Now that I had a baby, it was difficult enough to fit in the amount of physical activity I demanded of myself; what made it harder was the fact that I couldn't plan my workouts in advance but had to exercise on the spur of the moment, if and when time allowed. When Suzanne needed me, she needed me intensely, and as much as I loved her, taking care of her made my days less predictable than they had ever been. Interferences with my exercise program sometimes drove me to the point of panic. And when I perceived that I wasn't meeting my physical activity 'obligations,' my fears of weight gain skyrocketed to the point that I'd have an urge to reduce my food intake."

Some new moms who have had eating disorders need closer professional monitoring than others during the months following childbirth. Sybil tried to lose weight more quickly than was advisable and needed help understanding that this tendency can increase the likelihood of binge eating and purging. A minority of new moms—whether or not they have abnormal eating behaviors—develop postpartum depression, which is sometimes related to body image concerns. For those who experience postpartum depression, professional help is available and can make a world of difference.

## Helping Her Cope

Since every family situation is different and eating disorders are complex conditions, there is no one "right" way to reach out to your daughter during her pregnancy. Throughout this book, we have emphasized the importance of showing empathy; as with every other situation involving disordered behavior, you'll want to communicate to her that you sense what she is going through and that you're on her side. Chances are her eating disorder makes it difficult for her to see the size and shape of her pregnant body accurately. Her increased appetite, coupled with her misperception of her expanding body, may cause her distress. Statements such as the following are likely to be helpful:

- "It must be so hard to eat healthy these days."
- "I'd imagine the last few weeks have been nerve-racking/ overwhelming/scary for you."
- "I can understand why you feel conflicted about snacking/resting."

Claudia, Sybil's mom, describes how self-reflection increased her empathy for her daughter. "My weight-consciousness has followed me for a long time," she admits. "When Sybil first developed her eating disorder, I was going through menopause. One part of me realized that it is normal and natural for women my age to put on some pounds as their metabolisms slow. But another part of me felt that fat was bad and that if I gained weight, even just a few pounds, I would lose my value as a person. In a department store one day, I overheard the expression *middle-age spread* in a conversation between two women. My gut reaction—'I'm doomed to be fat and bad'—may have been similar to how Sybil felt in the face of the freshman 15. My point is that becoming aware of how I feel about my own body has helped me understand my daughter's experience on some level. My body image issue is not nearly as severe as an eating disorder. Since I find it challenging to cope with my body anxieties, I can only imagine how hard Sybil's experience must have been for her, especially when her illness was in full gear."

## Moving Forward

Claudia and Sybil's recollections illustrate some key points. Anorexia and bulimia generally improve with professional treatment and, for some individuals, tend to reawaken later in life, especially in response to challenges that involve body image. In addition to those who are afflicted with the illness, many women teeter on the edge. Others, including now-60-year-old Claudia, experience body dissatisfaction for many years but don't generally engage in extreme weight-loss practices.

Throughout this book, we have emphasized how hard it is for adolescents with anorexia or bulimia to seek help. This also holds true for adult patients who may be embarrassed to have what they perceive as a "teenager's problem" or feel too swamped in day-to-day responsibilities—including a career, parenting, or caring for elderly relatives—to take time for their own health. In her first five years as a mom, Sybil has stayed physically healthy. Her part-time teaching job, in addition to child-care responsibilities, keeps her busy. To all outward appearances, she's fine. Yet her struggles are not over. "My slips into abnormal eating behaviors have become shorter and less frequent," she says. "Yet I still feel haunted by 'I'm fat and bad'; it lurks in my mind. It's not that my negative body thoughts are constant. They come and go, and some are more forceful and stubborn than others. Having people to confide in has been an enormous help."

Whether your child is 15, 30, 45, or older—whether she's living with you, in a college dormitory, in her own apartment, or with a significant other—try to encourage her not to suffer in isolation. Even patients who have had eating disorders for a long time can make progress and feel better with treatment. For individuals who appear fine on the outside but feel uncomfortable on the inside, therapy will often help cut through the loneliness of these disorders and pave the way to greater self-acceptance. In our final chapter, we will discuss future directions in research and explore how individuals in recovery, their families, friends, and professionals in the field are joining together to improve the lives of all sufferers.

## CHAPTER 13

# Paving the Road to Tomorrow

"Deirdre has shown great courage in recovery," says her mom, Carolyn. "I hope she'll make further progress. I'm determined to help her all I can." Carolyn and Bradley first consulted us six years ago when their daughter, then 13, was suffering from anorexia. Their story allows us to underscore the importance of comprehensive treatment, explore barriers that stand in the way, and describe a national campaign to garner legislative support for these illnesses. This family's account also speaks to the future, pointing to what lies ahead for policy makers, scientists, and educators in their quest to understand eating disorders and find solutions.

Brad remembers, "When Deirdre's weight loss started, my job required a great deal of travel, and I wasn't aware that she had a problem. In my eyes, Deirdre was athletic and about average in weight. I saw her as a quiet child who studied hard and had an insatiable curiosity. I wasn't sure she was popular in school—she was too reserved to be the life of the party—but she was thoughtful of others and eager to please. Being her father, maybe I was prejudiced, but I remember thinking that she was the sort of person kids would want as a friend.

"One evening, I was on the road when Carolyn called and asked me to come directly home. Apparently, the guidance counselor at school had notified her that Deirdre was going off by herself at noon when the other seventh graders headed for the cafeteria. In addition, Carolyn had discovered that under our child's baggy clothes, she was nothing but skin and bones. I turned my truck around and drove straight through the night, meeting Carolyn and Deirdre at the pediatrician's office early the next morning. That's when I found out about my daughter's eating disorder and arranged for outpatient care.

"Once she started treatment, I tried to be firm about what she needed to eat. Her food worries seemed endless. She often had trouble sleeping, and on several occasions, I found her doing sit-ups in her room in the middle of the night. When I raised this topic in family therapy, she said that she did 100 sit-ups each night because something inside her told her she had to. She also said that every time she sensed one of her sit-ups was 'sloppy' or 'too slow,' she'd make herself repeat it until she was satisfied that she'd done it right."

## Ups and Downs

"With treatment, Deirdre began to feel better," says Brad. "She started to eat healthier, gained some weight, and continued to get top grades. This is not to say that her problems were over. Upon entering high school, she seemed to be doing so well that Carolyn and I became less diligent about watching her eating habits, and when her eating disorder began to creep in again, we weren't aware of it. Looking back, I think her transition to high school was harder than I knew. A wave of stress—new teachers, new students, bigger classes, higher academic expectations, more independence—may have played a role in the flare-up of her illness. And something else may have been involved in the relapse; Deirdre had been on an antidepressant known as an SSRI [selective serotonin reuptake inhibitor]. Thinking herself 'cured,' she had stopped taking it.

"Deirdre gradually climbed out of her relapse. Her weight never quite reached the point her doctors wanted, but what she did gain she was able to maintain for the remainder of high school. Throughout her junior and senior years, she participated on the cross-country track team and stayed healthy, continuing to see her therapists. Her appointments were less frequent than they had been when she was ill, and my sense was that she found the ongoing support helpful. During her senior year, she was accepted at several colleges. Of her anorexia, she said, 'Dad, that's all in the past.' But was it? After discussing the situation with the team, we agreed that Deirdre would need professional monitoring during her freshman year. The college of her choice had help for eating disorders right on campus, so we arranged for therapy and medical monitoring there."

## More Changes, More Challenges

"Deirdre's eating disorder hadn't been a problem during her last two years of high school," recalls Brad, "and I became convinced that she was out of the woods. Maybe that was just wishful thinking, but I loved her so much that I couldn't see it any differently. About a month into the fall semester, the college hosted a parents' visiting weekend, so we drove up to see her. Deirdre looked healthy, liked her roommates, and seemed to be in good spirits. She'd been studying hard, but that was not a bit unusual for her. All told, she seemed to be adjusting well to campus life. 'Are you going to therapy?' I asked. She assured me she was. 'And how's your eating?' 'Fine,' she answered, and we left it at that, just as we'd done for the previous two years. I remember looking for clues that her eating disorder might be moving in on her and how optimistic I felt when I found none.

"The call came in December. I relived the nightmare of five years earlier, as once again, I turned my truck around and headed home to learn that my daughter was sick. But this time, her condition was more serious because of her frequent purging. She'd set her mind on making the spring track team, and in the midst of her overtraining and undereating, her illness had taken over. In addition, she had returned to her habit of making small cuts in her arm, a behavior she had developed in ninth grade. I thought she'd overcome that problem later in high school, but apparently I was wrong. Deirdre's college physician felt she was too sick to continue as an outpatient and consulted her 'home' treatment team. Although Deirdre was not in a medical crisis and did not need admission to an acute care hospital, she was vomiting her meals and had become very undernourished. Her doctors felt that she required the round-the-clock monitoring and treatment that a residential center would provide. Admission to a residential program would offer her comprehensive care and probably a longer stay than would be feasible in a psychiatric hospital.

"In the residential treatment facility, Deirdre tried hard to cooperate with her nutrition program. Her team included a psychologist for individual therapy, a primary care doctor, a nutritionist, and a social worker. In addition, a psychiatrist who specialized in medication made adjustments in Deirdre's antidepressant dosage. She spent a lot of time in group therapy sessions that were led by mental health professionals and focused on particular themes, such as life transitions, conflict resolution, relaxation techniques, and assertiveness training. Art therapy was offered as well. Carolyn and I were eager to be involved in our daughter's recovery, so we were receptive when the social worker invited us to family therapy."

## Dealing with Health Insurance

Many factors will determine where and for how long your child receives treatment. Is she medically stable? How severe are her eating disorder behaviors? How well is she able to participate in school/work and family activities? What is her emotional state? How motivated is she to get well? Is there a treatment program in her geographic area that will meet her needs? Another set of questions relates to costs and payment. Does she have health insurance, and if so, will it cover the treatment she needs?

Health insurers' decisions about whether to pay for services can affect both inpatient and outpatient settings. Brad describes the financial problems that arose for him when Deirdre needed residential treatment. "Right after she was admitted, I met with a representative from the center's finance department, who said that he did not know how much of Deirdre's stay would be covered by our insurer. Deirdre was covered under a fully insured group plan offered by Carolyn's employer. Her insurance company had approved an initial few days of residential treatment, and coverage for a continued stay would likely last as long as the insurer determined the care Deirdre was receiving to be 'medically necessary.' Days beyond what her insurance company was willing to cover would be billed to me and Carolyn. The uncertainty surrounding the insurance payments rattled my nerves; but at the time, I was so scared I'd lose Deirdre that I would have agreed to just about anything that offered the slightest hope. Besides, Deirdre seemed to be having an unusually rough time compared to her other sieges. Was her care medically necessary? In my eyes, there was no question about it.

"Toward the end of Deirdre's third week of residential care, the center notified us that the insurance company would cover only 21 days. I had no doubt that our daughter had made progress. But while our insurer considered her well enough for discharge to outpatient care, Carolyn and I felt that she needed a longer residential stay because she remained underweight and unable to refrain from purging without staff support. Her anxiety about eating sometimes skyrocketed, and it was very hard to hear her in tears about a meal plan calling for two slices of toast instead of one or a tablespoon of jelly instead of a teaspoon. She didn't believe that she had an illness; she thought she was healthy and needed to lose weight. How did the insurance cutoff affect Deirdre? Certainly she did not want her care to burden us financially. And while we appreciated her thoughtfulness, her health and safety came first. To convince her to accept help had never been easy. Within the two or three days after we learned about the insurer's decision, she wavered back and forth between wanting to leave on the 21st day and wanting to stay longer."

"I was so upset about the insurance cutoff that I didn't know where to turn," remembers Carolyn. "What did the term *medi-*

*cally necessary* mean? Would three weeks in residential care leave Deirdre more vulnerable to relapse than five weeks? The thought of paying out of pocket for two weeks of residential treatment was daunting. The costs would wipe out our savings, and we'd probably have to take out a second mortgage on our house. What's more, there were no guarantees that the residential care would work. We wondered whether our insurance company's decision was final, or whether there was a way to overturn it."

## Appealing a Health Insurance Denial

Carolyn's sense of turmoil in the face of her insurance company's denial is understandable and expected. As illuminated in the film *Thin*, insurance cutoffs can pose financial as well as emotional hardships for patients and their families; the situation can be particularly challenging when the individual is ambivalent about whether to stay in the facility. It is important to note that more care is not necessarily better care. Defining what is "medically necessary" for a patient involves evaluating what level of improvement she has achieved, what her needs are, and what services will meet them.

Carolyn and Brad learned that there was a formal appeals process through which they could try to reverse their insurer's denial. The appeal would make the case that their child's care was medically necessary and therefore warranted insurance coverage.

If you are interested in getting a decision overturned on behalf of your child, here are the steps to follow:

1. Find out whether your child's treatment facility helps families appeal insurance denials.
2. Determine whether you are covered under a group plan (if you are insured through your employer) or a nongroup plan (if you are self-employed).
3. Obtain a copy of the health insurance plan document. It should include a definition of *medical necessity*, which is the criterion many companies use to decide on permissible coverage.

4. Discuss your plan to appeal the insurance company's denial of payment with your child's providers. To support your appeal, they can write a letter to the insurance company designating why your child's care is necessary.

5. Contact your employer's human resources department to find out whether your plan is fully insured or self-funded. This is important, because the appeals process is different for each category, the essential distinction being that state insurance laws (such as managed care reform and mental health parity laws) apply only to fully insured plans.

   If your plan is fully insured and your child's situation is dire, you have a right to an expedited appeal. This will be an internal appeal; that is, the decision will be made within the insurance company. If the denial is upheld on internal appeal, you can take your case to an independent review at the Office of Patient Protection, a state government program. This process may differ from one state to another, and it would be best to check with your state's insurance commission.

   If your health insurance is self-funded, the plan will spell out what your appeal rights are and what procedure you should follow. There is no Office of Patient Protection option for self-funded plans, and all decisions are made by your insurance company. If you and your child's physicians disagree with the outcome, you can sue in federal court for denial of benefits.

6. You'll want to prepare an appeal letter to send to the insurance company. Here's what Carolyn and Brad wrote:

Dear Mr. Brown,

We wish to appeal the denial of payment issued to our daughter, Deirdre Sims. She is 18 years old and first developed her eating disorder about five years ago. During high school, she received medical monitoring, psychotherapy, and nutrition counseling, which were covered by our policy. Our goal was to make sure Deirdre graduated high school and entered college. Deirdre did, in fact, enroll at a university about 150 miles from home. We were concerned that her eating disorder might reappear and arranged for therapy and medical monitoring through her college health center.

Unfortunately, Deirdre went downhill. Although she did well academically, her medical status quickly deteriorated as she became dehydrated and her blood test results were abnormal. As her doctors recommended, we had her admitted to residential care, where she gained some weight and began to learn how to cope with her disorder. Our policy covered the first three weeks of her residential care but denied payment for the additional 14 days that our daughter needed. We can submit Deirdre's medical records, as well as opinions from her treatment teams regarding her medical and psychological issues, in support of her five-week stay in residential care. We felt that discharging her after only three weeks would place her at risk for relapse, requiring readmission to residential care.

Thank you in advance for reconsidering payment for the final two weeks of her stay.

Sincerely,
Bradley Sims
Carolyn Kiley-Sims

"The more I thought about our appeal, the better I felt that we'd sent it," says Carolyn. "And I had to wonder: if my child's weight loss and vomiting had been part of a serious physical illness, such as cancer, would our insurance company have denied payment for the intense treatment necessary to make her well? Granted, anorexia and bulimia are considered mental disorders; but if there was one thing I'd learned from having a daughter with an eating disorder, it was that the illness affects not only the mind, but also the body."

## What is Mental Health Parity?

Traditionally, health insurance companies across the United States have provided far less coverage for mental illnesses than for illnesses deemed to be "physical." To resolve this discrepancy, most states have passed laws requiring insurance benefits for serious mental disorders to be equivalent to those for physical illnesses. Unfortunately, many mental health parity laws do not cover eating disorders. As a result, health insurance companies often deny payment for medically necessary services.

In some states, efforts are underway to correct this problem. For several years, we've been working to promote legislation in Massachusetts on behalf of eating disordered patients. Here, as in a number of states, a mental illness must be deemed "biologically based" in order to be included in the mental health parity law. Eating disorders meet this criterion on a number of counts. First, research has revealed that genetics play a role in the development of anorexia and bulimia. Second, neurochemical changes, especially those that occur at the beginning of puberty, are likely to contribute to the onset of the illness. Third, eating disorders often coexist with obsessive-compulsive disorder or depression, both of which have biological roots. Together, these features provide substantial evidence that eating disorders have a biological basis and merit insurance coverage.

Carolyn describes the outcome of her appeal: "It was an incredible relief to learn that our insurance company was responsible for covering all five weeks of Deirdre's residential care. The insurer's initial denial letter had given me such a scare that I could only imagine the horrors suffered by families who had little or no access to the intense kinds of treatment required by many patients with anorexia or bulimia. I had an urge to do something—to take some sort of action—so that others with eating disorders, like Deirdre, would have the chance to get better. That's when I found out about opportunities to support parity legislation for eating disorders in my home state, as well as about an exciting national advocacy movement."

# Eating Disorders Coalition for Research, Policy & Action

April 2000 marked a historic milestone in the field of eating disorders, as a number of professional and advocacy-based groups joined forces to champion these illnesses as a federal public health priority. Based in Washington, D.C., the Eating Disorders Coalition for Research, Policy & Action is a nonprofit organization that aims to raise national awareness of eating disorders; improve access to care; and promote prevention strategies, mental health parity, and research. Each year, the Coalition holds numerous events to educate members of Congress about eating disorders and boost support for legislation that will improve the lives of afflicted individuals and their families. "At 19, Deirdre seems to be on the upswing," notes Carolyn. "Her eating has improved a lot, and she seems more at ease with herself and others. But I worry that her disorder may again rear its ugly head. The worst part of it is that there's no telling if and when that will happen. It's comforting to know that my family is not alone and that the Coalition is giving eating disorders a strong voice in Washington. The Coalition's website keeps me in the know about pending legislation so that I can contact senators and representatives in support of eating disorder issues."

Carolyn also expressed an interest in the Friends/Family Action Council (FAC), which is the internal advocacy arm of the Coalition. By sharing their personal stories and voices with policy makers on Capitol Hill, FAC members—individuals in recovery from eating disorders, those with an active illness, families, and health care professionals—spread the word about anorexia and bulimia. "I know a mother who went to Washington to participate in one of the Coalition's lobby days," says Carolyn. "After a morning of training, she met with policy makers to describe her struggles to get affordable care for her son as an example of why federal legislation on behalf of eating disorders is so important. She told me that she found the lobbying energizing and that she benefited from chatting with the other activists."

## What Does the Future Hold?

The field of eating disorders (prevention, treatment, and research) is dynamic; it is always changing and growing in new and positive directions. Although knowledge has increased substantially over the last several decades, there is still a great deal to learn. As we've noted throughout this book, eating disorders are multifaceted, so the quest for solutions will continue to require collaboration among scientists, educators, clinicians, patients, families, and policy makers.

### Increasing Efforts in Prevention

Interest in preventing eating disorders is strong. Education programs—for preteens, adolescents, and college students—have been developed and proved to be helpful; more are on the way. In Chapter 11, we discussed some of the major themes covered in prevention programs: media literacy, healthy eating, self-appreciation, combating weight bias, listening to one's body, and letting go of negative body thoughts in favor of positive ones. Do the schools in your community offer such programs? If not, maybe you can help make that happen.

As you've seen in the preceding chapters, educators often play key roles in recognizing at-risk students and encouraging them to seek help. Teachers, guidance counselors, college residence advisers, community center leaders, summer camp personnel, and everyone who works with young people need to stay informed about eating disorders. As we discussed in Chapter 11, healthy involvement in physical activity can help girls feel good about their bodies. Yet athletic coaches and dance instructors must be aware of the dangers of eating disorders and conscientious about maintaining healthy training environments.

We've explained how idealized female body images, such as those in fashion magazines and on TV, undermine girls' self-confidence and may contribute to the development of eating disorders. To confront this problem, sustained media campaigns could focus on changing today's "thinness-equals-happiness" messages to images that focus on inner qualities, self-appreciation, and health. Efforts in this direction are under way, but there's still a great deal of work to be done in this area, and you can help! When you run across an advertisement that glorifies thinness, feel free to share your thoughts—either directly or through an eating disorder advocacy organization—with the company that sells the product.

## Increasing the Number of Clinicians and Researchers with Expertise in Eating Disorders

Fellowships in eating disorders are helping to draw talented under-graduate and graduate students into the field. Postdoctoral fellow-ships will bring in more specialists to teach, train, and consult with clinicians who have less expertise in eating disorders. Over the past decade, more medical schools, psychiatry residency programs, doctoral programs in psychology, and master's programs in social work have begun to offer formal curricula in eating disorders, and this positive trend needs to continue.

## Continuing the Search for Treatments

Ongoing efforts to unlock the mysteries of eating disorders will help pave the way to more effective treatments. Research is in progress regarding whether and to what degree eating disorders occur across different cultures. In addition, scientists will continue to investigate the genetics of eating disorders, as well as the roles of neurotransmitters such as serotonin. As we discussed in Chapters 3 and 7, it is not unusual for an individual with anorexia or bulimia to have an anxiety disorder that predated her eating problems. Further understanding of why someone who is prone to anxiety may be at risk of developing an eating disorder could open the door to improved treatment and prevention strategies. Advances in technology have given rise to neuroimaging techniques that may provide valuable insights into how the brains of eating disordered individuals work.

Experts are developing strategies to enhance cognitive behav-ioral treatment (replacing negative thoughts with positive ones), perhaps by adding components of other kinds of talk therapy, such as the dialectical behavior approach, which focuses on teaching the patient how to manage tumultuous feelings without resorting to unhealthy behaviors. Family-based (Maudsley) therapy for adolescents with anorexia or bulimia has shown promise, and studies on its effectiveness are ongoing. Efforts to formulate new drugs are under way, as are continued research projects to determine the benefits of treating patients with a combination of talk therapy and medication.

By participating in research studies, individuals with anorexia and bulimia can play a valuable role in expanding scientific knowledge about these illnesses. Entering a research study gives a person with an eating disorder an opportunity to be actively involved in her own care, to benefit from new discoveries, and to help others. Talk to your treatment team for more information about eating disorder research and to identify studies in which it would be most appropriate for you or your child to participate.

## In a Nutshell

What you can do to advocate for eating disorders:

- Write letters to national, state, and local policy makers in support of eating disorders legislation.
- See if your child's school has policies about weight-related teasing or body image concerns.
- Contact the schools and colleges in your community and suggest they offer eating disorder programs.
- Get involved in the development or implementation of prevention programs.
- Help with the activities of eating disorder advocacy organizations in your community/state.
- Encourage your child to consider opportunities to participate in eating disorder research studies that you and her treatment team feel are appropriate.
- Spread the word that there's a national organization—the Eating Disorders Coalition for Research, Policy & Action—

working every day to improve the lives of patients with eating disorders and their families.

- Visit the Coalition's website (eatingdisorderscoalition.org) often, and join the e-mail list to receive updates on what's happening in related legislation at the federal level.
- Join the Friends/Family Action Council, the advocacy branch of the Coalition.

Help keep the advocacy movement strong!

## Marching Forward

In the course of day-to-day life with your child, chances are you've wondered what she'll be like in 5, 10, or even 20 years. Try to remind yourself that, with treatment, most patients feel better over time. Recognizing and treating these illnesses in their early stages, before they take charge of the person's life, are of primary importance. But even patients who have suffered from an eating disorder for a long time can get better with the appropriate help. You'll probably have many other questions as well: "Will she continue to get better? How much better? And once she's better, how do I know whether her disorder will come back?" We wish we had all the answers. What is clear is that an eating disorder, no matter what its course, is not a personal weakness or failing on the part of the sufferer or her family. No one is to blame.

As you continue your journey, know that the field of eating disorders is on the move. Know that researchers will continue to ask questions, do their best to answer them, and then ask more. Know that a national advocacy campaign is on your side and gaining momentum. And know that, armed with what you've learned in this book, you will do the best you possibly can to help improve your child's health so she can experience the many joys that life has to offer.

# Resources

## Advocacy and Support Organizations

### Academy for Eating Disorders (AED)
60 Revere Drive, Suite 500
Northbrook, IL 60062
847-498-4274
aedweb.org
An international professional organization that strives to promote eating disorder research and prevention.

### The Anna Westin Foundation
P.O. Box 268
Chaska, MN 55318
952-361-3051
annawestinfoundation.org
Focuses on education and advocacy for people with eating disorders.

### Bodywhys—The Eating Disorders Association of Ireland
P.O. Box 105
Blackrock, County Dublin
Ireland
Phone: 01-283-4963 (administration); 1-890-200-444
   (helpline)
bodywhys.ie
Offers information about eating disorders, a phone hotline, online self-help, and a well-monitored message board.

### Dads and Daughters (DADS)

P.O. Box 3458

Duluth, MN 55803

888-824-DADS (3237)

dadsanddaughters.org; daughters.com

A national nonprofit organization offering tools to strengthen father-daughter relationships. Promotes messages that value daughters for who they are rather than for how they look. Programs include *Daughters*, a newsletter that supports parents in their efforts to raise healthy, confident girls.

### Eating Disorder Referral and Information Center

2923 Sandy Pointe, Suite 6

Del Mar, CA 92014-2052

858-792-7463

edreferral.com

Provides referrals to eating disorder practitioners, treatment facilities, and support groups. Offers information about the treatment and prevention of eating disorders.

### Eating Disorders Coalition for Research, Policy & Action (EDC)

611 Pennsylvania Avenue SE #423

Washington, DC 20003-4303

202-543-9570

eatingdisorderscoalition.org

Active on Capitol Hill since 2000, the EDC is a group of professional and advocacy-based organizations. The EDC is committed to raising national awareness of eating disorders; improving access to care; and promoting prevention strategies, parity, and research.

## Gürze Books

5145 B Avenida Encinas
Carlsbad, CA 92208
800-756-7533 (toll-free/24 hours), or 760-434-7533
bulimia.com
A publishing company that has specialized in publications
and education on eating disorders since 1980. Offers books,
newsletters, and links to websites of treatment facilities.

## Harris Center for Education and Advocacy in Eating Disorders

Massachusetts General Hospital
2 Longfellow Place
Boston, MA 02114
617-726-8470
harriscentermgh.org
Seeks new knowledge through interdisciplinary research
to better understand eating disorders and their detection,
treatment, and prevention and to share that knowledge with the
community at large.

## Health Law Advocates, Inc. (HLA)

30 Winter Street
Suite 940
Boston, MA 02108
617-338-5241
hla-inc.org/index.php
A nonprofit law firm that handles cases related to access to
treatment for eating disorders. Serving those who live or work
in Massachusetts, HLA's initiatives are an example of how
families facing health insurance denials can be helped.

### National Association of Anorexia Nervosa and Associated Disorders (ANAD)

P.O. Box 7
Highland Park, IL 60035
847-831-3438
anad.org/site/anadweb
Coordinates a nationwide network of free support groups. Provides treatment referrals, phone counseling, advocacy, and education programs.

### National Centre for Eating Disorders

54 New Road
Esher, Surrey KT10 9NU
United Kingdom
Phone: 0845-838-2040
eating-disorders.org.uk
Independent British counseling organization for the treatment of eating disorders. Offers help and support to sufferers, families, and friends.

### National Eating Disorder Information Centre (NEDIC)

ES 7-421, 200 Elizabeth Street
Toronto, ONT M5G 2C4
Canada
866-633-4220 (toll-free helpline), or 416-340-4156
nedic.ca
Canadian organization dedicated to raising awareness of eating disorders and food and weight preoccupation through public education.

### National Eating Disorders Association (NEDA)

603 Stewart Street, Suite 803
Seattle, WA 98101
206-382-3587, or 800-931-2237 (toll-free helpline)
nationaleatingdisorders.org

Dedicated to increasing public awareness of eating disorders. Provides prevention and outreach programs, educational materials, and treatment referrals, as well as a toll-free helpline.

**National Institute of Mental Health (NIMH)**
6001 Executive Boulevard
Room 8184 MSC 9663
Bethesda, MD 20892
866-615-6464 (toll-free), or 301-443-4513
nimh.nih.gov/publicat/eatingdisorders.cfm
NIMH Eating Disorder Fact Sheets discuss the characteristics, possible causes, and treatment of anorexia nervosa, bulimia nervosa, and binge eating disorder.

## Prevention Curricula

**The Positive Body Image**
National Council of Jewish Women
Essex County Section
513 West Mt. Pleasant Avenue
Livingston, NJ 07039
973-740-0588
A program for sixth-grade girls and boys focused on media literacy.

**Franko, Debra L., et al. "Food, Mood and Attitude: Reducing Risk for Eating Disorders in College Women."** *Health Psychology* **24 (2005): 567–78.**
A two-hour, interactive CD-ROM program designed to prevent eating disorders in college women who are at risk of developing these conditions. The program addresses interpersonal issues with family members and peers and draws from cognitive behavioral strategies (identifying erroneous thoughts). In addition, there is a strong media literacy component. The CD-ROM is available at Inflexxion.com.

**Kater, Kathy.** *Healthy Body Image: Teaching Kids to Eat and Love Their Bodies Too!* **Seattle: National Eating Disorders Association, 2005.**

Curriculum for grades four to six consisting of 11 lessons that help students feel good about their bodies and resist negative cultural messages.

**————.** *Real Kids Come in All Sizes: 10 Essential Lessons to Build Your Child's Body Esteem.* **New York: Broadway Books/Random House, 2004.**

A companion book to Kater's *Healthy Body Image* curriculum, aimed at parents and educators.

**Steiner-Adair, Catherine, and Lisa Sjostrom.** *Full of Ourselves: A Wellness Program to Advance Girl Power, Health and Leadership.* **New York: Teachers College Press, 2006.**

An eight-session, school-based eating disorder prevention program aimed at improving self-esteem and body attitude in adolescent girls.

## Parent Training Program

**Zucker, Nancy.** *Off the C.U.F.F. A Parent Skills Book for the Management of Disordered Eating.* **Durham, N.C.: Duke University Medical Center, 2006.**

Duke University's eating disorder program offers skills-training groups to assist parents as they try to help their adolescents improve their eating habits. *Off the C.U.F.F.* is the manual that is used with these groups. To purchase a manual or learn more about the groups, visit http://eatingdisorders.mc.duke.edu.

## Books

Bulik, Cynthia M., and Nadine Taylor. *Runaway Eating: The 8-Point Plan to Conquer Adult Food and Weight Obsessions.* Emmaus, Pa.: Rodale, 2005. Based on research; recommended for adult women of all ages.

Fairburn, Christopher. *Overcoming Binge Eating.* New York: Guilford Press, 1995. Based on research; recommended for older adolescents and adults.

Latner, Janet D., and G. Terence Wilson, eds. *Self-Help Approaches for Obesity and Eating Disorders: Research and Practice.* New York: Guilford Press, 2007. Based on research; recommended for older adolescents and adults.

Schaefer, Jenni, and Thom Rutledge. *Life Without Ed: How One Woman Declared Independence from Her Eating Disorder and How You Can Too.* New York: McGraw-Hill, 2004. Offers individuals suffering from eating disorders important tools to help them regain their health. Recommended for adolescents and adults.

Schmidt, Ulrike, and Janet Treasure. *Getting Better Bit(e) by Bit(e): A Survival Kit for Sufferers of Bulimia Nervosa and Binge Eating Disorders.* East Sussex, U.K: Psychology Press Ltd., 1993. Based on research; recommended for older adolescents and adults.

## Books

Andersen, Arnold, Leigh Cohn, and Thomas Holbrook. *Making Weight: Healing Men's Conflicts with Food, Weight & Shape.* Carlsbad, Calif.: Gürze Books, 2000. Reaches out to men with eating disorders and their families, exploring the different facets of these illnesses and shedding light on recovery.

Brumberg, Joan J. *The Body Project: An Intimate History of American Girls.* New York: Random House, 1997. Historical perspective on the relationship between women and their bodies.

———. *Fasting Girls: The History of Anorexia Nervosa.* New York: Vintage Books, 2000. Follows the history of anorexia nervosa from the Middle Ages to the 1980s.

Costin, Carolyn. *The Eating Disorder Sourcebook.* Chicago: McGraw-Hill, 2006. Written for both the general population and professionals. This comprehensive book is filled with helpful information about detection, treatment, and prevention.

Ginsburg, Richard D., Stephen Durant, and Amy Baltzell. *Whose Game Is It, Anyway? A Guide to Helping Your Child Get the Most from Sports.* Boston: Houghton Mifflin, 2006. Teaches parents to cope with the long- and short-term challenges that arise for girls and boys in the world of athletics. Outlines a three-step approach to affording one's child a healthy, positive sports experience.

Greenfield, Lauren. *Thin.* New York: Chronicle Books, 2006. The companion book to Greenfield's 2006 documentary film *Thin*, which tells the stories of young women in treatment at a residential care facility for eating disorders.

Kadison, Richard, and Theresa Foy DiGeronimo. *College of the Overwhelmed: The Campus Mental Health Crisis and What To Do About It.* San Francisco: Jossey-Bass, 2005. Helpful for parents, college guidance counselors, residence advisors, and students themselves. Describes the pressures today's college students are under and suggests how parents can help them cope.

Kirkpatrick, Jim, and Paul Caldwell. *Eating Disorders: Everything You Need to Know.* Buffalo, N.Y.: Firefly Books, 2001. Defines eating disorders and their possible causes, treatments, and complications.

Knapp, Caroline. *Appetites: Why Women Want.* New York: Counterpoint/Perseus Book Group, 2003. Draws on the author's own history of anorexia nervosa to support the theme that women have a great deal of difficulty recognizing and satisfying their appetites, one of which involves food. Others include the desire for joy, for relationships with others, and for inner peace.

Liu, Aimee. *Gaining: The Truth About Life After Eating Disorders.* New York: Warner Books, 2007. Describes the author's experiences of relapse and recovery and explores the perspectives of individuals she interviewed who have struggled with eating disorders.

Lock, James, and Daniel le Grange. *Help Your Teenager Beat an Eating Disorder.* New York: Guilford Press, 2005. Explains the family-based (Maudsley) model of therapy for adolescents.

Maine, Margo, and Joe Kelly. *The Body Myth: Adult Women and the Pressure to Be Perfect.* Hoboken, N.J.: John Wiley & Sons, 2005.

Challenges the popular perception that a woman's value is based on her physical appearance.

Neumark-Sztainer, Dianne. *"I'm, Like, So Fat!" Helping Your Teen Make Healthy Choices About Eating and Exercise in a Weight-Obsessed World.* New York: Guilford Press, 2005. Aimed at parents. This guide explores multiple dimensions of food-related problems and suggests strategies for teaching teenagers to respect and take care of their bodies.

Pope, Harrison G., Jr., Katharine A. Phillips, and Roberto Olivardia. *The Adonis Complex: The Secret Crisis of Male Body Obsession.* New York: The Free Press, 2000. It is widely known that mainstream Western culture supports a female body ideal that is unattainable by the vast majority of women. What many people don't realize is that the media also propagates unrealistic messages about the male physique. This book tracks the evolution of negative body image in males and suggests ways to help boys feel better about themselves.

Reindl, Sheila. *Sensing the Self: Women's Recovery from Bulimia.* Cambridge, Mass.: Harvard University Press, 2001. Recommended for individuals with bulimia and for all those who want to help them. This book is based on the author's interviews with women in recovery. Woven throughout patient experiences is the theme that growing self-awareness and self-acceptance are key parts of the journey from eating disorder to improved health.

Simmons, Rachel. *Odd Girl Out: The Hidden Culture of Aggression in Girls.* New York: Harcourt, Inc., 2002. Focuses on girl-to-girl bullying; explores how girls are socialized from an early age to be nice at all times. When a girl gets angry at a friend, she is unlikely to tell her face-to-face. Instead, she is apt to start a rumor about her, call her nasty names, or stop talking to her. Simmons's interviews with girls who have been bullied illustrate how devastating these forms of aggression can be.

Strober, Michael, and Meg Schneider. *Just a Little Too Thin: How to Pull Your Child Back from the Brink of an Eating Disorder.* Cambridge, Mass.: Da Capo Press, 2005. Helps parents recognize and cope with signs of eating problems in their children. Describes the different levels of severity of disordered eating and how to find appropriate treatment.

Thompson, Becky. *A Hunger So Wide and So Deep: A Multicultural View of Women's Eating Problems.* Minneapolis: University of Minnesota Press, 1996. Includes the voices of African American, Latina, and Caucasian women; explores the various emotional challenges faced by individuals with unhealthy eating habits.

Walsh, B. Timothy, and V. L. Cameron. *If Your Adolescent Has an Eating Disorder: An Essential Resource for Parents.* New York: Oxford University Press, 2005. Includes warning signs, what to expect when you take your child for a medical evaluation, treatment, how you can support her through recovery, and prevention.

Willett, Walter C., and P. J. Skerrett. *Eat, Drink and Be Healthy: The Harvard Medical School Guide to Healthy Eating.* New York: Free Press, 2005. Introduces the healthy eating pyramid for adults and offers a wealth of nutrition information in reader-friendly terms.

# Websites

**American Academy of Pediatrics** (http://aap.org/family/steroids.htm): "Steroids: Play Safe, Play Fair." A lucid, concise overview of the use of steroids in sports. Elucidates why these substances are particularly dangerous to adolescents.

**The Body Positive** (http://thebodypositive.org): Helps empower people of all ages, especially young people, to celebrate their natural size and shape instead of what society promotes as the ideal body. Offers educational programs and videos.

**Center for Media Literacy** (http://medialit.org): Nonprofit organization dedicated to helping people develop the skills necessary to critique media messages.

**The Center for Young Women's Health**, Children's Hospital, Boston (http://youngwomenshealth.org/about_us.html): Focuses on improving the lives of adolescent girls and young women through research, clinical services, health care advocacy, and education.

Girl Power! (http://girlpower.gov): Now in its seventh year, a national public education campaign sponsored by the U.S. Department of Health and Human Services. Focuses on building positive self-images in girls ages 9 to 13.

MySelfHelp.com (http://myselfhelp.com): Offers an interactive self-help program for individuals struggling with eating disorders. Also offers programs for depression, stress, and other mental health issues.

Neuroendocrine Clinical Research Studies in Anorexia Nervosa, Massachusetts General Hospital (http://massgeneral.org/an): Offers information about anorexia and osteoporosis; describes research studies aimed at finding treatment for patients with anorexia who have suffered bone loss.

New Moon Publishing (http://newmoon.org): Produces media that support girls in their authenticity and encourage creative expression. Through fiction, poems, letters, and artwork, *New Moon Magazine*—the winner of six Parents' Choice Gold awards—celebrates the lives of girls and women around the world.

# References

## Comprehensive Works

American Psychiatric Association. "Practice Guideline for the Treatment of Patients with Eating Disorders, Third Edition." *American Journal of Psychiatry* 163, no. 7 Suppl (2006): 4–54.

Berkman, N. D., C. M. Bulik, K. A. Brownley, K. N. Lohr, J. A. Sedway, A. Rooks, and G. Garhlehner. *The Management of Eating Disorders.* Rockville, Md.: Agency for Healthcare Research and Quality, 2006. (Copies of the report are available free of charge from the AHRQ Publications Clearinghouse. Call 800-358-9295 or send an e-mail to ahrq.gov/news/pubsix.htm.)

Brewerton, T. D., ed. *Clinical Handbook of Eating Disorders: An Integrated Approach.* New York: Marcel Dekker, 2004.

Commission on Adolescent Eating Disorders. "Eating Disorders." In *Treating and Preventing Adolescent Mental Health Disorders: What We Know and What We Don't Know; A Research Agenda for Improving the Mental Health of Our Youth,* edited by D. E. Evans, E. B. Foa, R. E. Gur, H. Hendin, C. P. O'Brien, M. E. P. Seligman, and B. T. Walsh, 258–81. New York: Oxford University Press, 2005.

Cooper, P. J., and A. Stein, eds. *Childhood Feeding Problems and Adolescent Eating Disorders.* New York: Routledge, 2006.

Fairburn, C. G., and K. D. Brownell, eds. *Eating Disorders and Obesity: A Comprehensive Handbook,* 2nd ed. New York: Guilford Press, 2000.

Keel, P. K. *Eating Disorders.* Upper Saddle River, N.J.: Pearson/Prentice Hall, 2005.

Thompson, J. K. *Handbook of Eating and Weight Disorders*. New York: Wiley, Inc., 2003.

Treasure, J., U. Schmidt, and E. van Furth, eds. *Handbook of Eating Disorders*. West Sussex, U.K.: Wiley, Inc., 2003.

Wonderlich, S., J. Mitchell, M. de Zwaan, and H. Steiger, eds. *Annual Review of Eating Disorders*, Part I-2007. Oxford: Radcliffe Publishing, 2007.

## Chapter 1

Bemporad, J. R. "Self-Starvation Through the Ages. Reflections on the Pre-History of Anorexia Nervosa." *International Journal of Eating Disorders* 19, no. 3 (1996): 217–37.

Frisch, M. J., D. B. Herzog, and D. L. Franko. "Residential Treatment for Eating Disorders." *International Journal of Eating Disorders* 39, no. 5 (2006): 434–42.

Hudson, J. I., E. Hiripi, H. G. Hope, and R. Kessler. "The Prevalence of Correlates of Eating Disorders in the National Comorbidity Survey." *Biological Psychiatry* 61, no. 3 (2007): 348–58.

Insel, Thomas R. National Institute of Mental Health, Department of Health and Human Services. Letter, October 5, 2006. http://nationaleatingdisorders.org/nedaDir/files/documents/NIMHLetter.pdf.

Kirkpatrick, J., and P. Caldwell. *Eating Disorders: Everything You Need to Know*. Buffalo, N.Y.: Firefly Books, 2001.

Miller, K. K., S. Grinspoon, S. Gleysteen, K. A. Grieco, J. Ciampa, D. B. Herzog, and A. Klibanski. "Preservation of Neuroendocrine Control of Reproductive Function Despite Severe Undernutrition." *Journal of Clinical Endocrinology and Metabolism* 89, no. 9 (2004): 4434–38.

Watson, T. L., and A. E. Andersen. "A Critical Examination of the Amenorrhea and Weight Criteria for Diagnosing Anorexia Nervosa." *Acta Psychiatrica Scandinavica* 109, no. 3 (2003): 175–82.

## Chapter 2

Andersen, A., L. Cohn, and T. Holbrook. *Making Weight: Healing Men's Conflicts with Food, Weight, and Shape.* Carlsbad, Calif.: Gürze Books, 2000.

Brumberg, J. J. *The Body Project: An Intimate History of American Girls.* New York: Random House, 1997.

———. *Fasting Girls: The History of Anorexia Nervosa.* New York: Vintage Books, 2000.

Croll, J., D. Neumark-Sztainer, M. Story, and M. Ireland. "Prevalence and Risk and Protective Factors Related to Disordered Eating Behaviors Among Adolescents: Relationship to Gender and Ethnicity." *Journal of Adolescent Health* 31, no. 2 (2002): 166–75.

Fairburn, C. G., Z. Cooper, H. Doll, and B. Davies. "Identifying Dieters Who Will Develop an Eating Disorder: A Prospective, Population-Based Study." *American Journal of Psychiatry* 162, no. 12 (2005): 2251–55.

Golden, N. H., D. K. Katzman, R. E. Kreipe, S. L. Stevens, S. M. Sawyer, J. Rees, D. Nicholls, and E. S. Rome. "Eating Disorders in Adolescents: Position Paper of the Society for Adolescent Medicine." *Journal of Adolescent Health* 33, no. 6 (2003): 496–503.

Gordon, R. A. *Eating Disorders: Anatomy of a Social Epidemic,* 2nd ed. Oxford: Blackwell, 2000.

Heatherton, T. F., P. Nichols, F. Mahamedi, and P. K. Keel. "Body Weight, Dieting, and Eating Disorder Symptoms Among College Students, 1982 to 1992." *American Journal of Psychiatry* 152, no. 11 (1995): 1623–29.

Keyes, A., J. Brozek, A. Henschel, O. Mickelsen, and H. L. Taylor. *The Biology of Human Starvation.* Minneapolis: University of Minneapolis Press, 1950.

Strober, M. A., and M. F. Schneider. *Just a Little Too Thin: How to Pull Your Child Back from the Brink of an Eating Disorder.* Cambridge, Mass.: Da Capo Press, 2005.

Woodside, D. B., P. E. Garfinkel, E. Lin, P. Goering, A. S. Kaplan, D. S. Goldbloom, and S. H. Kennedy. "Comparisons of Men with Full or Partial Eating Disorders, Men Without Eating Disorders, and Women with Eating Disorders in the Community." *American Journal of Psychiatry* 158 (2001): 570–74.

## Chapter 3

Adkins, E. C., and P. K. Keel. "Does 'Excessive' or 'Compulsive' Best Describe Exercise as a Symptom of Bulimia Nervosa?" *International Journal of Eating Disorders* 38, no. 1 (2005): 24–29.

Fulkerson, J. A., and S. A. French. "Cigarette Smoking for Weight Loss or Control Among Adolescents: Gender and Racial/Ethnic Differences." *Journal of Adolescent Health* 32, no. 4 (2003): 306–13.

Kaye, W. H., C. M. Bulik, L. Thornton, N. Barbarich, and K. Masters. "Comorbidity of Anxiety Disorders with Anorexia and Bulimia Nervosa." *American Journal of Psychiatry* 161, no. 12 (2004): 2215–21.

Lilenfeld, L. R., S. Wonderlich, L. P. Riso, R. Crosby, and J. Mitchell. "Eating Disorders and Personality: A Methodological and Empirical Review." *Clinical Psychology* 26, no. 3 (2006): 299–320.

Perry, C. L., M. T. Mcguire, D. Neumark-Sztainer, and M. Story. "Characteristics of Vegetarian Adolescents in a Multiethnic Urban Population." *Journal of Adolescent Health* 29, no. 6 (2001): 406–16.

Sundgot-Borgen, J., and M. K. Torstveit. "Prevalence of Eating Disorders in Elite Athletes Is Higher Than in the General Population." *Clinical Journal of Sports Medicine* 14, no. 1 (2004): 25–32.

Thompson-Brenner, H., and D. Westen. "Personality Subtypes in Eating Disorders: Validation of a Classification in a Naturalistic Sample." *British Journal of Psychiatry* 186 (June 2005): 517–24.

## Chapter 4

Cockell, S. J., J. Geller, and W. Linden. "The Development of a Decisional Balance Scale for Anorexia Nervosa." *European Eating Disorders Review* 10, no. 5 (2002): 359–75.

Grinspoon, S., L. Thomas, S. Pitts, E. Gross, D. Mickley, D. Miller, D. B. Herzog, and A. Klibanski. "Prevalence and Predictive Factors for Regional Osteopenia in Women with Anorexia Nervosa." *Annals of Internal Medicine* 133, no. 10 (2000): 790–94.

Herzog, D. B., D. L. Franko, S. C. Jackson, M. P. Manzo, K. K. Miller, and A. Klibanski. "Does Participation in Osteoporosis Treatment Studies Influence Eating Disorder Symptoms in Anorexia Nervosa?" Presented at the International Conference on Eating Disorders, Montreal, Ont., April 27–30, 2005. Also presented at the annual meeting of the American Association of Psychiatry, Atlanta, Ga., May 26, 2005.

## Chapter 5

Andersen, A. E. "Eating Disorders and Coercion." *American Journal of Psychiatry* 164, no. 1 (2007): 9–11.

Beresin, E. V., C. Gordon, and D. B. Herzog. "The Process of Recovering from Anorexia Nervosa." *Journal of the American Academy of Psychoanalysis* 17, no. 1 (1989): 103–30.

Guarda, A. S., A. M. Pinto, J. W. Coughlin, S. Hussain, N. A. Haug, and L. J. Heinberg. "Perceived Coercion and Change in Perceived Need for Admission in Patients Hospitalized for Eating Disorders." *American Journal of Psychiatry* 164, no. 1 (2007): 108–14.

Herzog, D. B., E. V. Beresin, and V. E. Charat. "Anorexia Nervosa." In *Textbook of Child and Adolescent Psychiatry*, edited by G. Wiener, 671–89. Washington, D.C.: American Psychiatric Press, 2004.

Herzog, D. B., P. Hamburg, and A. Brotman. "Psychotherapy and Eating Disorders: An Affirmative View." *International Journal of Eating Disorders* 6, no. 4 (1987): 545–50.

Lock, J., D. le Grange, W. S. Agras, and C. Dare. *Treatment Manual for Anorexia Nervosa: A Family-Based Approach.* New York: Guilford Press, 2001.

Rorty, M., J. Yager, and E. Rossotto. "Why and How Do Women Recover from Bulimia Nervosa? The Subjective Appraisals of Forty Women Recovered for a Year or More." *International Journal of Eating Disorders* 14, no. 3 (1993): 249–60.

Schmidt, U., S. Lee, J. Beecham, S. Perkins, J. Treasure, I. Yi, S. Winn, P. Robinson, R. Murphy, S. Keville, E. Johnson-Sabine, M. Jenkins, S. Frost, L. Dodge, M. Berlelowitz, and I. Eisler. "A Randomized Controlled Trial of Family Therapy and Cognitive Behavior Therapy Guided Self-Care for Adolescents with Bulimia Nervosa and Related Disorders." *American Journal of Psychiatry* 164, no. 4 (2007): 591–98.

Walsh, T., and V. Cameron. *If Your Adolescent Has an Eating Disorder: An Essential Resource for Parents.* New York: Oxford University Press, 2005.

Willumsen, T., and P. K. Graugaard. "Dental Fear, Regularity of Dental Attendance and Subjective Evaluation of Dental Erosion in Women with Eating Disorders." *European Journal of Oral Science* 113, no. 4 (2005): 297–302.

Yager, J., and A. E. Andersen. "Clinical Practice: Anorexia Nervosa." *New England Journal of Medicine* 353, no. 14 (2005): 1481–88.

## Chapter 6

American Dietetic Association. "Position of the American Dietetic Association: Nutrition Intervention in the Treatment of Anorexia Nervosa, Bulimia Nervosa, and Other Eating Disorders." *Journal of the American Dietetic Association* 106, no. 12 (2006): 2073–82.

Bridge, J. A., S. Iyengar, C. B. Salary, R. P. Barbe, B. Birma-
her, H. A. Pincus, L. Ren, D. A. Brent. "Clinical Response
and Risk for Reported Suicidal Ideation and Suicide Attempts
in Pediatric Antidepressant Treatment: A Meta-Analysis of
Randomized Controlled Trials." *Journal of the American Medical
Association* 297, no. 15 (2007): 1683–96.

Castro, J., J. Toro, L. Lazaro, F. Pons, and I. Halperin. "Bone
Mineral Density in Male Adolescents with Anorexia Nervosa."
*Journal of the American Academy of Child and Adolescent Psychiatry*
41, no. 5 (2003): 613–18.

Katzman, D. K., B. Christensen, A. R. Young, and R. B. Zipur-
sky. "Starving the Brain: Structural Abnormalities and Cognitive Impairment in Adolescents with Anorexia Nervosa."
*Seminars in Clinical Neuropsychiatry* 6, no. 2 (2001): 146–52.

Kerem, N. C., and D. K. Katzman. "Brain Structure and Function
in Adolescents with Anorexia Nervosa." *Adolescent Medicine* 14,
no. 1 (2003): 109–18.

Kotler, L. A., M. J. Devlin, M. Davies, and B. T. Walsh. "An
Open Trial of Fluoxetine for Adolescents with Bulimia Nervosa." *Journal of Child and Adolescent Psychopharmacology* 13, no.
3 (2003): 329–35.

Kreipe, R., and S. Yussman. "The Role of the Primary Care Practitioner in the Treatment of Eating Disorders." *Adolescent Medicine* 14, no. 1 (2003): 133–47.

Lask, B., I. Gordon, D. Christie, I. Frampton, U. Chowdhury,
and B. Watkins. "Functional Neuroimaging in Early-Onset
Anorexia Nervosa." *International Journal of Eating Disorders* 37
(2005) Suppl: S49–S51.

Mickley, D. "Medical Evaluation and Management of Eating Disorders in the Primary Care Setting." Presented at Primary Care
Symposium (Multidisciplinary Treatment of Eating Disorders
in Adolescents and Adults), Massachusetts General Hospital,
Boston, April 11, 2005.

Misra, M., A. Aggarwal, K. K. Miller, C. Almazan, M. Wor-
ley, L. A. Soyka, D. B. Herzog, and A. Klibanski. "Effects of

Anorexia Nervosa on Clinical, Hematologic, Biochemical, and Bone Density Parameters in Community-Dwelling Adolescent Girls." *Pediatrics* 114, no. 6 (2004): 1574–83.

Misra, M., and A. Klibanski. "Anorexia Nervosa and Osteoporosis." *Reviews in Endocrine and Metabolic Disorders* 7, no. 1–2 (2006): 91–99.

Shamim, T., N. H. Golden, M. Arden, L. Filiberto, and I. R. Shenker. "Resolution of Vital Sign Instability: An Objective Measure of Medical Stability in Anorexia Nervosa." *Journal of Adolescent Health* 32, no. 1 (2003): 73–77.

Sherman, B. J., C. R. Savage, K. T. Eddy, C. Connor, M. A. Blais, T. Deckersbach, S. C. Jackson, D. L. Franko, S. L. Rauch, and D. B. Herzog. "Strategic Memory in Adults with Anorexia Nervosa: Are There Similarities to Obsessive Compulsive Spectrum Disorders?" *International Journal of Eating Disorders* 39, no. 6 (2006): 468–76.

Walsh, T., and V. Cameron. *If Your Adolescent Has an Eating Disorder: An Essential Resource for Parents.* New York: Oxford University Press, 2005.

Walsh, T., A. Kaplan, E. Attia, M. Olmstead, M. Parides, J. Carter, M. Pike, M. Devlin, B. Woodside, C. Roberto, and W. Rockert. "Fluoxetine After Weight Restoration in Anorexia Nervosa." *JAMA* 295, no. 22 (2006): 2605–12.

## Chapter 7

Biro, F. M., R. H. Striegel-Moore, D. L. Franko, J. Padgett, and J. A. Bean. "Self-Esteem in Adolescent Females." *Journal of Adolescent Health* 39, no. 4 (2006): 501–7.

Corstorphine, E., G. Waller, R. Lawson, and C. Ganis. "Trauma and Multi-Impulsivity in the Eating Disorders." *Eating Behaviors* 8, no. 1 (2007): 23–30.

Kadison, R., and T. F. DiGeronimo. *College of the Overwhelmed: The Campus Mental Health Crisis and What to Do About It.* San Francisco: Jossey-Bass, 2005.

Robins, C. J., and A. L. Chapman. "Dialectical Behavior Therapy: Current Status, Recent Developments, and Future Directions." *Journal of Personality Disorders* 18, no. 1 (2004): 73–89.

Silberg, J. L., and C. M. Bulik. "The Developmental Association Between Eating Disorders Symptoms and Symptoms of Depression and Anxiety in Juvenile Twin Girls." *Journal of Child Psychiatry* 46, no. 12 (2005): 1317–26.

Stein, D., L. R. Lilenfeld, P. C. Wildman, and M. D. Marcus. "Attempted Suicide and Self-Injury in Patients Diagnosed with Eating Disorders." *Comprehensive Psychiatry* 45, no. 6 (2004): 447–51.

Wade, T. D., C. M. Bulik, M. Neale, and K. S. Kendler. "Anorexia Nervosa and Major Depression: Shared Genetic and Environmental Risk Factors." *American Journal of Psychiatry* 157, no. 3 (2000): 469–71.

## Chapter 8

Carter, J. C., M. P. Olmsted, A. S. Kaplan, R. E. McCabe, J. S. Mills, and A. Aime. "Self-Help for Bulimia Nervosa: A Randomized Controlled Trial." *American Journal of Psychiatry* 160, no. 5 (2003): 973–78.

Courturier, J., and J. Lock. "What Is Recovery in Adolescent Anorexia Nervosa?" *International Journal of Eating Disorders* 37, no. 7 (2006): 550–55.

Esplen, M. J., P. E. Garfinkel, M. Olmsted, R. M. Gallop, and S. Kennedy. "A Randomized Controlled Trial of Guided Imagery in Bulimia Nervosa." *Psychological Medicine* 28, no. 6 (1998): 1347–57.

Fairburn, C. G., M. D. Marcus, and G. T. Wilson. "Cognitive-Behavioral Therapy for Binge Eating and Bulimia Nervosa: A Comprehensive Treatment Manual." In *Binge Eating: Nature, Assessment, and Treatment*, edited by C. G. Fairburn and G. T. Wilson, 364–404. New York: Guilford Press, 1993.

Frisch, M. J., D. L. Franko, and D. B. Herzog. "Arts-Based Therapies in the Treatment of Eating Disorders." *Eating Disorders* 14, no. 2 (2006): 131–42.

Healing Quest, "Yoga for Eating Disorders," Season One transcripts, Ep. 9. http://healingquest.tv/YogaEatingTrans.html.

Herzog, D. B., D. J. Dorer, P. K. Keel, S. E. Selwyn, E. R. Ekeblad, A. T. Flores, D. N. Greenwood, R. A. Burwell, and M. B. Keller. "Recovery and Relapse in Anorexia and Bulimia Nervosa: A 7.5-Year Follow-Up Study." *Journal of the American Academy of Child and Adolescent Psychiatry* 38, no. 7 (1999): 829–837.

Johnson, C. L., and C. Taylor. "Working with Difficult-to-Treat Eating Disorders Using an Integration of Twelve-Step and Traditional Psychotherapies." *Psychiatric Clinics of North America* 19, no. 4 (1996): 829–41.

Keel, P. K., D. J. Dorer, D. L. Franko, S. C. Jackson, and D. B. Herzog. "Post-Remission Predictors of Relapse in Eating Disorders." *American Journal of Psychiatry* 162, no. 12 (2005): 2263–68.

Miller, J. J., K. Fletcher, and J. Kabat-Zinn. "Three-Year Follow-Up and Clinical Implications of a Mindfulness Meditation-Based Stress Reduction Intervention in the Treatment of Anxiety Disorders." *General Hospital Psychiatry* 17, no. 3 (1995): 192–200.

Nilsson, K., and B. Haggleof. "Patient Perspectives of Recovery in Adolescent Onset Anorexia Nervosa." *Eating Disorders* 14, no. 4 (2006): 305–11.

Norris, L., K. M. Boydell, L. Pinhas, and D. Katzman. "Ana and the Internet: A Review of Pro-Anorexia Websites." *International Journal of Eating Disorders* 39, no. 6 (2006): 443–47.

Rossoto, E., M. Rorty-Greenfield, and J. Yager. "What Causes and Maintains Bulimia Nervosa? Recovered and Nonrecovered Women's Reflections on the Disorder." *Eating Disorders* 4, no. 2 (1996): 115–27.

Strober, M., R. Freeman, W. Morrell. "The Long-Term Course of Severe Anorexia Nervosa in Adolescents: Survival Analysis of Recovery, Relapse, and Outcome Predictors Over 10–15

Years in a Prospective Study." *International Journal of Eating Disorders* 22, no. 4 (1997): 339–60.

Telch, C. F., W. S. Agras, and M. M. Linehan. "Dialectical Behavior Therapy for Binge Eating Disorder." *Journal of Consulting and Clinical Psychology* 69, no. 6 (2001): 1061–65.

Thiels, C., U. Schmidt, J. Treasure, and R. Garthe. "Four-Year Follow-Up of Guided Self-Change for Bulimia Nervosa." *Eating and Weight Disorders* 8, no. 3 (2003): 212–17.

Tozzi, F., P. F. Sullivan, J. L. Fear, J. McKenzie, and C. M. Bulik. "Causes and Recovery in Anorexia Nervosa: The Patient's Perspective." *International Journal of Eating Disorders* 33, no. 2 (2003): 143–54.

Vitousek, K. B., J. Daly, and C. Heiser. "Reconstructing the Internal World of the Eating-Disordered Individual: Overcoming Denial and Distortion in Self-Report." *International Journal of Eating Disorders* 10, no. 6 (1991): 647–66.

Wilson, J., R. Peebles, K. Hardy, and I. Litt. "Surfing for Thinness: A Pilot Study of Pro–Eating Disorder Web Site Usage in Adolescents with Eating Disorders." *Pediatrics* 118, no. 6 (2006): 1635–43.

## Chapter 9

Le Grange, D., and R. Binford. "Manualized Family-Based Treatment for Anorexia Nervosa: A Case Series." *Journal of the American Academy of Child and Adolescent Psychiatry* 44, no. 1 (2005): 41–46.

Le Grange, D., and J. Lock. *Treating Bulimia in Adolescents: A Family-Based Approach.* New York: Guilford Press, 2007.

Lock, J., D. le Grange, W. S. Agras, and C. Dare. *Treatment Manual for Anorexia Nervosa: A Family-Based Approach.* New York: Guilford Press, 2001.

Stewart, M. C., P. K. Keel, and R. S. Schiavo. "Stigmatization of Anorexia Nervosa." *International Journal of Eating Disorders* 39, no. 4 (2006): 320–25.

Zucker, N., M. Marcus, and C. M. Bulik. "A Group Parent-Training Program: A Novel Approach." *Eating and Weight Disorders* 11, no. 2 (2006): 78–82.

## Chapter 10

Becker, A. E., K. Fay, S. E. Gilman, and R. H. Striegel-Moore. "Facets of Acculturation and Their Diverse Relations to Body Shape in Fiji." *International Journal of Eating Disorders* 40, no. 1 (2006): 42–50.

Field, A. E., S. B. Austin, R. Striegel-Moore, C. B. Taylor, C. A. Camargo, Jr., N. Laird, and G. Colditz. "Weight Concerns and Weight Control Behaviors of Adolescents and Their Mothers." *Archives of Pediatric and Adolescent Medicine* 159, no. 12 (2005): 1121–26.

Field, A. E., C. A. Camargo, Jr., C. B. Taylor, C. S. Berkey, S. B. Roberts, and G. A. Colditz. "Peer, Parent, and Media Influences on the Development of Weight Concerns and Frequent Dieting Among Preadolescent and Adolescent Girls and Boys." *Pediatrics* 107, no. 1 (2001): 54–60.

Grabe, S., and J. S. Hyde. "Ethnicity and Body Dissatisfaction Among Women in the United States: A Meta-Analysis." *Psychological Bulletin* 132, no. 4 (2006): 622–40.

Halmi, K. A., S. R. Sunday, M. Strober, A. Kaplan, D. B. Woodside, M. Fichter, J. Treasure, W. H. Berrettini, and W. H. Kaye. "Perfectionism in Anorexia Nervosa: Variation by Clinical Subtype, Obsessionality, and Pathological Eating Behavior." *American Journal of Psychiatry* 157, no. 11 (2000): 1799–1805.

Johnson, C., P. S. Powers, and R. Dick. "Athletes and Eating Disorders: The National Collegiate 54 Athletic Association Study." *International Journal of Eating Disorders* 26, no. 2 (1999): 179–88.

Roberts, A., T. F. Cash, A. Feingold, and B. T. Johnson. "Are Black-White Differences in Females' Body Dissatisfaction Decreasing? A Meta-Analytic Review." *Journal of Consulting and Clinical Psychology* 74, no. 6 (2006): 1121–31.

Taylor, C. B., S. Bryson, A. A. Celio Doyle, K. H. Luce, D. Cunning, L. B. Abascal, R. Rockwell, A. E. Field, R. Striegel-Moore, A. J. Winzelberg, and D. E. Wilfley. "The Adverse Effect of Negative Comments About Weight and Shape from Family and Siblings on Women at High Risk for Eating Disorders." *Pediatrics* 118, no. 2 (2006): 731–38.

Treasure, J., G. Smith, and A. Crane. *Skills-Based Learning for Caring for a Loved One with an Eating Disorder: The New Maudsley Method.* Oxford: Routledge, 2007.

Wade, T. D., and C. M. Bulik. "Shared Genetic and Environmental Risk Factors Between Undue Influence of Body Shape and Weight on Self-Evaluation and Dimensions of Perfectionism." *Psychological Medicine* 1–10 (2006, Dec. 19) [Epub ahead of print].

## Chapter 11

Bell, C., and M. J. Cooper. "Socio-Cultural and Cognitive Predictors of Eating Disorder Symptoms in Young Girls." *Eating and Weight Disorders* 10, no. 4 (2005): e97–e100.

Fallon, A., and P. Rozin. "Sex Differences in Perceptions of Desirable Body Shape." *Journal of Abnormal Psychology* 94, no. 1 (1985): 102–5.

Field, A. E., S. B. Austin, R. Striegel-Moore, C. B. Taylor, C. A. Camargo, Jr., N. Laird, and G. Colditz. "Weight Concerns and Weight Control Behaviors of Adolescents and Their Mothers." *Archives of Pediatric and Adolescent Medicine* 159, no. 12 (2005): 1121–26.

Field, A. E., C. A. Camargo, Jr., C. B. Taylor, C. S. Berkey, S. B. Roberts, and G. A. Colditz. "Peer, Parent, and Media Influences on the Development of Weight Concerns and Frequent Dieting Among Preadolescent and Adolescent Girls and Boys." *Pediatrics* 107, no. 1 (2001): 54–60.

Franko, D. L., L. B. Mintz, M. Villapiano, T. C. Green, D. Mainelli, L. Folensbee, S. F. Butler, M. M. Davidson, E. Hamilton, D. Little, M. Kearns, and S. H. Budman. "Food, Mood, and Attitude: Reducing Risk for Eating Disorders in College Women." *Health Psychology* 24, no. 6 (2005): 567–78.

Knapp, C. *Appetites: Why Women Want*. New York: Counterpoint/Perseus Book Group, 2003.

Nichter, M. *Fat Talk: What Girls and Their Parents Say About Dieting*. Cambridge, Mass.: Harvard University Press, 2000.

Pope, H. G., R. Olivardia, A. J. Gruber, and J. Borowiecki. "Evolving Ideals of Male Body Image as Seen Through Action Toys." *International Journal of Eating Disorders* 26, no. 1 (1999): 65–72.

Simmons, R. *Odd Girl Out: The Hidden Culture of Aggression in Girls*. New York: Harcourt, Inc., 2002.

Steiner-Adair, C., and L. Sjostrom. *Full of Ourselves: A Wellness Program to Advance Girl Power, Health and Leadership*. New York: Teachers College Press, 2006.

Taylor, C. B., S. Bryson, K. Luce, D. Cunning, A. Doyle, L. Abascal, R. Rockwell, P. Dev, A. Winzelberg, and D. Wilfley. "Prevention of Eating Disorders in At-Risk College-Age Women." *Archives of General Psychiatry* 63, no. 8 (2006): 881–88.

Willett, Walter C., and P. J. Skerrett. *Eat, Drink and Be Healthy: The Harvard Medical School Guide to Healthy Eating*. New York: Free Press, 2005.

Zucker, N. *Off the C.U.F.F. A Parent Skills Book for the Management of Disordered Eating*. Durham, N.C.: Duke University Medical Center, 2006.

## Chapter 12

Bulik, C. M., L. Reba, A. M. Siega-Riz, and T. Reichborn-Kjennerud. "Anorexia Nervosa: Definition, Epidemiology, and Cycle of Risk." *International Journal of Eating Disorders* 37 (2005) Suppl: S2–S9.

Bulik, C. M., and N. Taylor. *Runaway Eating: The 8-Point Plan to Conquer Adult Food and Weight Obsessions*. Emmaus, Pa.: Rodale, 2005.

Franko, D. L. "Eating Disorders in Pregnancy and the Postpartum: Empirically-Informed Treatment Guidelines." In *Psychiatric Disorders in Pregnancy and the Postpartum: Principles and Treatment*, edited by V. Hendrick, 179–96. Totowa, N.J.: The Humana Press, 2006.

Franko, D. L., M. A. Blais, A. E. Becker, S. S. Delinsky, D. N. Greenwood, A. T. Flores, E. R. Ekeblad, K. T. Eddy, and D. B. Herzog. "Pregnancy Complications and Neonatal Outcomes in Women with Eating Disorders." *American Journal of Psychiatry* 158, no. 9 (2001): 1461–66.

Franko, D. L., and E. B. Spurrell. "Detection and Management of Eating Disorders During Pregnancy." *Obstetrics and Gynecology* 95, no. 6, part 1 (2000): 942–46.

Maine, M., and J. Kelly. *The Body Myth: Adult Women and the Pressure to Be Perfect*. Hoboken, N.J.: John Wiley & Sons, 2005.

Mathieu, J. "Disordered Eating Across the Life Span." *Journal of the American Dietetic Association* 104, no. 8 (2004): 1208–10.

Zerbe, K. "Eating Disorders in Middle and Later Life: A Neglected Problem." *Primary Psychiatry* 10 (2003): 80–83.

## Chapter 13

Cogan, J. C., D. L. Franko, and D. B. Herzog. "Federal Advocacy for Anorexia Nervosa: An American Model." *International Journal of Eating Disorders* 37, Suppl 1 (2005): S101–S102.

Greenfield, Lauren. *Thin*. Directed by Lauren Greenfield. Time Warner, Inc./HBO, New York, 2006.

Steinglass, J., and B. T. Walsh. "Habit Learning and Anorexia Nervosa." *International Journal of Eating Disorders* 39, no. 4 (2006): 267–75.

Strober, M. "Pathological Fear Conditioning and Anorexia Nervosa: On the Search for Novel Paradigms." *International Journal of Eating Disorders* 35, no. 4 (2004): 504–8.

# Index

Abdominal discomfort, 92
Abdul, Paula, 12
Actonel (risedronate), 96
Acute care hospitalization,
    68–70. *See also* Treatment
Adolescence
    striving for individuality
        and, 21–22, 25
    weight worries and, 19–21
Adulthood
    coping and, 229–31
    eating disorders and, 215–23
Advocacy, for eating disorders,
    245–46
Aftercare, residential treatment
    centers and, 73–74
Alcohol use, medications and,
    100
Alendronate (Fosamax), 96
Amenorrhea, 9, 55
American culture
    mainstream, boys in, 207
    as risk factor for eating
        disorders, 170–71, 176
American lifestyles, changes
    in, eating disorders and, 25

Anabolic steroids, 26
Anorexia nervosa, 4, 5–7. *See
    also* Eating disorders
    antidepressants for treatment
        of, 101
    common signs to, 38–45
    key signs of, 4
    medical consequences of,
        97
    warning signs of, 29–34
Antidepressants
    for treating anorexia, 101
    for treating bulimia nervosa,
        98–101
Antipsychotic drugs, 101–2
Anxieties, 42–43
Appearance, physical,
    maintaining positive
        attitudes toward,
        202–7
Arts-based therapies, 139
Athletics, 183–84
    competitive, risk of eating
        disorders and, 40, 183
    healthy environments for,
        208–9

Backpack snacks, 199

BED. *See* Binge eating disorder (BED)

Binge eating, 8

Binge eating disorder (BED), 4, 10–11

Biology, as part of puzzle of eating disorders, 170–71, 188–89

Bisphosphonates, 96

Blood pressure, 68–69

Body dysmorphic disorder, 21

Body image, 19, 192–95
  discussing, for motivation for treatment, 56
  learning positive, 202–5

Bone health
  amenorrhea and, 55
  bone density and, 96
  bone loss and, 93–94
  discussing, 93–96

Boys
  bone loss in, 94
  eating disorders and, 38
  emotions and, 205–8
  muscle dysmorphia and, 24–26
  puberty and, 20
  societal pressure and, 23
  warning signs of eating disorders for, 38
  weight worries and, 20

Brain structure/function, eating disorders and, 92
  neurotransmitters and, 99

Bulimia nervosa, 4, 7–9. *See also* Eating disorders
  antidepressants for treatment of, 98–101
  challenges of recognizing, 34–38
  common signs to, 38–45
  key signs of, 45
  medical consequences of, 97–98
  social activity and, 60
  use of antidepressants and, 98–99

Bullies, 136, 172–76

Carbohydrates, restricting, 198

Catherine of Siena, Saint, 6

Causes, of eating disorders, 169, 170–71, 188–89. *See also* Risk factors, for eating disorders

CBT. *See* Cognitive behavioral therapy (CBT)

Childbirth, eating disorders and, 223–27

Cigarette smoking, 108

Cliques, coping with, 174–79

Cognitive behavioral therapy (CBT), 77, 79–80

College campuses, eating problems on, 20–21

Communication, parent-child, improving, 116–17

Community support groups, 141

Competitive athletics, risk of eating disorders and, 40, 183–84

Coping
with cliques, 174–78
day-to-day, 159–60

Creative treatments. *See also* Treatment
arts-based therapies, 139
community support groups, 141
guided imagery, 142–43
journaling, 79, 113, 140–41
mindfulness training, 139–40
pet therapy, 143
self-help on Internet, 142
self-help workbooks, 141
yoga, 140

Cues, for recognizing hunger/satiety, 84, 200–201

Culture, eating disorders and, 170–71, 188–89. *See also* American culture

Curricula, for preventing eating disorders, 212

Cutting, 37–38, 108

Dangers. *See* Medical dangers, of eating disorders

Day treatment, 74–75

Dental problems, eating disorders and, 84–85

Depression, 43–44

Determinants of eating disorders, 169, 170–71, 188–89. *See also* Risk factors, for eating disorders

Dialectical behavior therapy, 77

Dietary fats, 197

Dieting
as disordered eating, 13–14
recognizing hunger signals and, 201
as risk factor for developing eating disorders, 171

Disappointments, handling of, 180–81

Discussion groups, 141
online, 142

Disordered eating. *See also* Eating disorders
dieting as, 13–14
eating disorders and, 14–15

Drugs
alcohol use and, 100
antidepressant, 98–101
antipsychotic drugs, 101–2
suicide risk and, 101

Eating, healthy, 195–98
backpack snacks for, 199
food pyramid for, 195–96
learning sensory quality of, 201

Eating disorders, 170. *See also* Anorexia nervosa; Bulimia nervosa; Disordered

eating; Eating disorders not otherwise specified (EDNOS); Risk factors, for eating disorders; Treatment; Treatment teams
abdominal discomfort and, 92–93
advocacy efforts for, 245–46
after childbirth and, 227–28
causes of, 170–71, 188–89
changes in American lifestyles and, 25
complexity of, 18–19
components of, 144–45
culture and, 170–71
curricula for preventing, 212
dental problems and, 84–85
determinants of, 169
early trauma and, 109
ethnic groups and, 171–72
family history and, 184–87
future research efforts for preventing, 243–45
honesty and, 33–34
informing others about, 60–63, 112, 163
interpersonal relationships and, 17
medical dangers of, 97–98
medical risks of, discussing, 54–56
monitoring, 87–92
mother-daughter perspective of, 49–51

need for hospitalization and, 68–70
obtaining medical evaluations and, 51–53
pregnancy and, 223–27
reaching out to students with, 58–59
research on, 11–12, 243–45
secrecy about, 27–28
self-esteem and, 19, 23–24, 207
self-identity and, 24–26
throughout life, 215–23
treatment-reluctant children and, 63
12-step programs, 141
uniqueness of, 122–23
Eating Disorders Coalition for Research, Policy & Action, 12, 242
Eating disorders not otherwise specified (EDNOS), 4, 9–11. *See also* Eating disorders
Eating problems on college campuses, 20–21
EDNOS. *See* Eating disorders not otherwise specified (EDNOS)
Effexor (venlafaxine), 100
Electrolyte imbalances, 69
Emotions
boys and, 207–8
eating disorders and, 22–23
visualization of, 160–61
Empathy, 26–27

Ethnic groups, eating disorders and, 171–72

Examinations, medical, 51–53

Exercise, excessive, 39–41

Families, effects of eating disorders on, 147–54. *See also* Parents

Family-based (Maudsley) treatment, 18, 82–83, 152–53, 160, 245

Family history, eating disorders and, 184–87

Family therapy, 114–17
  for food management, 129–30

Fats, dietary, 197–98

Fluoxetine (Prozac), 100

Fonda, Jane, 12

Food, learning sensory quality of, 201

Food groups, 195–97

Food intake, deciding amount of, 198–202

Food intake logs, 79, 113, 140–41

Food management, family therapy for, 129–30

Food pyramid, for healthy eating, 195–96

Food thoughts, brain and, 15–16

Food-thoughts-feelings records, 79

Food and weight worries, 15–16, 21–22

Fosamax (alendronate), 96

Genetic predisposition, eating disorders and, 188–89

Girls
  bone loss and, 93–95
  cliques and, 174–79

Grinspoon, Steven, 96

Group therapy, 74, 77, 81–82

Guided imagery, 142–43

Health insurance, 236–38
  appealing denial of, 238–41
  mental healthy parity and, 241

Healthy eating, 195–98
  backpack snacks for, 199
  determining amount for, 198–202
  food pyramid for, 195–96

Heart rates, 68–69

Homosexual males, eating disorders and, 38

Honesty, eating disorders and, 33–34

Hospitalization
  acute care, recognizing need for, 68–70
  partialization, 74–75

Hunger, recognizing cues for, 84, 200–201

Identity, search for, adolescents and, 24–26

Individual psychotherapy, 77, 80–81

Information, sharing, 60–61, 163–66

Interactions, improving, with children, 116–17

Internet
pro-anorexia websites, 138, 142
self-help on, 141

Interpersonal relationships, eating disorders and, 17

Interpersonal therapy, 77

Intuition, 26

Isolation, 57–60

Journals, keeping, 79, 113, 140–41

Keys, Ancel, 15

Klibanski, Anne, 96

Lapses, 133–34. *See also* Relapses

Life-threatening aspects of eating disorders. *See* Medical dangers, of eating disorders

Lifestyles, changes in American, eating disorders and, 25

Logs, for food intake, 79, 113, 140–41

Males, eating disorders and, 38. *See also* Boys

Malnutrition, 68

Maudsley treatment, 18, 82–83, 152–53, 160, 245

Media literacy, 209–11

Medical dangers, of eating disorders, 92, 97–98
of anorexia, 97
bone health, 93–96
of bulimia, 97–98
dental problems, 84–85
monitoring, 87–93

Medical evaluations, for eating disorders, 51–53

Medical professionals, choosing, 66–67. *See also* Treatment teams

Medical risks
of anorexia, 97
of bulimia, 97–98
discussing, to enhance motivation for treatment, 54–56

Medications, for eating disorders, 98–102
alcohol use and, 100
antidepressants, 98–101
antipsychotic drugs, 101–2
suicide risk and, 101

Menstruation, 20

Mental health parity, defined, 241

Miller, Karen, 96

Mindfulness training, 139–40

Misra, Madhusmita, 96
Monitoring
  eating disorders, 87–92
  professional, 143–44
Moodiness, as sign of eating
  disorders, 43–44
Motivation for treatment,
  enhancing, 53–60. *See also*
  Treatment
  by discussing body image,
    56
  by discussing medical risks,
    54–56
  by discussing social activity,
    57–58
  unsuccessful attempts and,
    63
Moving forward, recovery
  and, 163–66, 230–31
Muscle dysmorphia, 24–26

Neurotransmitters, eating
  disorders and, 99
Nutrition, cornerstones of,
  195–96
Nutrition counseling, 84. *See
  also* Healthy eating

Obesity, 10–11
Olanzapine (Zypexa), 102
Online support systems, 142
Osteopenia, 93–94. *See also*
  Bone health
Outpatient treatment, 75–76.
  *See also* Treatment

Parents
  day-to-day coping and,
    159–60
  effects of child's eating
    disorders on, 147–54
  helping children to choose
    health, 154–57
  hiding of eating disorders by
    children and, 27–28
  involvement in child's
    treatment and, 82–84
  openness to different
    strategies and, 151–54
  responses of, to children's
    needs, 26–27
  setting examples for
    children, 195–96
  sharing information and,
    163–64
  taking care of other children
    and, 157–59
  taking time off and, 161–62
Partial hospitalization
  programs, 74–75. *See also*
  Treatment
Perfectionism, 41–42, 179–80,
  179–82
Personality, as part of puzzle of
  eating disorders, 170–71,
  188–89
Pets, for recovery, 143, 162–63
Physical appearance,
  maintaining positive
  attitudes toward, 202–7
Praiseworthy behaviors, 181

Pregnancy, eating disorders and, 223–27

Privacy, eating disorders and, 60–63, 112, 163–66

"Pro-anorexia" websites, 138, 142

Professional monitoring, 143–44

Professionals, medical, choosing, 66–67. *See also* Treatment teams

Progress, recognizing signs of, 144–45

Prozac (fluoxetine), 100

Psychodynamically oriented therapy, 77

Psychotherapy, 76–81

Puberty, 20

Purging, 8

Recovery
addressing patient withdrawal during, 114–17
addressing social life of patient during, 117–21
building on patient strengths during, 112–14
day-to-day coping with, 159–60
defined, 125
father's perspective during, 121–22
moving forward and, 163–66

pets for, 143, 162–63
riding emotional wave of, 160–61
supporting patient through, 105–12

Relapses
defined, 134–35
managing, 133–34
preventing, 135–37
professional monitoring and, 143–44

Relationships, 170, 188
building positive, with one's body, 202–5
improving, with children with eating disorders, 116–17
interpersonal, eating disorders and, 17
parent-child, strengthening, 26–27

Religious starvation, 6

Research, on eating disorders, 11–12, 243–45

Residential treatment facilities, 70–71. *See also* Treatment
aftercare and, 73–74
questions to ask about, 71–76

Risedronate (Actonel), 96

Risk factors, for eating disorders, 188. *See also* Causes, of eating disorders
American culture and, 170–71

bullying and, 172–74
child's view of parents and,
    181–82
cliques and, 174–79
competitive athletics, and,
    183–84
ethnic background and,
    171–72
family history and, 184–87
genetic predisposition and,
    188–89
managing disappointments
    and, 180–81
perfectionism and, 179–80
summary of, 188
teasing and, 172–74

Satiety, recognizing cues for,
    84, 200–201
Secrecy, about eating
    disorders, 27–28
Selective serotonin reuptake
    inhibitors (SSRIs), 98–100
Self-esteem, 23–24
    adolescence and, 19
    building, with positive
        activities, 207
Self-help
    on Internet, 141
    workbooks, 141
    groups, 82
Self-imposed starvation, 6
Self-starvation, 6. *See also*
    Anorexia nervosa
Setbacks. *See* Lapses; Relapses

Siblings, effects of eating
    disorders on, 157–59
Snacks, backpack, 199
Social activities
    bulimia nervosa and, 60
    discusssing, for motivationf
        or treatment, 57–60
    patient, during recovery,
        117–21
    during recovery, 117–22
Sports, healthy environments
    for, 208–9. *See also*
    Athletics
SSRIs. *See* Selective serotonin
    reuptake inhibitors (SSRIs)
Starvation, self. *See* Anorexia
    nervosa
Steroids, anabolic, 26
Students, reaching out to,
    58–59
Suicide risk, medications and,
    101
Support groups, 82

Teams. *See* Treatment teams
Teasing, 172–74
Therapies. *See* Creative
    treatments; Recovery;
    Treatment
Time delays, 113
Time off, taking, 161–62
Trauma, early, eating disorders
    and, 109
Treatment. *See also* Creative
    treatments; Motivation

for treatment, enhancing;
Treatment teams
acute care hospitalization,
68–70
day, 74–75
dental care and, 84–85
group therapy, 81–82
Maudsley, 18, 82–83, 152–
53, 160, 245
nutrition counseling, 84
outpatient, 75–76
parental involvement in,
82–83
partial hospitalization,
74–75
psychotherapy, 76–81
residential, 70–74
therapy activities during,
74–75
Treatment facilities,
residential, 70–71
aftercare and, 73–74
questions to ask about,
71–76
Treatment-reluctant children,
63
Treatment teams, 65–66. *See
also* Treatment
choosing professionals for,
66–67
hospitalization of child and,
68–70
introducing child to, 67–70
treatment settings and, 67
12-step programs, for eating
disorders, 141

University campuses, eating
problems on, 20–21

Vegetarianism, individuals
with eating disorders and,
32–33
Venlafaxine (Effexor), 100
Visualization of emotions,
160–61
Vitamin D, 96

Warning signs
of anorexia, 29–34, 38–44
of bulimia, 34–38, 38–45
of eating disorders in males,
38
Waves, emotional,
visualization of, 160–61
Websites
pro-anorexia, 138, 142
self-help, 141
Weight bias, 172–73
Weight loss, as warning sign of
anorexia, 30
Weight worries
adolescence and, 19–21
emotions and, 21–23
Withdrawal, of child from
parents, addressing, 114–17
Workbooks, self-help, 141
Worthiness, eating disorders
and. *See* Self-esteem

Yoga, 140

Zypexa (olanzapine), 102